関正生の

The Rules 英語長文問題集 3

入試難関

別冊 問題編

旺文社

大学入試

関正生の The Rules 英語長文問題集 3 入試難関

別冊 問題編

Contents
問題編 目次

Lesson 1

運動と睡眠の関係

科学技術のおかげで日々の生活が楽になる反面,「健康・病気」などへの関心はますます高まっています。それは入試の世界にも如実に反映されており，頻出テーマの1つとなっています。この長文には,「具体例の発見」「因果表現」「テーマの把握」「強調構文」など, 難関大攻略のための重要事項が詰め込まれています。少し難しく感じるかもしれませんが，このレベルの問題を把握・体感するのにとてもよい素材です。

目標

⇒「因果関係」をきちんと把握する！

語数：944語　　**出題校：中央大学**

Lesson 1

試験本番での目標時間 23分　この本での目標時間 32分

▶解答・解説 本冊 p.12

次の英文を読み，設問に答えなさい。文章は，それぞれ数段落をまとめた4つのブロックに分けられており，各ブロックの先頭には番号［Ⅰ］～［Ⅳ］が付してあります。なお，＊印のついた語には注があります。

［Ⅰ］——

1 If you're one of the third of all Americans who suffer from insomnia*1 — roughly 108 million of us — put away your sleeping pills. Science has a much safer solution. "There has been more and more research in the last decade showing exercise can reduce insomnia," Rush University clinical psychologist Kelly Glazer Baron said. "In one study we did, for example, older women suffering from insomnia said their sleep improved from poor to good when they exercised. They had more energy and were less depressed."

2 "There are more solid studies recently that looked at people clinically diagnosed*2 with insomnia disorder, rather than self-described poor sleepers," agreed the University of Pittsburgh's Christopher Kline, who studies sleep through the lens of sports medicine. "The results show exercise improves both self-reported and objective measures of sleep quality, such as what's measured in a clinical sleep lab."

3 Exercise is not quite as effective as sleeping pills, admits Arizona State University sleep researcher Shawn Youngstedt, but if you consider the potential problems of pharmaceutically*3 induced sleep, one's thinking changes. "Sleeping pills are extremely dangerous," Youngstedt said. "They are as bad as smoking a pack of cigarettes a day. Not to (　A　) they cause infections, falling and dementia*4 in the elderly, and they lose their effectiveness after a few weeks. It's less expensive, healthier and just as easy to exercise," he said, "and there's an added bonus. Research suggests those who are physically active have a lower risk of developing insomnia in the first place."

［Ⅱ］——

4 There's more good news for the 18 million Americans who struggle with sleep apnea, a dangerous disorder in which you temporarily stop breathing for up to a minute during the night. Exercise can help with that, too. "For sleep apnea, exercise has always been recommended," Kline said, "mostly to jump-start weight loss from dieting, because those with sleep apnea are normally overweight or

obese. But we did a study where the participants didn't diet, and exercise alone led to a 25% reduction of sleep apnea symptoms over a 12-week period."

5 "Exercise has also been shown to help with restless-leg symptoms across all age groups," Youngstedt said. Restless-leg syndrome, a disorder of the nervous system, occurs when the legs — or other parts of the body like the arms or face — itch, burn or move involuntarily. The irresistible urge to move often happens at night, which disrupts sleep.

6 Finding a safe, healthy type of treatment for sleep disorders like insomnia, sleep apnea and restless legs is critical, these experts say, because disturbed sleep is a key risk factor for diseases and (B) conditions such as stroke, heart attack and high blood pressure.

7 "There is a large amount of literature*5 showing that people who exercise have better sleep," Baron said. "People who exercise reported an increase in deep sleep and a decrease in the number of awakenings. Plus, people felt less depressed, and their mood was better."

[Ⅲ] ——

8 How much exercise is needed to get a good night's rest? Most sleep studies have focused on the recommended amount: two and a half hours a week of moderate-intensity aerobic exercise, along with strength or resistance training that targets every muscle group two days a week. Kline says "brisk walking, light biking ... anything that increases your heart rate so that you can still talk while exercising but have to catch your breath every few sentences or so, is considered moderate exercise."

9 "I think trying to do it outside is also helpful, because bright light can help promote sleep," Youngstedt added. "Light exposure helps regulate the body clock."

10 Other studies show that people who exercise less than the recommended amount, and those who go way beyond in time and intensity, see moderate benefits. <u>It's only when you are training to the level of an elite athlete that exercise can actually interfere with sleep quality.</u> "High-level athletes, who may overtrain for a certain event, do have issues with sleep when traveling and under stress," Youngstedt said. "But for the vast majority of us, that's not a factor."

[Ⅳ] ——

11 What's the best time of day to do this sleep-enhancing movement? Experts used to say morning was best; in fact, any exercise within six hours of bedtime was strongly discouraged. On that topic, the science has changed. "One common

myth is that exercise should be avoided at night," Youngstedt said. "There are about 10% of us for whom exercise at night does disturb sleep, but I personally think that's because they aren't accustomed to it. For most of us, exercise at night, even if it ends just a couple of hours before bedtime, will help with sleep."

12 Destroying that myth is especially helpful for those who tend to stay up later. "Night owls have problems getting up in the morning; they just can't do it," Baron said. "Their mood and ability to apply effort just isn't there. If you're sacrificing sleep for exercise, is that a good idea?"

13 However, one of the benefits of staying with a morning exercise routine, she adds, is that you are less likely to cancel. "Morning exercisers are more consistent," she explained. "So many of us have competing demands in our day, so if we leave it to the evening, we might not follow through."

14 Staying the course is important to keep sleep benefits in place. "They have to keep it up," Youngstedt said. "I think it helps to have a consistent schedule, so figure out what works best for you and then stick to it."

15 "If you have insomnia or sleep apnea, it's even more important to exercise," Baron said. "You will likely feel even less inclined to exercise when you are fatigued, but keep with it, because it can really help."

語注 ＊1 insomnia 不眠症　＊2 diagnosed 診断された　＊3 pharmaceutically 薬剤的に
＊4 dementia 認知症　＊5 literature 研究文献

A 問1〜問2：本文中の空所（ A ）と空所（ B ）に入る最も適切なものを，各組の①〜④の中から1つ選びなさい。

問1 （ A ）

① believe　② know　③ mention　④ expect

問2 （ B ）

① beneficial　② desirable　③ unknown　④ unhealthy

B 問3〜問6：それぞれ指定したブロックの内容に照らして最も適切なものを①〜④の中から1つずつ選びなさい。

問3 ブロック［Ⅰ］（第1〜3段落）

① Kelly Glazer Baron has read a lot about insomnia, but has never been personally involved in a study related to this problem.

② According to Christopher Kline, relatively good studies have shown that exercise has no effect on the quality of sleep people get.

③ Shawn Youngstedt does not view sleeping pills as being safe.

④ According to Youngstedt, one advantage of sleeping pills is their cost.

問4 ブロック［Ⅱ］（第4〜7段落）

① Exercise should be avoided if one suffers from sleep apnea.

② In a study that Kline was involved in, exercise alone led to a decline in the number of sleep apnea symptoms.

③ Restless-leg syndrome is a problem caused by people who like to move around throughout the night.

④ According to Baron, a lot of literature shows that people wake up with increasing frequency as a result of exercise.

問5 ブロック［Ⅲ］（第8〜10段落）

① It is generally recommended that in order to sleep well, one should get an unlimited amount of exercise.

② Kline does not consider walking quickly to be moderate exercise.

③ Youngstedt thinks exercising outside on a sunny day leads to the elimination of the body clock.

④ Some studies indicate that getting some exercise, but less than the recommended amount, leads to moderate sleep benefits.

問6 ブロック［Ⅳ］（第11〜15段落）

① Baron discusses a benefit of exercise in the morning.

② Nobody recommends exercising at night.

③ According to Baron, sleep apnea makes sleeping problems improbable.

④ Baron makes it clear that being tired will probably increase one's desire to exercise.

C 問7 ブロック［Ⅲ］（第8〜10段落）の下線部を和訳しなさい。

Lesson 2

我々は現実をありのまま見ているのか?

「認識と現実」に関する英文です。今回の英文は多くの受験生にとって抽象的で難解に感じられるでしょう。しかし内容が難しいときこそ，本書で学ぶルールが役立ちます。例えば，Lesson 1で学んだ「疑問文の役割」はテーマを把握する上で今回も役立ちますし，内容一致問題の典型的なひっかけパターンを見抜くルールも大いに役立ちます。さらに, Lesson 6で学ぶ「消えたbutに気づく」方法も大活躍します。
さらに，この英文を通して，感情表現や「重要な」という意味の重要単語などをマスターしておきましょう。

目標
⇒「テーマ」「因果関係」「『重要』と示す語句」を意識する！

語数：622語　　**出題校：関西学院大学**

Lesson 2

試験本番での目標時間 18 分　この本での目標時間 25 分　▶解答・解説 本冊 p.33

次の英文を読み，設問に答えなさい。

When you open your eyes, do you see the world as it really is? Do you see reality? Humans have been asking themselves this question for thousands of years. The notion that what we see might not be what is truly there has (　1　) and annoyed us. Great minds of history have taken up this puzzling question again and again. They all had theories, but now neuroscience*1 has an answer.

The answer is that we don't see reality. The world exists. It's just that we don't see it. We do not experience the world as it is because our brain didn't evolve to do so. It is a kind of paradox: Your brain gives you the impression that your perceptions are objectively real, yet the sensory processes*2 that make perception possible actually separate you from ever accessing that reality directly. Our five senses are like a keyboard to a computer — they provide the means for us to process information from the world, but they have very little to do with what is then experienced in perception. They are in essence just mechanical media, and therefore (　2　) only a limited role in what we perceive. In fact, (ア) <u>in terms of</u> the number of connections that our brain makes, just 10 percent of how we process sight comes from our eyes. The other 90 percent comes from other parts of our brains. Perception derives not only from our five senses (　3　) from our brain's seemingly infinitely refined network that makes sense of all the incoming information. The new findings of perceptual neuroscience reveal why we don't perceive reality, and why this can lead to creativity and innovation at work, at home, or at play.

Given this, why does this matter to you? Why might you need to depart from the way you currently perceive? After all, it feels like we see reality accurately, at least most of the time. Clearly our brain's model of perception has served our species well, allowing us to successfully survive in the world and its ever-shifting complexity, from our days as hunter-gatherers to our current existence (　4　) on our smartphones. We are able to find food and shelter, hold down a job, and build meaningful relationships. We have built cities, launched astronauts into space, and created the Internet. We must be doing something right, so who cares that we don't see reality?

Perception (イ) <u>matters</u> because it serves as the basis of everything we think, know, and believe — our hopes and dreams, the clothes we wear, the professions we choose, the thoughts we have, and the people whom we trust ... and don't trust. Perception is the taste of an apple, the smell of the ocean, the enchantment of spring, the glorious noise of the city, the feeling of love, and even conversations about the impossibility of love. Our sense of self, our most essential way of understanding existence, begins and ends with perception. The death that we all fear is less the death of the body and more the death of perception, as many of us would be quite happy to know that after "bodily death" our ability to engage in perception of the world around us continues. This is because perception is what allows us to experience life itself; to see it as alive. Yet most of us don't know how or why perceptions work, or how or why our brain evolved to perceive the way it does.

Fortunately, the neuroscience of perception (5) us a solution. The answer is essential because it will lead to future innovations in thought and behavior in all aspects of our lives, from love to learning. What is the next greatest innovation? It's not a technology. It's a way of seeing.

語注　＊1 neuroscience 神経科学　＊2 sensory process 感覚過程（物事を認識する過程）

問1　本文中の空所（1）～（5）に入れるのに最も適当なものを，それぞれ下記（①～④）の中から1つ選びなさい。

(1)	① denied	② made	③ ignored	④ troubled
(2)	① access	② notify	③ play	④ tap
(3)	① and	② away	③ but	④ so
(4)	① bills paying	② bills paid	③ payment of bills	④ paying bills
(5)	① deprives	② helps	③ offers	④ takes

問2　本文中の下線部（ア）・（イ）の文中での意味に最も近いものを，それぞれ下記（①～④）の中から1つ選びなさい。

ア in terms of

① by the way to　② from the perspective of

③ for the sake of　④ on account to

イ matters

① is clear　② is difficult　③ is important　④ is questionable

問3　次の英文（①〜⑥）の中から本文の内容と一致するものを2つ選びなさい。ただし，その順序は問いません。

① The people of ancient times all believed that the reality of the world could only be seen with their own eyes.

② The sensory processes interfere with our perceptions even when we feel they are objectively real.

③ Our five senses are different from a computer keyboard in that they are just mechanical media.

④ Our perception has enabled us to survive in the complex world, from primitive ages to our modern times.

⑤ Many people hope that death of perception is caused by bodily death.

⑥ The neuroscience of perception will lead to various technological innovations in the future.

Lesson 3

「黄金比」と「わびさび」

今回は「美しいとは何か？」を探る英文で，単に「美しさは変化する」という事実にとどまらず，日本や西洋での違いまで踏み込んでいます。こういった抽象的な内容に対処するための読解ルールとして,「対比」や「具体例」の合図などを学んでいきます。「For example を見たら具体例」と考える受験生が多いのですが，実際の英文ではFor exampleが使われないことがよくあります。その「消えたFor exampleに気づく方法」を習得していきましょう。

目標

⇒「対比」や「具体例」の合図に反応しよう！

語数：667 語　　**出題校：宇都宮大学**

Lesson 3

試験本番での目標時間 27分　この本での目標時間 37分　▶解答・解説 本冊 p.49

次の英文を読み，設問に答えなさい。

Beauty is in the eye of the beholder.*1

This proverb was first recorded in the English language in its current form in the 19th century. However, (1) <u>the concept of people viewing beauty differently from their own points of view has been around in most cultures of the world since ancient times.</u> But what exactly is beauty, and is it really subjective? The definition in the Merriam-Webster dictionary is "the qualities in a person or a thing that give pleasure to the senses or the mind." This definition, however, does not mention whether there is a universal standard for beauty, or whether each individual person views beauty based on a totally different set of standards. Some of the arts seem to suggest the (2) if we consider the fact that everybody has their own favorite piece of music or painting that they consider to be beautiful. Nature, on the other hand, consistently comes up with scenes that are universally considered to be beautiful.

(3) <u>There is little doubt that physical beauty, or beauty based on physical appearance of people, is personal.</u> The ideal "beautiful woman" differs between cultures, and in many cases is based on fashion. Some cultures appreciate fatness, while others believe that body mutilation*2 represents beauty. For example, body art in the form of piercings and tattoos is recognized as a sign of beauty in many countries of the world today, although there are also many people in these same countries who continue to (4) with this assessment.

Certain ancient Greek philosophers, including Pythagoras, believed that beauty was based on symmetry and regularity, and they were therefore convinced that mathematics was at the core of true beauty. (5) <u>This concept</u> was discovered when they noticed that objects which matched the golden ratio*3 appeared to be more attractive than objects that were more random in shape. Symmetry and regularity also seem to play a part in (6) beauty. At the end of the 19th century, British anthropologist Francis Galton discovered that "averaging" out human faces by mixing them to form one image achieved a level of regularity that was more attractive than each of the individual components.

Despite this, there are many forms of art that are considered beautiful, yet are not based on symmetry and regularity. Some examples of this include

Cubism, Expressionism and many other forms of modern art. And, one of the deepest concepts of beauty does not lie in symmetry, harmony and regularity, but focuses on objects not being perfect, permanent or complete; *wabi-sabi*.

Wabi-sabi is a Buddhist concept introduced to Japan from China, where it (7) evolved into a distinctly Japanese idea of beauty. The word *wabi* originally referred to the loneliness of nature, and *sabi* referred to something that is simplistic. The meaning gradually changed over time, and by the 14th century *wabi* meant "rough simplicity" and *sabi* "beauty" or "calmness." Nowadays this concept is usually described as "natural simplicity" or "imperfect beauty."

Wabi-sabi is based on the three Buddhist views of existence, which are impermanence, pain and emptiness. It was thought that understanding the beauty contained within emptiness and imperfection was the first step to achieving a state of enlightenment*4. *Wabi-sabi* places the emphasis on simplicity, economy, modesty, asymmetry and roughness, and (8) the main message that it includes is that nothing is finished, nothing is perfect and nothing lasts forever. A fallen autumn leaf, for example, could be considered to be *wabi-sabi* because it expresses the beauty of nature while at the same time emphasizing its imperfection and impermanence. In its artistic form, *wabi-sabi* is best expressed in pottery. Asymmetric bowls with natural base colors, showing a rough style of imperfection, stimulate the mind into considering the beauty of the three Buddhist views of existence.

Whether the true essence of beauty lies in mathematics, as believed by the ancient Greeks, or in the artistic emptiness of *wabi-sabi*, as believed by the Japanese, remains open to question, but one thing is certain. Beauty will always remain in the eye of the beholder.

語注　＊1 beholder 見る者　＊2 mutilation 切断　＊3 golden ratio 黄金比（美術や建築などで美しいとされる比率）　＊4 enlightenment 悟り

（Adapted from *Transculture*, 2017 by Christopher Belton and Koshi Odashima）

問1　下線部（1）を日本語に訳しなさい。

問2　空所（2）に入る語として最も適切なものを以下の中から選び，記号で答えなさい。

① former　② latter　③ opposite　④ other

問3　下線部（3）を日本語に訳しなさい。

問4　空所（4）に入る語として最も適切なものを以下の中から選び，記号で答えなさい。

① cope　② disagree　③ encounter　④ hold

問5　下線部（5）はどのようなことか，日本語で簡潔に述べなさい。

問6　空所（6）に入る語として最も適切なものを以下の中から選び，記号で答えなさい。

① emotional　② inner　③ negative　④ physical

問7　下線部（7）の表す意味に最も近いものを以下の中から選び，記号で答えなさい。

① broke　② developed　③ dived　④ divided

問8　下線部（8）はどのようなメッセージか，50字以内の日本語で述べなさい。

				5					10					15
				20					25					30
				35					40					45
				50										

問9　次のそれぞれの英文について，本文の内容に合う場合は○を，合わない場合は×を記入しなさい。

① Sayings that have the same meaning as "beauty is in the eye of the beholder" have been shared across cultures since ancient times.

② Ancient Greek philosophers believed that beauty was based on simplicity and asymmetry.

③ The concept of *wabi-sabi*, which refers to the loneliness of nature and weakness, has never changed.

④ *Wabi-sabi* is a Buddhist concept introduced to China from Japan.

⑤ Some examples of beautiful art which does not rely on symmetry and regularity include Cubism and Expressionism.

Lesson 4

発音指導の難しさと大切さ

言語論は昔からの頻出テーマです。そもそも「英語」という言語の試験ですし，言語論は「言語習得（教育）・言語の消滅・文化とのかかわり・コミュニケーション」など様々な側面があるため，入試では非常によく出題されるわけです。

また，今回は英文がさほど難しくないのでなんとなく読めてしまい，その結果，記述答案も「なんとなく」のものになりがちです。それでは部分点はもらえても，合格点に届くとは限りませんし，他の受験生でも取れる程度の得点しかもらえないでしょう。より精密な答案を作り上げるために，どう考えるべきなのか，記述の方法論を習得していきます。

目標

⇒「説明問題」の合格答案を作る！

語数：467語　　**出題校**：福島大学

Lesson 4

試験本番での目標時間 22分　この本での目標時間 32分

▶解答・解説 本冊 p.68

次の英文を読み，設問に答えなさい。

Most learners at every level are keen to learn how to speak as well as how to read and write in English, and beginners are no exception. They are very keen to learn how to pronounce English in a way that makes themselves understood easily. (1) <u>This</u> became very clear to Vicki, a colleague of ours with considerable experience teaching adult learners. At the time, Vicki was working with a class of beginning-level learners from very diverse backgrounds. Because she is always conscientious*1 about meeting the needs of her students, she decided to collect feedback about different aspects of her classes on a regular basis. This feedback consistently indicated that her students were pleased with her teaching but they wanted to learn how to speak in their daily lives. At first, she responded to these requests by not only increasing the opportunity for her students to speak in class, but also devising assignments that encouraged them to speak outside the class and advising them of community-based facilities where they could practice. However, even after (2) <u>these changes</u>, the students still reported that they wanted to learn to speak in their daily lives.

Vicki gradually came to understand that what the students really wanted was not an increased opportunity to speak, but explicit instruction on how to speak, that is, explicit instruction in pronunciation. She realized she had been avoiding actually teaching pronunciation because she was a little unsure how to go about it. Once she started to incorporate pronunciation instruction into her classes, however, (3) <u>the need to learn to speak no longer featured in the feedback from students</u>. In addition, former students who had moved to higher levels came back to attend her beginner classes, so much so that, at times, her classes would be overflowing with past students as well as current class members. They obviously felt they were learning to speak!

When teaching beginner adult learners of English, we are faced with a seemingly daunting task. There are so many things they need to learn. They need to learn how to speak, listen, read, and write in English, and proficiency in each of these skills requires the mastery of many different sub-skills. It can therefore be difficult to establish priorities when deciding what to teach in a beginning-level classroom. Unfortunately, pronunciation is often overlooked as a teaching priority at this level because other aspects of English are deemed[*2] to be more important. Some teachers may even feel that instruction in pronunciation is too threatening or challenging for beginners who are already struggling with so many different aspects of English. Other teachers may have the idea that pronunciation is too difficult or complicated for them to teach. We disagree! (4) Such views are based on misconceptions of pronunciation and its role in how we learn to speak a language.

語注　＊1 conscientious 誠実な　　＊2 deem ～とみなす
（出典：“Pronunciation instruction is not appropriate for beginning-level learners,” *Pronunciation Myths*.）

問1　下線部（1）が指している内容を，本文に基づいて日本語で説明しなさい。

問2　下線部（2）が指している内容を，本文に基づいて日本語で説明しなさい。

問3　下線部（3）について，このようなことが起こったのはなぜか，以前のフィードバックの内容を踏まえて，本文に基づいて日本語で説明しなさい。

問4　下線部（4）が指している内容を，本文に基づいて日本語で説明しなさい。

Lesson 5

才能や知識以外に大切なものは何?

イノベーションを起こすためには何が必要だと思いますか？　才能や知識以外に，もう1つ欠かせない要素について，今回の英文が教えてくれます。その「ある要素」をテーマにした英文は入試の定番ですが，今回の英文は過去の偉人を例に出し，大変説得力のある論を展開しています。
このLessonでは「主張」と「具体例」の把握がポイントになります。これまで学んだルールが存分に使えますので，ルールを使いこなす練習を積んでいきましょう。さらに，新たな「具体例の発見方法」や「空所補充問題の解法」も紹介していきます。

目標
⇒「主張」と「具体例」を見つけ出す！

語数：716語　　**出題校：大阪府立大学**

Lesson 5

試験本番での目標時間 30分　この本での目標時間 38分　▶解答・解説 本冊 p.82

次の英文を読んで，設問に答えなさい。

When I was in high school, a man came to speak about Winston Churchill. Mostly, it was the usual mix of historical events and anecdotes, but what I remember best was how the talk ended. The speaker concluded by saying that if we were to remember one thing about Churchill, it should be that (1)(A)(B)(C)(D)(E)(F) his power to communicate. I didn't understand that at the time. Growing up, I had always heard about the importance of hard work, honesty and other things, but never communication.

Yet now, thirty years later, I've begun to understand what he meant. As Walter Isaacson argues, the ability to work together effectively is decisive. (2)In order to make innovation possible, it's not enough to just come up with big ideas. You also need to work hard to communicate them clearly.

Today, (3)we take electricity for granted. We switch on lights, watch TV and enjoy connected devices without a second thought. It's hard to imagine an earlier age in which we had to use smoky, smelly candles in order to see at night and didn't have the benefit and convenience of basic household appliances.

Michael Faraday, probably more than anyone else, transformed electricity from an interesting curiosity into the workhorse of the modern age. Yet Faraday was more than just a talented scientist. He was also a very effective communicator. As Nancy Forbes and Basil Mahon write, "(4)His scientific genius lay not simply in producing experimental results that were beyond everyone's understanding but in explaining them too." This wasn't a natural talent; he worked hard at it, taking plentiful notes on his own lectures and those of others. (5)The effort paid off. His regular lectures at the Royal Institution made him, and the Institution itself, well-known in the scientific world.

A more recent genius was Richard Feynman. He won the Nobel Prize for Physics in 1965, but also made important discoveries in biology and was an early pioneer of parallel and quantum computing. His talent, in fact, was so remarkable that even other elite scientists considered him to be a magician. Yet like Faraday, Feynman was not content to (あ) his tricks. He insisted on teaching an introductory class for undergraduates — exceedingly rare for top academics. With his Brooklyn accent, ironic sense of humor and talent for explaining things in practical, everyday terms, he was a student favorite.

Perhaps the best example of how Feynman combined brilliance with exceptional communication skills was a talk he gave a few days after Christmas in 1959. Starting from a basic question about what it would take to shrink the Encyclopedia Britannica to fit on the head of a pin, he moved step by step until, in less than an hour, he had invented the field of nanotechnology.

Schopenhauer once said that, "talent hits a target no one else can hit; Genius hits a target no one else can see." Feynman was a genius who wanted us to see it too.

We tend to (い) knowledge and communication as two separate spheres. We act as if having the skills of an expert was a private matter, earned through quiet study. Communication, on the other hand, is often reduced to the realm of the social, a tool we use to interact with others of our species. Yet, as Wittgenstein argued decades ago, that position is logically unsound because it assumes that we are able to communicate to ourselves in a private language. (6) In truth, we can't really know anything that we can't communicate. To assert that we can possess knowledge, but are unable to explain what it is, makes no sense.

And so it is curious that we (う) communication little or no attention. Schools don't teach communication. They teach math, some science and history, but provide very little guidance on how to express ideas clearly. When we enter professional life, we rarely put serious effort toward expressing ourselves in a language that can be understood by those outside our own group. When our efforts and achievements fail to receive a sympathetic response, we are left wondering why. The fact is that although it may be fashionable to say that our present era is an information age, we (え) in a communication age and it's time we start taking it seriously.

問1 下線部（1）の空所（ A ）～（ F ）を下の①～⑥で埋め，本文の内容に最もふさわしい英文を完成させるとき，空所（ A ）（ C ）（ F ）に入るものをそれぞれ記号で答えなさい。ただし，いずれの記号も1回ずつしか使えない。

① effective　② him　③ made　④ so　⑤ was　⑥ what

問2　下線部（2）を日本語に訳しなさい。

問3　下線部（3）に意味が最も近いものを下の①～④から選び，記号で答えなさい。

① we believe that electricity is not always available
② we fail to fully appreciate electricity
③ we grant the use of electricity to everyone
④ we recognize that electricity is convenient

問4　下線部（4）を日本語に訳しなさい。

問5　下線部（5）に意味が最も近いものを下の①～④から選び，記号で答えなさい。

① The effort earned a lot of money.
② The effort was free of debt.
③ The effort was successful.
④ The effort was worthless.

問6　空所（ **あ** ）～（ **え** ）のそれぞれに当てはまる語として最も適切なものを下の①～④から選び，記号で答えなさい。ただし，いずれの記号も1回ずつしか使えない。

① give　　② hide　　③ live　　④ treat

問7　下線部（6）を日本語に訳しなさい。

問8　本文の内容に最もよく当てはまる文を下の①～④から選び，記号で答えなさい。

① Having enough knowledge allows us to be understood by other people.
② It is important to convey our understanding in a clear way.
③ We can learn to communicate through quiet study in our field.
④ We cannot pursue knowledge and communication at the same time.

Lesson 6

そんなに急いで食事するのはナゼ?

皆さんの中にも，勉強や部活で忙しくて「ゆっくり食べる時間がない」と嘆いている人がいることでしょう。これは大人にも，そして世界中でも当てはまる話ですが，今回の英文では「時間がなくなったことが本当の原因なのか？」と掘り下げて議論をしています。これは皆さんも自分の生活を考え直すよいきっかけになるかもしれません。
また，この長文をとおしてこれまで習得した様々なルールが役立つことが実感できるでしょう。さらに，新たに〈SV 人 to 原形〉の訳し方など，従来の問題集ではあまり触れられることのなかったルールを扱います。「〈cause 人 to 原形〉は『人が～することを引き起こす』と訳す」とこだわっているうちは解けない設問にどう対処していくかを具体的に示していきます。

目標

⇒抽象的な内容は「形」から考える

語数：749語　　**出題校：**学習院大学

Lesson 6

試験本番での目標時間 26分　この本での目標時間 36分　▶解答・解説 本冊 p.101

次の英文を読み，設問に答えなさい。

There are no chairs in the cafeteria at one high school in central China. They disappeared during the summer so that students could store up a few precious extra minutes of study time. (1) With the chairs gone, there was no risk of spending too much time over lunch. Students eat standing at tables before rushing back to class. "We learnt this from other places," an official said in a Chinese newspaper, adding that it should be possible to shorten the time students spent on eating their lunch down to just 10 minutes.

After the story of this chairless cafeteria became known, the school's policy was widely criticized. "It's a terrible idea to make students eat while standing," stated an editorial*1 in the same newspaper. "It (2) sacrifices the students' health for academic scores. It's unacceptable." A medical doctor said that this practice would be very bad for the digestion and could set children up for a lifetime of illnesses.

Most of us dislike the notion of a chairless cafeteria that makes children eat faster. Yet the disturbing thing about dining arrangements at the Chinese high school is that they are not so different from (3) millions of other children and adults now consume meals around the world. Is the student in China quickly eating a 10-minute lunch so different from the office worker who lunches on a protein bar because there are too many emails and not enough hours in the day?

What makes the chairless cafeteria at the school seem shocking is that the lack of time for eating is so deliberate and calculated. In the rest of the world, by contrast, many of us do not quite understand why we are eating in such an irritated state so often. For decades, people have complained that modern life does not leave enough time to cook. The new worry is that we often feel we do not even have the time to eat.

How else can we explain the successful marketing of products such as liquidized*2 breakfast cereal to drink? A bowl of cornflakes with milk used to be what you ate when you lacked the time to cook a proper breakfast. But now, even sales of breakfast cereals have become a victim of time pressure.

According to research in 2015, 40 per cent of people surveyed said that cereal was an inconvenient breakfast because it takes time to clean up the bowl after eating. Sales of breakfast cereal in Britain fell by 3.6 million kilograms.

A lack of time — or what we think is a lack — is one of the main reasons why modern food habits differ from those of previous generations. It makes it impossible for us to pursue our desires and forces us into (4) compromises we never quite intended. There is evidence that when someone feels lacking in time, he or she will cook less, enjoy meals less and yet end up eating more food.

(5) Sliced bread was only the start. Everywhere you look, there are products promising to save you time, from two-minute rice to quick-cook pasta. All this talk about time is a clever marketing device too, because it can convince us that there is no point even trying to cook anything that takes longer than 20 minutes — even though those same 20 minutes feel like nothing when we are browsing online shopping. (6) Feeling rushed causes us to spend less time preparing our meals. When we say we lack time to cook — or even time to eat — we are not making a simple statement of fact. We are talking about cultural values and (7) the way our society tells us that our days should be divided.

There is something paradoxical*3, however, in the way we think that we have too little time to eat properly. By objective standards, most of us in wealthy countries have far more free time on average than workers did a hundred years ago: nearly 1,000 more hours a year, in fact. In 1900, the average American worked 2,700 hours a year. By 2015 the average American worked just 1,790 hours a year. Compared with many of the workers of the past, the average worker today (8) has so much time on their hands. Except, it seems, for time to eat. Many of us are trapped in a lifestyle in which eating well seems all but impossible. Yet this is partly because we live in a world that places a higher value on time than it does on food.

語注　＊1 editorial 社説　＊2 liquidized 液化した　＊3 paradoxical 逆説的な，矛盾した

問1　下線部（1）の意味に最も近いものを次の①～④の中から1つ選びなさい。

① Providing the chairs did not help the students take a long enough lunch break.

② Providing the chairs helped the students take a long enough lunch break.

③ Removing the chairs did not keep the students from taking too long a lunch break.

④ Removing the chairs kept the students from taking too long a lunch break.

問2　下線部 (**2**) の意味に最も近いものを次の①～④の中から1つ選びなさい。

① contributes neither to the students' health nor to their academic scores

② keeps the students healthy and at the same time improves their academic scores

③ worsens the students' academic scores in order to improve their health

④ worsens the students' health in order to improve their academic scores

問3　空所 (**3**) に入る語句として最も適切なものを次の①～④の中から1つ選びなさい。

① the fortunate fact that

② the unfortunate fact that

③ the hurried manner in which

④ the unhurried manner in which

問4　下線部 (**4**) の例として最も適切なものを次の①～④の中から1つ選びなさい。

① a proper breakfast

② a protein bar for lunch

③ not enough hours

④ too many emails

問5　下線部 (**5**) の意味に最も近いものを次の①～④の中から1つ選びなさい。

① Many other examples followed sliced bread.

② Sliced bread had just appeared on the market.

③ The bread was sliced in the first place.

④ The first thing to do was slice the bread.

問6　下線部 (**6**) を与えられた語句に続けて，句読点を含め25字以内の日本語に訳しなさい。

私たちは気持ちが

				5					10					15
				20					25					

問7　下線部（7）の意味に最も近いものを次の①～④の中から1つ選びなさい。

① people's ideas about how a person should spend his or her time

② people's sense that they must frequently check their calendar

③ the government's plan of how events should be scheduled on the calendar

④ the government's recommendation on how a person should spend his or her time

問8　下線部（8）の意味に最も近いものを次の①～④の中から1つ選びなさい。

① has plenty of leisure time

② has plenty of work to do

③ mostly works full time

④ mostly works with their hands

問9　本文の内容と一致するものを次の①～⑦の中から2つ選びなさい。ただし，3つ以上選んだ場合は得点を認めません。

① A doctor says that eating while standing is good for you and helps prevent disease.

② For decades we have felt that we do not have enough time to eat properly.

③ More and more people in Britain are buying breakfast cereal because of time pressure.

④ It is known that when feeling pressed for time you eat more than when feeling relaxed.

⑤ People tend to think that time is better used cooking than browsing the Internet.

⑥ The average American today works far longer hours than his or her ancestors.

⑦ Ours is a society in which time is considered to be more important than food.

Lesson 7

アメリカで大問題の「竜巻」

日本で発生する竜巻は1年に25件程度ですが，アメリカでは平均で1,300件ほど確認されています。竜巻はアメリカ全土で甚大な被害をもたらし，大きな問題となっているのです。こういった異常気象や気候変動は入試頻出のテーマであり，今後もますます増えると予想されます。それゆえ「災害」関係の表現は非常に大事です。ところが，こういった内容の英文はあまり見慣れないせいか，苦手とする受験生がものすごく多いのです。

さらに今回の英文は，箇条書きのリストや図表がある，共通テストや資格試験で見られる形です。今までのLessonとはちょっと違ったパターンですが，慣れていない受験生が多いので，ここでルールをまとめて対策をしていきます。

目標

⇒「自然・災害」の英文／共通テスト型の問題対策

語数：470語　　**出題校：信州大学**

Lesson 7

試験本番での目標時間　この本での目標時間

分

分

▶解答・解説 本冊 p.122

次のアメリカにおける竜巻（Tornado）の防災対策に関する英文を読んで設問に答えなさい。

Tornadoes are nature's most violent storms. Spawned from powerful thunderstorms, tornadoes can cause fatalities and devastate a neighborhood in seconds. A tornado appears as a rotating, funnel-shaped cloud that extends from a thunderstorm to the ground with whirling winds that can reach 300 miles per hour (MPH). Damage paths can be in excess of one mile wide and 50 miles long. Every state is at some risk from this hazard.

Some tornadoes are clearly visible, while rain or nearby low-hanging clouds obscure others. Occasionally, tornadoes develop so rapidly that little, if any, advance warning is possible. Before a tornado hits, the wind may die down and the air may become very still. A cloud of debris can mark the location of a tornado even if a funnel is invisible. Tornadoes generally occur near the trailing edge of a thunderstorm. It is not uncommon to see clear, sunlit skies behind a tornado.

The following are facts about tornadoes:

- They may strike quickly, with little or no warning.
- They may appear nearly transparent until dust and debris are picked up or a cloud forms in the funnel.
- The average tornado moves Southwest to Northeast, but tornadoes have been known to move in any direction.
- The average forward speed of a tornado is 30 MPH, but may vary from stationary to 70 MPH.
- Tornadoes can accompany tropical storms and hurricanes as they move onto land.
- Waterspouts are tornadoes that form over water.
- Tornadoes are most frequently reported east of the Rocky Mountains during spring and summer months.
- Peak tornado season in the southern states is March through May; in the northern states, it is late spring through early summer.
- Tornadoes are most likely to occur between 3 p.m. and 9 p.m., but can occur at any time.

If you are under a tornado WARNING, seek shelter immediately!

If you are:	Then:
In a structure (e.g. residence, small building, school, nursing home, hospital, factory, shopping center, high-rise building)	Go to a pre-designated shelter area such as a safe room, basement, storm cellar, or the lowest building level. If there is no basement, go to the center of an interior room on the lowest level (e.g. closet, interior hallway) away from corners, windows, doors, and outside walls. Get under a sturdy table and use your arms to protect your head and neck. Do not open windows.
Outside with no shelter	Lie flat in a nearby ditch or depression and cover your head with your hands. Be aware of the potential for flooding. Do not get under an overpass or bridge. You are safer in a low, flat location. Never try to outrun a tornado in urban or congested areas in a car or truck. Instead, leave the vehicle immediately for safe place. Watch out for flying debris. Flying debris from tornadoes causes most fatalities and injuries.

⇒設問は次ページにあります。

問1　本文中の下線部の transparent と同じような意味を表す語を本文中から抜き出しなさい。

問2　次の図は地下室の無い一軒家の見取り図です。本文によると①～⑥の中で竜巻が発生した際の避難場所として最も適切な場所はどこかを選びなさい。また，その根拠となる一文を本文から探して最初の2つの単語を抜き出して書きなさい。

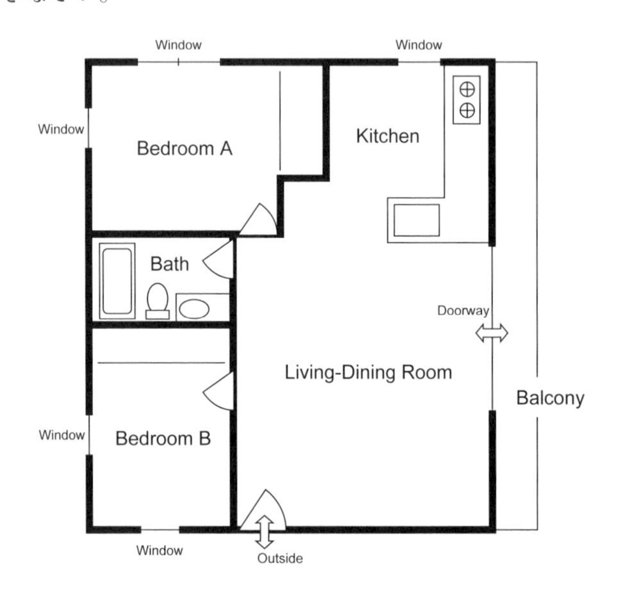

① Bedroom A　　② Bath　　③ Bedroom B
④ Kitchen　　⑤ Living-Dining Room　　⑥ Balcony

問3　次の英文の内容が，本文の内容と合致している場合には○を，合致していない場合には×をつけなさい。

① Sometimes tornadoes hit before a warning can be issued.
② Most tornadoes have no connection with other natural disasters.
③ It is impossible to know exactly which course a tornado will take.
④ Tornadoes arise most frequently early in the morning.
⑤ Vehicles may help you to escape from tornadoes in urban areas.
⑥ Broken objects caught in tornadoes can cause injuries.

Lesson 8

伝統は残すべき?

今回はアメリカ人が英語に関するとあることに対して，歴史を遡って考察する興味深い英文です。
また，5問中4問が「説明問題」になっています。漠然と解く人が多い説明問題にも，きちんとした解き方がありますので，正しい解法を身につけていきましょう。さらに，これまでに学んできた「イコール表現」や「具体例の発見方法」の確認にもうってつけの問題です。

目標
⇒説明問題を攻略しよう！

語数：541語　　**出題校**：九州大学

Lesson 8

試験本番での目標時間 25分　この本での目標時間 33分

▶解答・解説 本冊 p.134

Read the following passage and answer the questions below.

(1) It's a familiar complaint. Parents lament that technology is turning good, clear handwriting into a lost art form for their kids. In response, lawmakers in state after state — particularly in the South — are making time in classrooms to keep the graceful loops of cursive writing*1 alive for the next generation. Alabama passed a law requiring it in 2016. That same year, Louisiana passed its own cursive law. Others like Arkansas, Virginia, California, Florida and North Carolina, have similar laws. Texas is the latest state in which educators are pushing to bring back cursive writing in elementary schools. Each state's curriculum differs in subtle ways. (2) The guideline described in the Texas Education Code, for instance, includes requirements for instruction to begin with teaching second-graders how to form cursive letters with the "appropriate strokes when connecting letters." Third-graders would focus on writing complete words, thoughts, and answers to questions, and fourth-graders would need to be able to complete their assignments outright in cursive.

Anne Trubek, the author of "The History and Uncertain Future of Handwriting," told CNN*2 that efforts to emphasize cursive have been ongoing "for years." And debates about whether we should preserve handwriting in general are not strictly modern phenomena, as various periods in history featured disagreements between (3) historical traditionalists and those who favored new writing and communication technologies. In ancient Greece, Socrates had strongly opposed writing, a form of communication perceived new at that time, Trubek noted. The philosopher preferred the Greeks' oral tradition and felt those who didn't write things down would preserve a "better memory," she said. Later, religious scholars in the Middle Ages protested against the invention of the printing press, which threatened to make their beautiful, hand-copied texts out of date. As inventions like the printing press and the Internet throw humanity forward, "there will be a loss," Trubek said.

In the history of handwriting, we're in a unique place in which most Americans alive learned cursive writing, and efforts to spread cursive again among a new generation of youth represent a new "reaction" to ongoing change, she said. Today, (4) debates in favor of cursive take the form of "tradition strangely joined with patriotism," she said, noting that some lawmakers complained that if students didn't learn how to write in cursive, then they wouldn't be able to read the Declaration of Independence. Trubek, who is also a professor at Oberlin College, said she herself can't read the original flowing script of the Declaration of Independence, and there was nothing wrong with students reading the nation's founding documents in typed versions with fonts readable to modern eyes.

Trubek also said students didn't necessarily need cursive to come up with their own signature that gives them their "individuality" and "uniqueness" in signing legal forms either. She said technologies like the chips in credit cards were more effective in preventing crimes than pen-and-paper signatures that can be faked. "I don't think children should be required to learn cursive if they don't want to," Trubek said.

But, still, Trubek said being careful and thoughtful has its virtues. "It's a fine motor skill," and taking time to skillfully perfect the art has positive effects on students' cognitive development. "Handwriting is slower," she said, "And sometimes you just want to slow down."

Notes :

*1 cursive writing : a style of handwriting where the characters written in sequence are joined. An example is given below.

Cursive writing

*2 CNN (Cable News Network) : a broadcasting company in the United States which specializes in news delivery

Q1. Explain in Japanese what a "familiar complaint" in underlined part (1) refers to.

Q2. Regarding underlined part (2), summarize in Japanese the cursive writing curriculum for second-graders in Texas.

Q3. Give two examples of "historical traditionalists" in underlined part (3), and explain why each of them was reluctant to accept a new form of communication. Answer these questions in Japanese.

Q4. Regarding underlined part (4), identify the specific debate related to patriotism and describe it in Japanese.

Q5. Choose the one statement which best summarizes Trubek's opinion. Write the number (①, ②, ③, or ④) of your choice.

① The lack of cursive writing skill is very serious because American students need at least to learn how to read the US founding documents.

② Historical arguments have stressed the importance of inventing and teaching a new handwriting skill to young children.

③ It is not necessary to require all the students to learn cursive writing, while acquiring it can have some positive impacts.

④ Signatures in cursive can give more authenticity to legal forms than advanced technologies such as credit card chips.

Lesson 9

本当の「アメリカンドリーム」とは?

皆さんは「アメリカンドリーム」と聞いたら，何を思い浮かべますか？　今回の英文では，多くの受験生が想像する意味とは異なる「本来のアメリカンドリーム」を説明してくれます。アメリカ史は昔から入試長文で定番のテーマです。「独立の歴史」などの出題頻度は減りましたが，今回は「価値観」といった異なる側面からアプローチする英文です。
実は本書の中でもかなり難しい英文なのですが，設問の考え方は基本的かつ重要なものばかりです。Lesson 6で学んだルール「消えたbutにどうやって気づくか？」がポイントになるとてもよい素材です。正解率は気にしなくて大丈夫ですので，今できる力をすべて使ってトライしてみてください。

目標
⇒「消えたbut」に気づいて，「主張・対比」を把握する！

語数：963語　　**出題校：法政大学**

Lesson 9

試験本番での目標時間 28 分　この本での目標時間 38 分　▶解答・解説 本冊 p.150

次の英文を読んで，設問に答えなさい。

James Truslow Adams coined the phrase "American dream" in his 1931 book *The Epic of America*, which he published in the depths of the Great Depression*1. Adams argued for a view of the American dream that〔　A　〕of his time: "It is not a dream of motor car and high wages merely, but a dream of social order in which each man and each woman shall be able to attain to the fullest stature of which they are innately capable, and be recognized by others for what they are,〔　B　〕."

For people to realize the potential they were born with: this was the original concept of the American dream. It was not about becoming rich or famous; it was about having the opportunity〔　C　〕, and being appreciated for who you are as an individual, not because of your type or rank. Though America was one of the first places where this was a possibility for many of its citizens, the dream is not limited to any one country or people; it is a universal dream that we all share. And this dream has been corrupted by what I call "averagarianism," the idea that individuals can be evaluated, sorted, and managed by comparing them to the average.

Adams originally coined his term in direct response to the growing influence of Frederick Winslow Taylor's theory of scientific management, which valued efficient systems but gave "no regard for the individuals to whom alone any system could mean anything." For Adams, Taylor's view of the world was not only altering the fabric of society, but it was altering the way people viewed themselves and one another, the way they determined their priorities, and the way they defined the meaning of success. As averagarianism reshaped the educational system and workplace, the American dream came to signify〔　D　〕and changed into a belief that even the lowliest of citizens could climb to the top of the economic ladder.

It is easy to see why this shift in values occurred, and it is not nearly as straightforward as simple materialism. We all feel the weight of the one-dimensional thinking that has spread so widely in our averagarian culture: a standardized educational system that always sorts and ranks us; a workplace that hires us based on these educational rankings, then frequently imposes new rankings at every annual economic performance; a society that gives out rewards, esteem, and praise according to our professional ranking. When we look up at these artificial and meaningless steps that we are expected to climb, we worry that we might not fully ascend them and that we will be denied those opportunities that (1) <u>are only afforded to those who muscle their way up the one-dimensional ladder.</u>

We worry that if we, or our children, are labeled "different," we will have no chance of succeeding in school and will be destined to a life on the lower position. We worry that if we do not attend a leading school and earn high grades, the employers we want to work for may not even look at us. We worry that if we answer a personality test in the wrong way, we may not get the job we want. (2) <u>We live in a world that 〔 1 〕〔 2 〕〔 3 〕 the 〔 4 〕〔 5 〕〔 6 〕 else, only better,</u> and reduces the American dream to a narrow ambition to be *relatively* better than the people around us, rather than the best version of ourselves.

The principles of individuality present a way to restore the original meaning of the American dream — and, even better, the chance for everyone to attain it. If we overcome the barriers of one-dimensional thinking, if we demand that social institutions value individuality over the average, then (3) <u>〔 1 〕〔 2 〕〔 3 〕 we 〔 4 〕〔 5 〕〔 6 〕 opportunity,</u> but also we will change the way we think about success — not in terms of how different we are from the average, but of how close we are 〔 E 〕.

We are not talking about a future utopia; we are talking about a practical reality that is already happening all around us today. Our healthcare system is moving toward personalized medicine. Competency-based evaluation is being tried out — successfully — at leading universities. In the evaluation, instead of awarding grades for never being absent in a course, completing all your homework on time, and getting an A on your midterm exam, credits*2 would be given if, and only if, you demonstrate competency in the relevant skills, abilities, and knowledge needed for the fulfillment of that particular course. Enterprises that have committed themselves to valuing the individual are achieving global success, like Costco, Zoho, and Morning Star. These are the places that provide us with a glimpse of what designing a flexible system fit for all will actually look like. It's time for *all* institutions to embrace individuality and adopt this relationship between people and the system as the necessary principle to restore the dream.

The ideal that we call the American dream is one that we all once shared — the dream of becoming the best we can be, on our own terms, and of living a life of excellence as we define it. It's a dream worth striving for and while it will be difficult to achieve, it has never been closer to becoming a reality than it is right now. We no longer need to be limited by the constraints imposed on us by the Age of Average. We can break free of the rule of averagarianism by choosing to value individuality over conformity to the rigid system. We have a bright future before us, and it begins where the average ends.

語注 ＊1 the Great Depression 世界大恐慌　＊2 credits 学習要件を満たしたことを証明する単位

問1 空所〔 A 〕，〔 B 〕，〔 C 〕，〔 D 〕，〔 E 〕に入る最も適切なものを，次の①～④からそれぞれ1つずつ選びなさい。

〔 A 〕
① amounted to more than the materialism
② denied any materialistic success
③ illustrated the materialism
④ promoted the materialistic culture

〔 B 〕
① according to the position privileged by their birth
② based on their birth as well as their inherited social status
③ because of the dream which was a product of their birth and position
④ regardless of the circumstances of their birth or position

〔 C 〕
① of demonstrating your acquired skills
② of reflecting on your learned abilities
③ to develop all your possibilities
④ to suppress your whole potential

〔 D 〕
① less individual attachment
② less personal fulfillment
③ more distinct individuality
④ more unique subjectivity

〔　E　〕 ① to the model popularized in our culture
② to the principles of individuality approved in our society
③ to the one-dimensional thinking we created by ourselves
④ to the standard we set for ourselves

問2　下線部（1）are only afforded to those who muscle their way up the one-dimensional ladder の内容に最も近いものを，次の①〜④から1つ選びなさい。

① are only given to the people who have enough physical strength to move up the one-dimensional ladder
② are only given to the people who push other people out of their way in moving up the one-dimensional ladder
③ are only granted to those who can build the one-dimensional ladder that they want to climb
④ are only granted to those who want to become more muscular by climbing the one-dimensional ladder

問3　下線部（2）We live in a world that〔　1　〕〔　2　〕〔　3　〕the〔　4　〕〔　5　〕〔　6　〕else の空所に当てはまる語を，次の①〜⑥から選びなさい。ただし，解答は〔　3　〕と〔　5　〕に入る語の記号のみを，それぞれ書きなさい。各語は1回しか使用できない。

① be　② as　③ demands　④ same　⑤ everyone　⑥ we

問4　下線部（3）〔　1　〕〔　2　〕〔　3　〕we〔　4　〕〔　5　〕〔　6　〕opportunity の空所に当てはまる語を，次の①〜⑥から選びなさい。ただし，解答は〔　3　〕と〔　5　〕に入る語の記号のみを，それぞれ書きなさい。各語は1回しか使用できない。

① have　② will　③ individual　④ not　⑤ more　⑥ only

⇒設問は次ページに続きます。

問5　本文の内容に合致するものを，次の①〜④から1つ選びなさい。

① Adams created the phrase "American dream" in order to support Taylor's theory that argued for the importance of individuals working in efficient systems.

② The one-dimensional thinking widespread in our culture of averagarianism has kept us from becoming the best we could possibly be.

③ Competency-based evaluation implies that class attendance and homework are the most important factors for awarding grades.

④ The end of the Age of Average depends on whether or not we can set up a new style of averagarianism, which is being tested in several fields.

Lesson 10

「話が上手い」って何だろう?

最近の入試では世界の変化を反映した新しいテーマがよく出ますが，昔から変わらず超頻出なのが「言語論」です。世の中が変化しても言語がコミュニケーションの基盤であることに変わりはなく，今後も出題され続けるでしょう。さらに，今回テーマになる「つなぎ言葉・言いよどみ」は実は入試頻出テーマで，たとえば似た内容が立教大学の問題などでも出ています。
今回の英文は，内容・設問ともに「着実に読む訓練」として最適です。特に「代名詞の特定」がポイントになる問題が3問もあります。代名詞の解法をきちんと学んでいない受験生が多いので，「普段から代名詞を確実に特定しながら読む」という姿勢をこのLessonで身につけていきます。

目標
⇒「主張と具体例」「対比」に加えて，「代名詞」を正しく把握する

語数：814語　　**出題校**：立命館大学

Lesson 10

試験本番での目標時間 25分　この本での目標時間 32分　▶解答・解説 本冊 p.168

次の英文を読んで，設問に答えなさい。

Imagine standing up to give a speech in front of an audience. While you are speaking, someone in the room uses a clicker to count your every stumble and hesitation — every one of your *ums* and *uhs**1. Once you've finished, this person loudly announces how many of these have spoiled your presentation. (ア) This is the method used by the Toastmasters public-speaking club*2. As part of the training, one person has the job of counting the speaker's *uhs*. The club's measures may be extreme, but they reflect the folk wisdom that *ums* and *uhs* are the mark of a nervous, ignorant, and careless speaker, and should be〔　A　〕at all costs. Many scientists, though, think our cultural obsession*3 with eliminating what they call "disfluencies*4" is〔　B　〕. Saying *um* is no weakness of character, but a natural feature of speech; far from distracting listeners, there's evidence that it focuses their attention in ways that improve comprehension.

Disfluencies arise mainly because of the〔　C　〕speakers face. Speakers have to talk and think at the same time, launching into speech with only a vague sense of how a sentence will unfold, confident that by the time they've finished the earlier parts of the sentence, they'll have worked out exactly what to say in the later parts. Mostly the timing works out, but occasionally it takes longer than expected to〔　D　〕. Saying *um* is the speaker's way of signaling that processing is still going on. People sometimes have more disfluencies while speaking in public, ironically*5, because they are trying hard not to make mistakes.

Since disfluencies show that a speaker is thinking carefully about what she is about to say, they provide useful information to listeners, helping them to focus attention on what's being said. One famous example comes from the movie *Jurassic Park*. When Jeff Goldblum's character is asked whether a group of only female animals can breed, he replies, "No, I'm ..., I'm simply saying that life, uh ... finds a way." The disfluencies emphasize that he's coming to grips with*6 something not easy to explain — an idea that turns out to be a key part of the movie.

Experiments with *ums* or *uhs* either added to or taken out of speech show that when words are accompanied by disfluencies, listeners recognize (イ) them faster and remember them more accurately. In some cases, disfluencies allow listeners to make useful predictions about what they're about to hear.

Disfluencies can also improve our comprehension of longer pieces of content. Psychologists Scott Fraundorf and Duane Watson experimented with recordings of a speaker retelling passages from *Alice's Adventures in Wonderland* and compared how well listeners remembered versions from which all disfluencies had been removed as opposed to ones that contained an average number of *ums* and *uhs*. They found that hearers remembered details better after listening to 〔 E 〕. Stripping a speech of *ums* and *uhs*, as Toastmasters aim to do, appears to be doing listeners no favors.

Moreover, there's reason to question the assumption that disfluencies reveal a speaker's lack of knowledge. In a study led by Kathryn Womack, experienced physicians and newly qualified doctors looked at images of various skin conditions while talking their way to a diagnosis*7. Not surprisingly, the expert doctors were more accurate in their diagnoses than the new doctors. They also produced more complex sentences, and a greater number of disfluencies, calling into question the idea that disfluencies reflect a lack of control over one's material. 〔 F 〕, the authors of the study suggest that the experienced doctors had more disfluent speech because they had a larger body of knowledge to work with and were constructing more detailed explanations while planning their speech.

If disfluencies appear to help communication, why are they so stigmatized*8? Language expert Michael Erard argues in his book *Um ...* that historically, public speakers were unconcerned with disfluencies until the 20th century — possibly because neither hearers nor speakers consciously noticed them until it became possible to record and replay spoken language. The aversion*9 to disfluencies may well have arisen from speakers' horror at hearing their own recorded voices.

Perhaps there's an argument to be made that public speaking is different from day-to-day communication. It's (ウ) a performance in which the speaker is meant to demonstrate mastery over language and make speaking look easy precisely because of the absence of signals like disfluencies that reveal its complexity. Maybe so. But the removal of *ums* should be recognized for what it is — a display focused on presenting the speaker in a favorable light — and not a kindness directed at the listener. In fact, designers of synthesized*10 voice systems have begun adding naturalistic disfluencies into artificial speech. It's an irony of our age that robots, unconcerned with ego, may be busy putting disfluencies into their speech just as humans, occupied with their self-images, are undergoing tough training to (エ) take them out.

語注 ＊1 um/uh うーん，えーっと　＊2 Toastmasters public-speaking club トーストマスターズクラブ（パブリックスピーチや話し方，リーダーシップスキルの上達を目的とする世界的な団体）
＊3 obsession 強迫観念　＊4 disfluency 流ちょうでないこと，言いよどみ
＊5 ironically 皮肉なことに　＊6 come to grips with ～ ～に取り組む　＊7 diagnosis 診断
＊8 stigmatized 非難された　＊9 aversion 嫌悪感　＊10 synthesized 合成された

問1 本文の〔 A 〕～〔 F 〕それぞれに入れるのに最も適当なものを①～④から1つ選びなさい。

〔 A 〕 ① avoided　② ignored　③ practiced　④ preserved

〔 B 〕 ① deeply mistaken　② fundamentally important
③ only natural　④ sometimes forgotten

〔 C 〕 ① comprehension difficulties　② general criticism
③ lengthy training　④ time pressures

〔 D 〕 ① check for disfluencies　② find the right phrase
③ read to the end　④ remember the time

〔 E 〕 ① a better recording
② *Alice's Adventures in Wonderland*
③ the disfluent versions
④ the story without *ums* and *uhs*

〔 F 〕 ① For instance　② Nevertheless
③ On the contrary　④ On the other hand

問2　下線部（**ア**）～（**エ**）それぞれの意味または内容として，最も適当なものを①～④から1つ選びなさい。

（**ア**）　This

① Loudly announcing presentations
② Strictly monitoring *ums* and *uhs*
③ Speaking in front of an audience
④ Using a clicker to help time a speech

（**イ**）　them

① words
② *ums* or *uhs*
③ disfluencies
④ experiments

（**ウ**）　a performance

① an argument
② public speaking
③ mastery over language
④ day-to-day communication

（**エ**）　take them out

① improve their self-images
② speak without disfluencies
③ create better forms of artificial speech
④ develop robots who express themselves like humans

Lesson 11

我々は本当に幼少期の記憶がないのか?

科学技術が発達した現在でも,「脳」に関する謎は尽きません。脳は「言語・思考・記憶・心」など様々な分野とかかわるため，いろいろな切り口の英文が出題されます。
今回の英文は，今まで習得してきた様々なルールを少し抽象的な英文で使いこなすためのよい練習になります。「過去と現在の対比」「因果表現」「具体例の発見方法」「〈this + 名詞〉の考え方」「名詞構文」など，ポイントが盛りだくさんです。「ルールが実際に使えるか？」も意識しながらトライしましょう。

目標

⇒「対比関係」を正しく把握する！

語数：851語　　**出題校**：立命館大学

Lesson 11

試験本番での目標時間 25分　この本での目標時間 32分 ▶解答・解説 本冊 p.186

次の英文を読んで，設問に答えなさい。

Think back to your earliest memory. Perhaps images of a birthday party or scenes from a family vacation come to mind. Now think about your age when that event occurred. Chances are that your earliest recollection extends no further back than your third birthday. In fact, most adults can probably come up with no more than a handful of memories from between the ages of 3 and 7 — although family photo albums or other things may trigger more — and most likely none before that. Psychologists refer to (ア) this inability of most adults to remember events from early life, including their birth, as childhood amnesia*1.

For a long time, the theory behind childhood amnesia rested on the assumption that the memory-making parts of babies' brains were undeveloped, and that around age 3, children's memory capabilities rapidly developed to adult levels. 〔　A　〕, psychologists have recently discovered that children as young as 3 months old and 6 months old can form long-term memories. The difference lies in which memories stay with us. For instance, it appears that babies are born with more implicit*2, or unconscious, memories. At the same time, the explicit*3 memory that records specific events does not carry information over that three-year gap, explaining why people do not remember their births. But why does this happen and what changes take place in those first years? And if we can form memories as babies, why don't we retain them into adulthood? Let's look at some of the research.

Recent studies have largely 〔　B　〕 the long-held thinking that babies cannot encode*4 information that forms the foundation of memories. For instance, in one experiment involving 2- and 3-month-old infants, the babies' legs were attached by a ribbon to a mobile, a toy that hung above the baby's bed. By kicking their legs, the babies learned that the motion caused the mobile to move. Later, placed under the same mobile without the ribbon, the infants remembered to kick their legs. When (イ) the same experiment was performed with 6-month-olds, they picked up the kicking relationship much more quickly, indicating that their encoding ability must develop 〔　C　〕 instead of in one significant burst around 3 years old.

This memory encoding could relate to a baby's development of the prefrontal cortex*5 at the forehead. This area, which is active during the encoding and retrieval*6 of explicit memories, is not fully functional at birth. However, by 24 months, the number of synapses*7 in the prefrontal cortex has reached adult levels. Also, the size of the hippocampus*8 at the base of the brain steadily grows until your second or third year. (ウ) This is important because the hippocampus determines what sensory*9 information to transfer into long-term storage.

But what about implicit memory? It is essential for newborns, allowing them to associate feelings of warmth and safety with the sound of their mother's voice, and to instinctively know how to feed. Confirming this early presence, studies have revealed few developmental changes in unconscious memory as we age. Even in many adult amnesia cases, implicit skills such as riding a bicycle or playing a piano often survive the brain damage. Now we know that babies have a strong implicit memory and can encode explicit ones as well, which indicates that childhood amnesia may stem from faulty explicit memory retrieval. However, unless we're thinking specifically about a past event, it takes something to 〔 D 〕 an explicit memory in all age groups.

Our earliest memories may remain blocked from our consciousness because we had no 〔 E 〕 at that time. A 2004 study traced the verbal development in 27- and 39-month-old boys and girls as a measure of how well they could recall a past event. The researchers found that if the children didn't know the words to describe the event when it happened, they couldn't 〔 F 〕 it later after learning the appropriate words.

Expressing our personal memories of events in words contributes to our autobiographical memories*10. Memories of these types help to define our sense of self and our relationship to people around us. Closely linked to (エ) this is the ability to recognize yourself. Some researchers have proposed that children do not develop self-recognition skills and a personal identity until 16 or 24 months. In addition, we develop knowledge of our personal past when we begin to organize memories into a context of time and place. Many preschool-age children can explain the different parts of an event in sequence, such as what happened when they went to a circus. But it isn't until their fifth year that they can understand the ideas of time and the past, and are able to place that trip to the circus on a mental time line.

Parents play a central role in developing children's autobiographical memory as well. Research has shown that the way parents verbally recall memories with their small children influences their style for retelling memories later in life.

〔　G　〕, children whose parents tell them about past events in detail, such as birthday parties or trips to the zoo, will be more likely to vividly describe their own memories when they grow up.

語注　＊1 amnesia 記憶喪失　＊2 implicit 潜在的な　＊3 explicit 顕在的な
＊4 encode 記号化する，意味づけをする　＊5 prefrontal cortex　前頭前野（額の内側にある脳の中枢部）　＊6 retrieval 取り戻すこと，回復　＊7 synapse シナプス（神経細胞の連接部）
＊8 hippocampus 海馬（脳の記憶形成に関与する部位）　＊9 sensory 感覚の，知覚の
＊10 autobiographical memory 自分についての記憶

問1　本文の〔　A　〕～〔　G　〕それぞれに入れるのに最も適当なものを①～④から1つ選びなさい。

〔　A　〕 ① Consequently　② Evidently　③ However　④ Moreover

〔　B　〕 ① ignored　② recognized　③ rejected　④ supported

〔　C　〕 ① as fast as possible
② as soon as they are born
③ before they are 3 months old
④ gradually with time

〔　D　〕 ① block　② eliminate　③ form　④ trigger

〔　E　〕 ① childhood experiences　② ideas
③ interest　④ language skills

〔　F　〕 ① explain　② invent　③ plan　④ reject

〔　G　〕 ① Besides　② In other words
③ Nevertheless　④ On the other hand

問2 下線部（**ア**）～（**エ**）それぞれの意味または内容として，最も適当なものを①～④から1つ選びなさい。

（**ア**） this inability
① the inability to recall our first experiences
② the inability to express memories in words
③ the inability to use photo albums to help with memory
④ the inability to remember special events throughout life

（**イ**） the same experiment
① testing whether babies can kick their legs when in bed
② testing whether babies needed a ribbon to move a mobile
③ testing whether babies can pull a ribbon connected to a toy
④ testing whether babies can relate kicking with moving a mobile

（**ウ**） This
① The functioning of specific memories
② The development of implicit memory
③ The number of synapses in the brain
④ The growth of a key part of the brain

（**エ**） this
① making contact with people around us
② teaching children appropriate vocabulary
③ identifying who we are in connection to others
④ defining our personal memories to describe past events

Lesson 12

「貧困」と「不平等」ではどっちが問題?

世界中で貧富の差はますます拡大しており，OXFAM Internationalの報告Public Good or Private Wealth?（January 21, 2019）によると「世界の富裕層トップ26人の資産の合計は，世界人口の下位50％（約38億人）の資産総額とほぼ同じ」だそうです。現代において「経済格差」は避けられない問題であり，入試でもよく出題されます。さらに，今回は「サルの実験」の話から普遍的な話題に展開していますが，これはCNN（アメリカのニュースチャンネル）でもまったく同じ実験の話，そして同じ展開で報道されたことがある，実は知っておくべきテーマなんです。
本書の最後を締めくくる早稲田大学の問題でも，本書で学んできたルールで攻略できることを実感してほしいと思います。さらに今回はchallengeや命令文など，「ちょっとした語句」に反応することで，「深く正しく読める」ルールを習得していきます。

目標
⇒「ちょっとした語句」が実は重要

語数：892語　　**出題校：早稲田大学**

Lesson 12

試験本番での目標時間 24分　この本での目標時間 36分

▶解答・解説 本冊 p.203

Read this article and answer the questions below.

Monkeys were taught in an experiment to hand over small stones in exchange for cucumber slices. They were happy with this deal.

Then the researcher randomly offered one monkey — within sight of a second monkey — an even better deal: a grape for a stone. Monkeys love grapes, so this fellow was thrilled.

The researcher then returned to the second monkey, but presented just some cucumber for the pebble. Now, this offer was insulting. Some monkeys would throw the cucumber back at the researcher in anger and disgust.

In other words, the monkeys cared deeply about fairness. What mattered to them was not just what they received but also what others got.

It is not only monkeys that are offended by inequality. For example, two scholars examined data from millions of flights to identify what factors resulted in "air rage" incidents, in which passengers become angry or even violent. One huge factor: a first-class cabin.

An incident in an economy section was four times as likely if the plane also had a first-class cabin; a first-class section increased the risk of a disturbance as much as a nine-hour delay did. (　A　)

Keith Payne, a professor of psychology at the University of North Carolina at Chapel Hill, tells of this research in a brilliant new book, *The Broken Ladder*, about how inequality destabilizes societies. It's an important, fascinating work arguing that inequality creates a public-health crisis in America.

The data on inequality reveals the shocking truth. The top 1 percent in America owns more than the bottom 90 percent. The annual Wall Street bonus pool alone is more than the annual year-round earnings of all Americans working full time at the minimum wage of $7.25 an hour, according to the Institute for Policy Studies. And what's becoming clearer is the weakening of the ties that hold society together.

Payne challenges a common perception that the real problem isn't inequality but poverty, and he's persuasive that societies are shaped not just by disadvantage at the bottom but also by inequality across the spectrum. Addressing inequality must be a priority, for we humans are social creatures, so society begins to break down when we see some receiving grapes and others cucumbers.

The breakdown affects not only those at the bottom, but also the lucky ones at the top. Consider baseball: Some team owners pay players a much wider range of salaries than others do, and one might think that pay inequality creates incentives for better performance and more wins.

In fact, economists have analyzed the data and (B). Teams with greater equality did much better, perhaps because the players felt a closer bond with each other.

What's more, it turned out that even the stars did better when they were on teams with flatter pay. "Higher inequality seemed to have a negative effect on the superstar players it was meant to motivate, which is what you would expect if you believed that the chief effect of pay inequality was to reduce cooperation and team unity," Payne notes.

Something similar emerges in national statistics. Countries with the widest gaps in income, including the United States, generally have worse health, more killings, and a greater range of social problems.

People seem to understand this truth instinctively, for they want much less inequality than we have. In a study of people in 40 countries, liberals said company presidents should be paid four times as much as the average worker, while conservatives said five times. In fact, the average president at the largest American public companies earns about 350 times as much as the average worker.

Presented with unlabeled charts depicting income distributions of two countries, 92 percent of Americans said they would prefer to live with the modest inequality that exists in Sweden. Republicans and Democrats, rich and poor alike, all chose Sweden by similar margins.

"When the level of inequality becomes too large to ignore, everyone starts acting strange," Payne notes. "Inequality affects our actions and our feelings in the same systematic, predictable fashion again and again."

"It makes us believe odd things, superstitiously clinging to the world as we want it to be (C)," he says. "Inequality divides us, splitting us into camps not only of income but also of ideology and race, eating away at our trust in one another. It generates stress and makes us all less healthy and less happy."

Think of those words in the context of politics today: Don't the terms "stress," "division," and "unhappiness" sound familiar?

So much of the national conversation gets focused on individuals such as

Donald Trump — for understandable reasons. But I suspect that such people are a symptom as well as a cause, and that to uncover the root of these problems we must go deeper than politics, deeper than poverty, deeper than race, and confront the inequality that is America today.

(*Adapted from https://www.nytimes.com/2017/06/ 03/opinion/sunday/ what-monkeys-can-teach-us-about-fairness.html*)

Q1. Choose the most suitable answer from those below to complete the following sentence.

The monkeys that threw slices of cucumber back at the researcher

① disliked the type of cucumbers they were being given.
② failed to understand the importance of fairness.
③ felt upset that other monkeys were getting better treatment.
④ had no more stones they could throw at the researcher.
⑤ thought the researcher wanted to have them.

Q2. Choose the most suitable order of sentences from those below to fill in blank space (A).

① However, in some flights, they get on in the middle of the plane.
② Looking at these two scenarios, the researchers found that an air-rage incident in economy was three times as likely when economy passengers had to walk through first class compared with when they bypassed it.
③ When there is a first-class section, it is at the front of the plane, and economy passengers typically walk through it to reach their seats.

Q3. Choose the most suitable answer from those below to complete the following sentence.

Keith Payne suggests that we are mistaken to think that

① data regarding matters of inequality accurately reflects the true situation.
② earning the minimum wage will strengthen family relationships.
③ humans can best be described as social creatures.
④ poverty is the reason for the weakening of social ties.
⑤ the disadvantage of being poor changes our perception of the value of food.

Q4. Choose the most suitable answer from those below to fill in blank space (B).

① discovered that the owners were right
② found that the opposite was true
③ revealed that this helped to raise wages
④ saw little value in their findings
⑤ were unable to establish a relationship

Q5. Use six of the seven words below to fill in blank space (C) in the best way. Indicate your choices for **the second, fourth, and sixth** positions.

① is　② it　③ rather　④ so　⑤ than　⑥ the　⑦ way

Q6. Choose the most suitable answer from those below to complete the following sentence.

The writer concludes that dealing with the problems he describes requires us to

① distinguish between the causes and symptoms of unhappiness.
② focus on how unequal American society has become.
③ increase the income of those at the bottom of society.
④ remove controversial individuals from public office.
⑤ understand the importance of racial tension in the U.S.

MEMO

出典一覧

Lesson 1：*The healthiest way to improve your sleep: exercise* by Sandee LaMotte, May 30, 2017. From CNN.com. Ⓒ 2017, Turner Broadcasting Systems, Inc.. All rights reserved. Used under license.　Lesson 2：*Deviate: The Science of Seeing Differently* by Beau Lotto, April 25, 2017 Ⓒ 2017, Beau Lotto, The Orion Publishing Group, London.　Lesson 3：*Transculture : Transcending Time, Region and Ethnicity* by Christopher Belton, Koshi Odashima（小田島 恒志）, March 1, 2017 © 2017, Christopher Belton, Koshi Odashima（小田島 恒志), 金星堂.　Lesson 4：*Pronunciation Myths: Applying Second Language Research to Classroom Teaching* by Linda Grant, February 21, 2014 Ⓒ 2014, Linda Grant, University of Michigan Press.　Lesson 5：*Why Communication Is Today's Most Important Skill* by Greg Satell, February 6, 2015. From Forbes. Ⓒ 2015, Forbes. All rights reserved. Used under license.　Lesson 6：*Are we really too busy to eat well?* by Bee Wilson, April 19, 2019 Ⓒ 2019, Financial Times.　Lesson 7：*Are You Ready? An In-depth Guide to Citizen Preparedness*, January 23, 2013 Ⓒ 2013, U.S. Department of Homeland Security, Federal Emergency Management Agency.　Lesson 8：*Cursive writing is making a comeback in classrooms in several states -- and Texas is the latest* by Ryan Prior, April 12, 2019. From CNN.com. Ⓒ 2019, Turner Broadcasting Systems, Inc.. All rights reserved. Used under license.　Lesson 9：From *The End of Average* by Todd Rose. Copyright Ⓒ 2016 by L. Todd Rose. Used by permission of Harper Collins Publishers.　Lesson 10：*Your Speech Is Packed With Misunderstood, Unconscious Messages* by Julie Sedivy. Originally published in Nautilus magazine on December 16, 2015.　Lesson 11：*Can a person remember being born?* by Cristen Conger, May 06, 2008. From HowStuffWorks.com. Ⓒ 2008 HowStuffWorks.com. All rights reserved. Used under license.　Lesson 12：*What Monkeys Can Teach Us About Fairness* by Nicholas Kristof, June 3, 2017. Ⓒ 2017, New York Times.

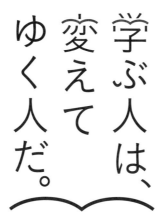

大学入試

関正生のThe Rules 英語長文問題集 3 入試難関

はじめに

長文読解に必要な3つの力をルールにまとめました

大学入試の長文読解には，3つの知的作業が求められると考えます。一文をしっかり把握する「構文力」，英文の展開を理解する「読解力」，設問の狙いを見抜いて解く「解法力」です。この3つの力は目新しいものではありません。しかしながらこの3つの力に関して，明確な手順・ルールに従って「読み・解き進めている」受験生はかなり少ないと思います。その場しのぎの作業で乗り切ってしまっているのではないでしょうか。

そういった場当たり的な勉強では，「英語力の経験値」が蓄積されないので，そのままでは，世間でよく聞く「たくさん長文やってるんだけど，どうも伸びない」という状態になってしまうのです。

「なんとなく読み解く」の対極が，「確固たるルールに基づいて読み解く」ことです。この本では，大学入試に出る長文対策として，僕の30年ほどの英語講師としての経験から練り上げ，極限まで洗練させた法則を“RULE”としてまとめました。

本書のタイトルで使われている，The Rulesは〈the＋複数形〉の形で，これを英文法の観点から解説すると，〈the＋複数形〉は「特定集団」を表すと言えます。昔はバンド名などによく使われました（The Beatlesなど）。また，the United States of America「アメリカ合衆国」は「(50の州が集まった）特定集団」ですし，the United Arab Emirates「アラブ首長国連邦（UAE)」は「ドバイなどの首長国が集まった特定集団」です。

本書のルールはその場しのぎのものではありません。僕自身が30年前から洗練させてきたもので，それが近年の問題でも通用することを本書の解説で証明していきます。英文を正しく読む，つまり英語の真の姿を理解するために受験で大活躍し，さらにその先でも使える，「厳選された，強力なルールの特定集団」という意味を持つのが，The Rulesです。

関 正生

Contents

関 正生 せき・まさお

1975年東京生まれ。埼玉県立浦和高校，慶應義塾大学文学部（英米文学専攻）卒業。TOEIC® L&Rテスト990点満点取得。現在はオンライン予備校『スタディサプリ』講師として，毎年，全国の中高生・大学受験生140万人以上に授業，全国放送CMで「英語の授業」を行う。著書に『英単語Stock3000』（文英堂），『英語長文ポラリス』（KADOKAWA），『サバイバル英文法』（NHK出版），『東大英語の核心』（研究社）など100冊以上。

編集協力：日本アイアール株式会社
校正：株式会社友人社，入江 泉，大河恭子，
Jason A. Chau
組版：日新印刷株式会社
録音：ユニバ合同会社
ナレーション：Ann Slater, Guy Perryman
装幀・本文デザイン：相馬敬徳（Rafters）
装幀写真撮影：曳野若菜
編集担当：須永亜希子

本書の特長

どのレベルでも使える長文読解のための「ルール」

学んだことは，試験本番で「再現」できないと意味がありません。本書で扱うルールは，大学や英文のレベル・問題形式を問わず再現性が高い，一生モノのルールです。

わかりやすい圧倒的な解説力

本書をスムーズに進めるために，そして入試問題を解くうえで必要十分な解説を施しました。これは実際に解説を読んでいただければすぐに実感できると思います。

解説でも英語力を高められる

解説中では，できるだけ本文から「英文」を引用していますので，本文に戻らずスムーズに解説を読めます。また，本シリーズ4つのうちレベル1・2では「英文と共に和訳」を入れますが（基礎力完成を目指す段階なので），レベル3・4では「英文のみ」です。これによって日本語を読んで理解した気になることがなくなり,「英語で考える」習慣が養成されます。

「思考力問題」対策も万全

具体的に「どういった思考を要するのか」を「ここが思考力！」のコーナーで解説しています（⇒「思考力を問う問題」について詳細はp.5）。

全文の「文構造の分析」と「音読用白文」

英文すべてに構文の解析をつけてありますので, 精読の練習としても使えます。また, 音読用の白文も用意しました（⇒音読と音声についての詳細はp.10，11）。

記述問題も豊富に収録

記述問題も多く採用しています。「自分の志望校には記述問題はないから」という受験生も，ぜひトライしてみてください。どれも「英語の実力」をつけるのに効果的なものばかりで，記述の力をつけておくと，マーク問題の精度も格段に上がります。

本書の使い方

❶まずは目標時間を意識して問題にトライ!

「この本での目標時間」を目指して問題を解いてみてください。その後, 時間を気にせず気になるところ，辞書で確認したいところなどにじっくり取り組むのも実力養成になります。

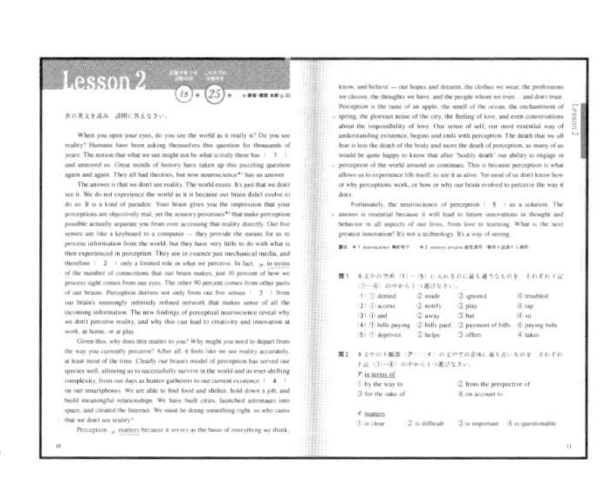

Lesson 2

15 分 25 分

次の英文を読み，設問に答えなさい。

When you open your eyes, do you see the world as it really is? Do you see reality? Humans have been asking themselves this question for thousands of years. The notion that what we see might not be what is truly there has （ 1 ） and annoyed us. Great minds of history have taken up this puzzling question again and again. They all had theories, but now neuroscience*1 has an answer.

The answer is that we don't see reality. The world exists. It's just that we don't see it. We do not experience the world as it is because our brain didn't evolve to do so. It is a kind of paradox: Your brain gives you the impression that your perceptions are objectively real, yet the sensory processes*2 that make perception possible actually separate you from ever accessing that reality directly. Our five senses are like a keyboard to a computer — they provide the means for us to process information from the world, but they have very little to do with what is then experienced in perception. They are in essence just mechanical media, and therefore （ 2 ） only a limited role in what we perceive. In fact, (ア) in terms of the number of connections that our brain makes, just 10 percent of how we process sight comes from our eyes. The other 90 percent comes from other parts of our brains. Perception derives not only from our five senses （ 3 ） from our brain's seemingly infinitely refined network that makes sense of all the incoming information. The new findings of perceptual neuroscience reveal why we don't perceive reality, and why this can lead to creativity and innovation at work, at home, or at play.

Given this, why does this matter to you? Why might you need to depart from the way you currently perceive? After all, it feels like we see reality accurately, at least most of the time. Clearly our brain's model of perception has served our species well, allowing us to successfully survive in the world and its ever-shifting complexity, from our days as hunter-gatherers to our current existence （ 4 ） on our smartphones. We are able to find food and shelter, hold down a job, and build meaningful relationships. We have built cities, launched astronauts into space, and created the Internet. We must be doing something right, so who cares that we don't see reality?

Perception (イ) matters because it serves as the basis of everything we think, know, and believe — our hopes and dreams, the clothes we wear, the professions we choose, the thoughts we have, and the people whom we trust ... and don't trust. Perception is the taste of an apple, the smell of the ocean, the enchantment of spring, the glorious noise of the city, the feeling of love, and even conversations about the impossibility of love. Our sense of self, our most essential way of understanding existence, begins and ends with perception. The death that we all fear is less the death of the body and more the death of perception, as many of us would be quite happy to know that after "bodily death" our ability to engage in perception of the world around us continues. This is because perception is what allows us to experience life itself, to see it as alive. Yet most of us don't know how or why perceptions work, or how or why our brain evolved to perceive the way it does.

Fortunately, the neuroscience of perception （ 5 ） us a solution. The answer is essential because it will lead to future innovations in thought and behavior in all aspects of our lives, from love to learning. What is the next greatest innovation? It's not a technology. It's a way of seeing.

語注 ＊1 neuroscience 神経科学　＊2 sensory process 感覚過程

問1 本文中の空所（1）～（5）に入れるのに最も適当なものを，それぞれ下記①～④の中から1つ選びなさい。

（1）①denied ②made ③ignored ④troubled
（2）①access ②notify ③play ④tap
（3）①and ②away ③but ④so
（4）①bills paying ②bills paid ③payment of bills ④paying bills
（5）①deprives ②helps ③offers ④takes

問2 本文中の下線部（ア）・（イ）の文中での意味に最も近いものを，それぞれ下記①～④の中から1つ選びなさい。

ア in terms of
①by the way to ②from the perspective of
③for the sake of ④on account to

イ matters
①is clear ②is difficult ③is important ④is questionable

10　11

❷解説をじっくりと読み，ルールを身に付ける！

正解した問題も，解説を読むことで，正しい考え方・解き方・補足事項などが身に付きます。解説中に出てくる長文読解のルール（⇒詳細はp.7）を自分のものにしていきましょう。

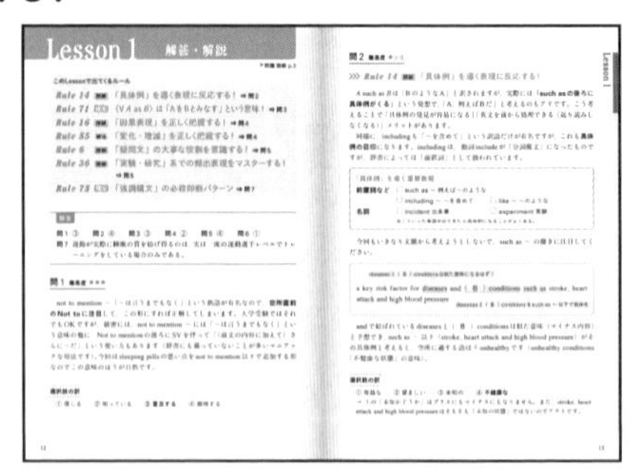

Lesson 1 解答・解説

このLessonで出てくるルール

Rule 14 「具体例」を導く表現に反応する！ ⇒問2
Rule 71 〈V A as B〉は「AをBとみなす」という意味！ ⇒問3
Rule 16 「因果表現」を正しく把握する！ ⇒問4
Rule 55 「変化・増減」を正しく把握する！ ⇒問4
Rule 6 「疑問文」の大事な役割を意識する！ ⇒問5
Rule 36 「実験・研究」系での頻出表現をマスターする！ ⇒問5
Rule 73 「強調構文」の必殺即断パターン ⇒問7

問1 ③　問2 ④　問3 ③　問4 ②　問5 ④　問6 ①

問1 難易度★★★

not to mention ～「～は言うまでもなく」という熟語が有名なので，[illegible]

問2 難易度★☆☆

>>> Rule 14 「具体例」を導く表現に反応する！

A such as B は「BのようなA」と訳されますが，実際には「such asの後ろに具体例がくる」という発想で，「A，例えばBだ」と考えるのもアリです。[illegible]

a key risk factor for diseases and (悪) conditions such as stroke, heart attack and high blood pressure

[illegible]

思考力……「思考力を問う問題」に付しています。

難易度★★★……設問ごとの難易度を，★～★★★の３段階で表示しています。

※難易度はあくまでそれぞれのレベルでターゲットとする大学を基準にしています。

❸「文構造の分析」で構文と語句をチェック！

わからない英文は，ここでじっくりと確認してください。

文構造の分析

1 [1] When you open your eyes, do you see the world as it really is? [2] Do you see reality? [3] Humans have been asking themselves this question for thousands of years. [4] The notion that what we see φ might not be what is truly there has troubled and annoyed us. [5] Great minds of history have taken up this puzzling question again and again. [6] They all had theories, but now neuroscience has an answer.

[illegible]

as it really is ありのままに／notion 名 考え／trouble 動 困らせる／annoy 動 悩ませる／mind 名（特定の分野において）聡明な人／take up 取り上げる／puzzling 形 難解な [illegible]

[illegible]

2 [1] The answer is that we don't see reality. [2] The world exists. [3] It's just that we don't see it. [4] We do not experience the world as it is because our brain didn't evolve to do so. [5] It is a kind of paradox: Your brain gives you the impression that your perceptions are objectively real, yet the sensory processes that make perception possible actually separate you from ever accessing that reality directly. [6] Our five senses are like a keyboard to a computer — they provide the means for us to process information from the world, but they have very little to do with what is then experienced in perception. [7] They are in essence just mechanical media, and therefore play only a limited role in what we perceive φ. [8] In fact, in terms of the number of connections that our brain makes φ, just 10 percent of how we process sight comes from our eyes. [9] The other 90 percent comes from other parts of our brains. [10] Perception derives not only from our five senses but from our brain's seemingly infinitely refined network that makes sense of all the incoming information. [11] The new findings of perceptual neuroscience reveal why we don't perceive reality, and why this can lead to creativity and innovation at work, at home, or at play.

[illegible]

exist 動 存在する／It's just that S V ただS Vなだけだ／experience 動 経験する，知覚する／evolve 動 進化する／paradox 名 パラドックス，逆説，矛盾 [illegible]／impression 名 印象／perception 名 知覚，認識／objectively 副 客観的に／yet 接 しかし／sensory 形 感覚［知覚］上の／process 名 過程，処理／separate A from B AをBから引き離す／access 動 到達する，アクセスする／five senses 五感 [illegible]／means 名 手段，方法／process 動 処理する／have little to do with ～ ～とはとんど関係がない／in essence 本質的には／media (medium の複数形) 名 媒体 [illegible]／play a role 役割を演じる／perceive 動 知覚する／in terms of ～ ～の観点から／connection 名 接続，結合／sight 名 視覚／derive from ～ ～に由来する／seemingly 副 一見したところ／infinitely 副 無限に／refined 形

〈　〉……名詞句・節
［　］……形容詞句・節
（　）……副詞句・節
S V O C……主節の要素
S′ V′ O′ C′……従属節の要素
(S)(V)(O)(C)……節中のさらなる細かい要素
□……従属接続詞　▒……相関表現
┆┆……等位接続詞　｛　｝……省略可能
φ……関係詞節内で目的語が欠ける場所（名詞が本来ある場所）

❹「音読」で仕上げ！

英文の仕上げは音読です。まず音声を聞いて，正しい発音・英文のリズムなどを確認し，声に出して読みましょう。英文を読むスピードアップや理解力の向上につながります（⇒詳細はp.10）。

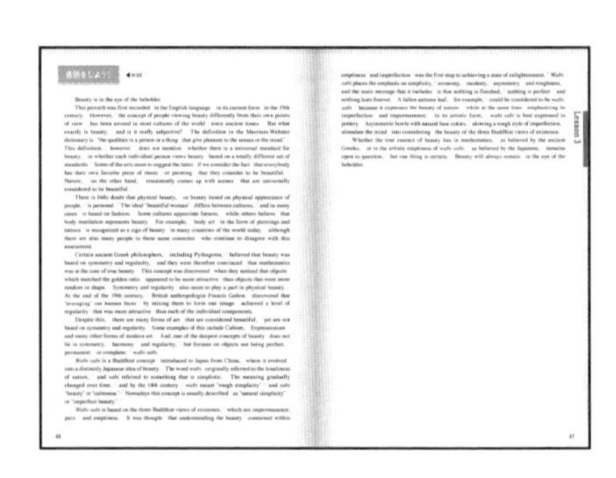

音読をしよう　◀03

Beauty is in the eye of the beholder.

This proverb was first recorded in the English language in its current form in the 19th century. However, the concept of people viewing beauty differently from their own points of view has been around in most cultures of the world since ancient times. But what exactly is beauty, and is it really subjective? The definition in the Merriam-Webster dictionary is "the qualities in a person or a thing that give pleasure to the senses or the mind." This definition, however, does not mention whether there is a universal standard for beauty, or whether each individual person views beauty based on a totally different set of standards. Some of the arts seem to suggest the latter if we consider the fact that everybody has their own favorite piece of music or painting that they consider to be beautiful. Nature, on the other hand, consistently comes up with scenes that are universally considered to be beautiful.

There is little doubt that physical beauty, or beauty based on physical appearance of people, is personal. The ideal "beautiful woman" differs between cultures, and in many cases is based on fashion. Some cultures appreciate fatness, while others believe that body mutilation represents beauty. For example, body art in the form of piercings and tattoos is recognized as a sign of beauty in many countries of the world today, although there are also many people in these same countries who continue to disagree with this assessment.

Certain ancient Greek philosophers, including Pythagoras, believed that beauty was based on symmetry and regularity, and they were therefore convinced that mathematics was at the core of true beauty. This concept was discovered when they noticed that objects which matched the golden ratio appeared to be more attractive than objects that were more random in shape. Symmetry and regularity also seem to play a part in physical beauty. At the end of the 19th century, British anthropologist Francis Galton discovered that "averaging" out human faces by mixing them to form one image achieved a level of regularity that was more attractive than each of the individual components.

Despite this, there are many forms of art that are considered beautiful, yet are not based on symmetry and regularity. Some examples of this include Cubism, Expressionism and many other forms of modern art. And, one of the deepest concepts of beauty does not lie in symmetry, harmony and regularity, but focuses on objects not being perfect, permanent or complete: *wabi-sabi*.

Wabi-sabi is a Buddhist concept introduced to Japan from China, where it evolved into a distinctly Japanese idea of beauty. The word *wabi* originally referred to the loneliness of nature, and *sabi* referred to something that is simplistic. The meaning gradually changed over time, and by the 14th century *wabi* meant "rough simplicity" and *sabi* "beauty" or "calmness." Nowadays this concept is usually described as "natural simplicity" or "imperfect beauty."

Wabi-sabi is based on the three Buddhist views of existence, which are impermanence, pain and emptiness. It was thought that understanding the beauty contained within emptiness and imperfection was the first step to achieving a state of enlightenment. *Wabi-sabi* places the emphasis on simplicity, economy, modesty, asymmetry and roughness, and the main message that it includes is that nothing is finished, nothing is perfect and nothing lasts forever. A fallen autumn leaf, for example, could be considered to be *wabi-sabi* because it expresses the beauty of nature while at the same time emphasizing its imperfection and impermanence. In its artistic form, *wabi-sabi* is best expressed in pottery. Asymmetric bowls with natural hue colors, showing a rough style of imperfection, stimulate the mind into considering the beauty of the three Buddhist views of existence.

Whether the true essence of beauty lies in mathematics, as believed by the ancient Greeks, or in the artistic emptiness of *wabi-sabi*, as believed by the Japanese, remains open to question, but one thing is certain. Beauty will always remain in the eye of the beholder.

//……必ず切りたい
/ ……切ってもOK

採用した英文について

「語数」にこだわらず，レベルに応じた「優れた英文」を採用

語数と難易度は関係ない

「短いから易しい」「長いから難しい」というのは思い込みです。東京大・大阪大・早稲田大では必ず短い文章が出ますが，難易度はかなり高いです。本書では長さにとらわれることなく「優れた英文・設問」を採用しました。

中堅大学であっても，長文はすごく「長い」

基礎・標準レベルの問題集は，とにかく短めの文章を採用しがちですが，志望校が決まっていれば，ぜひその過去問を見てください。想像以上に「長い」ことがほとんどだと思います。本書はあくまで実際の入試に沿っているので，結果的に他の問題集よりも長い文章が多くなりますが，それは現実を踏まえた結果だと考えています。

英文の掲載順について

ルールを習得するために，一番効率的な順番に載せています。最初は「読む」が中心になるため，どうしても難しい英文が前半にきます（難しい英文でも「読める」ルールを解説するため）。その後，「解く」や「細かいこと」を扱うルールが増えるため，後半のほうに易しい英文がくることもありますが，それは本文が全体で1つの授業，1つのストーリーになっていることの結果です。

※そもそも同レベルの大学の問題を収めているので，不都合なほど差が出ることはありません。

「思考力を問う問題」について

これからの入試で重要となる「思考力を問う問題」には 思考力 マークを付けています。ただし，本書では「要約問題」や「タイトル選択問題」などの「形式」だけで「思考力を要する問題」だと判断することこそ思考力の欠如とみなしており，たとえ普通の四択問題であっても，そこに複雑な思考を要するものは ここが 思考力 として補足説明をしています。具体的には,「暗記事項を当てはめるとミスするもの／受験生の知識レベルを超えているものの, 英文の構造や文脈から考えれば解答を導けるもの／単純な直訳では対応できないもの」などに「どんな思考が求められるのか」という解説を追加しています。

補足　近年（特に2019年以降）の入試問題は，英字新聞・ネット記事などからの出題が増えており,「情報を提供する」英文が主流をなしています（早稲田大・慶應大などを中心に）。そういった英文はそもそも要約に向かないので，大学側も設問として出題していません。そこに無理やり要約問題を追加したり，英文の展開図を示すことは，受験生をいたずらに惑わせることになると思います。
※決して「要約問題なんていらない」ということではなく,「要約に向かない英文を（出題者の意図を無視して）要約させることは効果的な勉強とは言えない」ということです。

「ルール」について

3種類のルール

本書に出てくるルールは，大きく次の3種類に分類できます。

読解　読解ルール……「英文の主張・具体例などをつかむ」ための，英文のつながり・展開などに関するルール
解法　解法ルール……「読めても解けない状態を解消する」ための，設問解法のルール
構文　構文ルール……「一文をしっかり読む」ための，構造把握に必要な文法・構文に関するルール

1冊の中で同じルールが何度も出てくる

この1冊の中で，何度も出てくるルールもあります。その理由と目的は以下のとおりです。

- **その解法がさまざまな問題で使えることを実際の入試問題の中で実感できる**
- **大事なルールの復習になる**
- **入試の「偏っている現実」がわかる**：例えば固有名詞は「具体例」の合図！（***Rule 12***）や，〈this＋名詞〉はまとめを作る！（***Rule 4***）は，ものすごくたくさんの入試問題で使えるルールです。そのようなルールは，本書の中でも何度も出てくるので「入試の現実」を体感できます。

※ちなみに，ルールが最初に出てきたときに「詳しくは後ほど」と言う場合もあります。これは「そこで扱うと冗長になる／あとのLessonで扱うほうがそのルールを詳しく解説できる」などの理由で，常にルールを最大限に効率よくマスターするためです。

レベルが違っても同じルールが出てくる

本シリーズは4レベルありますが，ルールはどのレベルの英文にも通用するものなので，レベル1に出てきたルールがレベル2，3，4（のいずれか，もしくはすべて）に出てくることも多々あります。

他のレベルでも同じルールが出てくるメリットは次のとおりです。

- どんなレベルの入試問題でも，同じルールが通用する（その場限りのルールではない）ことを実感できる。
- 1冊を終えて次のレベルの本に進んだときにも同じルールが使えることで復習にもなる。

『The Rules』全84ルール一覧

●本書に収録されているルールは色文字で示されているものです。(⇒ L00) は掲載Lessonを示しています。
●1 2 3 4 はそれぞれ次の本を表しています。1：1入試基礎，2：2入試標準，3：3入試難関，4：4入試最難関。
●同じルールNo.でも，種類が複数あるものもあります。
例）Rule 46「過剰」選択肢のパターン…「all系」と「only系」の2種類

Rule	分野	内容	収録
Rule 1	読解	消えたbutに気づいて「主張」を発見する！ ⇒ **L6**	1 2 3 4
Rule 2	読解	「重要な」という意味の重要単語に注目！⇒ **L2**	1 2 3 4
Rule 3	読解	In factを意識する！⇒ **L12**	1 2 3 4
Rule 4	読解	〈this＋名詞〉は「まとめ」を作る！⇒ **L4**	1 2 3 4
Rule 5	読解	「まとめ単語」による言い換えを見抜く！⇒ **L7**	1 2 3 4
Rule 6	読解	「疑問文」の大事な役割を意識する！⇒ **L1**	1 2 3 4
Rule 7	読解	「クオーテーションマーク」の役割を意識する！	1 2 3 4
Rule 8	読解	〈A＋名詞〉を見たら「具体例」と考える！⇒ **L5**	1 2 3 4
Rule 9	読解	Ifを見たら「具体例」と考える！	1 2 3 4
Rule 10	読解	命令文は「具体例」の合図！⇒ **L12**	1 2 3 4
Rule 11	読解	具体物や行動の羅列は「具体例」と考える！	1 2 3 4
Rule 12	読解	固有名詞は「具体例」の合図！⇒ **L3**	1 2 3 4
Rule 13	読解	数字を見たら「具体例」だと考える！⇒ **L6**	1 2 3 4
Rule 14	読解	「具体例」を導く表現に反応する！⇒ **L1**	1 2 3 4
Rule 15	読解	「イコール」関係を作る表現に反応する！⇒ **L3**	1 2 3 4
Rule 16	読解	「因果表現」を正しく把握する！⇒ **L1**	1 2 3 4
Rule 17	読解	「前後関係」の表現に注目！⇒ **L6,10**	1 2 3 4
Rule 18	読解	「従属接続詞」に反応する！	1 2 3 4
Rule 19	読解	「総称のyou」の意味に注意！⇒ **L5**	1 2 3 4
Rule 20	読解	「感情表現」に注目する！⇒ **L2**	1 2 3 4
Rule 21	読解	「一般論」と「主張」を把握する！	1 2 3 4
Rule 22	読解	「対比」を表す表現に反応する！⇒ **L3,11**	1 2 3 4
Rule 23	読解	「対比」は繰り返される！⇒ **L10**	1 2 3 4
Rule 24	読解	過去と現在の「対比」を予測する！⇒ **L3,4,6**	1 2 3 4
Rule 25	読解	「同じ形」なら「同じ意味」だと考える！⇒ **L6**	1 2 3 4
Rule 26	読解	「似ている・同じ」と明示する反復表現を意識する！	1 2 3 4

Rule	分類	内容	レベル
Rule 27	読解	evenは「反復」の目印!	1 2 3 4
Rule 28	読解	本文の前に「タイトル」に目を通す!	1 2 3 4
Rule 29	読解	本文の前に「語句の注釈」と「設問」をチェック!	1 2 3 4
Rule 30	読解	provide型の動詞は意味が類推できる!	1 2 3 4
Rule 31	読解	more than ~ は3つの意味を考える!⇒**L9**	1 2 3 4
Rule 32	読解	無生物主語・第3文型は「受動態」で訳す!⇒**L8**	1 2 3 4
Rule 33	読解	省略は「機械的に」補う!	1 2 3 4
Rule 34	読解	“-ly”で終わる単語は「すごく」と考えてみる!	1 2 3 4
Rule 35	読解	長文単語・語句をマスターする!⇒**L4,9,10,11,12**	1 2 3 4
Rule 36	読解	「実験・研究」系での頻出表現をマスターする!⇒**L1**	1 2 3 4
Rule 37	読解	「実験・研究」を主語にとる動詞をマスターする!	1 2 3 4
Rule 38	読解	「自然・災害」関係の語彙をマスターする!⇒**L7**	1 2 3 4
Rule 39	読解	「広告」の頻出表現をマスターする!	1 2 3 4
Rule 40	読解	グラフ特有表現をマスターする!	1 2 3 4
Rule 41	解法	まずは「形」から考える!⇒**L2**	1 2 3 4
Rule 42	解法	NOT問題の解法	1 2 3 4
Rule 43	解法	内容一致でnotを見たら隠してみる!⇒**L3**	1 2 3 4
Rule 44	解法	プラス0.5回読みをする!	1 2 3 4
Rule 45	解法	「強調」系の語句に反応する!	1 2 3 4
Rule 46	解法	「過剰」選択肢のパターン⇒**L2**	1 2 3 4
Rule 47	解法	「入れ替え」選択肢のパターン⇒**L2,6**	1 2 3 4
Rule 48	解法	「数字」を使ったひっかけパターン	1 2 3 4
Rule 49	解法	印象の強い単語・同じ単語を使ったひっかけパターン⇒**L5**	1 2 3 4
Rule 50	解法	指示語・代名詞の表す内容を特定する!⇒**L4**	1 2 3 4
Rule 51	解法	指示語の答えは「前」! ヒントは「後ろ」!	1 2 3 4
Rule 52	解法	意外と訳しづらいwhatを攻略!	1 2 3 4
Rule 53	解法	下線部和訳のパターンを知る!	1 2 3 4
Rule 54	解法	関係詞の「訳し方」を整理する!	1 2 3 4
Rule 55	解法	「変化・増減」を正しく把握する!⇒**L1**	1 2 3 4

Rule 56	解法	知らない熟語は「正しい直訳」から攻める!	1 2 3 4
Rule 57	解法	設問文を正確に把握する!	1 2 3 4
Rule 58	解法	広告問題では「注意事項」に反応する!	1 2 3 4
Rule 59	解法	空所補充問題の解法⇒**L5**	1 2 **3** 4
Rule 60	解法	下線部解釈問題の解法	1 2 3 4
Rule 61	解法	記述問題の心構え⇒**L3**	1 2 **3** 4
Rule 62	解法	説明問題の解法⇒**L8**	1 2 **3** 4
Rule 63	解法	文整序・段落整序問題の解法	1 2 3 4
Rule 64	解法	要約問題の取り組み方	1 2 3 4
Rule 65	解法	ビジュアル問題を解く手順	1 2 3 4
Rule 66	構文	andは「対等の品詞」を結ぶ!	1 2 3 4
Rule 67	構文	使役・知覚動詞とSVOCを徹底マスター!	1 2 3 4
Rule 68	構文	〈名詞+S′V′〉を見たら関係代名詞の省略!	1 2 3 4
Rule 69	構文	「同格のthat」をとる名詞⇒**L3**	1 2 **3** 4
Rule 70	構文	〈SV that～〉は「Sは～と思う・言う」の意味!⇒**L8**	1 2 **3** 4
Rule 71	構文	〈V *A* as *B*〉は「AをBとみなす」という意味!⇒**L1**	1 2 **3** 4
Rule 72	構文	分詞構文の訳し方のコツ⇒**L2**	1 2 **3** 4
Rule 73	構文	「任意倒置」のパターン⇒**L11**	1 2 **3** 4
Rule 74	構文	「強制倒置」のパターン⇒**L9**	1 2 **3** 4
Rule 75	構文	「強調構文」の必殺即断パターン⇒**L1**	1 2 **3** 4
Rule 76	構文	〈S out+動詞 O〉はS>Oの関係になる!	1 2 3 4
Rule 77	構文	「数字表現」の意味を正確にとる!	1 2 3 4
Rule 78	構文	第1文型は「存在・移動」と考える!⇒**L4**	1 2 **3** 4
Rule 79	構文	「動名詞の意味上の主語」の要注意パターン⇒**L3**	1 2 **3** 4
Rule 80	構文	SVOCになる形に注意!⇒**L5,6**	1 2 **3** 4
Rule 81	構文	「接続詞as」の識別をマスターする!⇒**L12**	1 2 **3** 4
Rule 82	構文	〈SV+人+to ～〉を使いこなす!	1 2 3 4
Rule 83	構文	名詞構文に注目して意訳する!	1 2 3 4
Rule 84	構文	特殊なSVMに注意!	1 2 3 4

音読について

●音読で意識すること

❶文法・構文を意識して10回

文構造を意識しながら，ときには日本語訳を確認しながら10回音読してください。ゆっくりでOKです。

❷内容を意識して10回

「意味・内容が浮かぶように」10回音読してください。これをこなしていくうちに，日本語を介さずに英文を理解できるようになっていきます。その英文が伝える内容が「画像として浮かぶくらい」まで音読できればベストです。内容優先ですから，自分で理解できるスピードでOKです。

❸スピードを意識して10回

「自分が本番で読むときの理想のスピード(自分が理解できる範囲でのマックスのスピード)」に徐々に近づけながら，10回読んでみてください。

●スケジュール

❶目安は1日30分

3カ月くらいで効果が出るはずです。ただ読むだけの「ダラダラ音読」は絶対にしないように，集中して取り組みましょう！

❷分配

同じ英文を一気に30回も読む必要はありません。1日5回×6日＝合計30回が目安です。

●音読の「注意点」

音読は必ず声に出してください。黙読だと難しい箇所を無意識のうちに飛ばしてしまうからです。ただし，声の大きさは無関係なので，ボソボソで十分です。ボソボソでも声を出すことによって，息継ぎが必要になります。英文を適切なところで区切るときに息継ぎをすることで，より自然な読み方が身に付くようになります。

●音読用白文について

❶2種類のスラッシュ

// ……必ず切りたい	/ ……切ってもOK

❷スラッシュを入れる方針

英文にスラッシュを入れること自体は昔からあるものです。本書でも基本方針は同じですが，従来のものと違うのは次の2点です。

● 英語ネイティブとアメリカで生まれ育った帰国子女の協力により「本物の感覚」でスラッシュを入れたこと。
● 英文を広く捉えるために，スラッシュを「あまり入れすぎない」こと。

従来は文法的区切り（例えば前置詞の前）に機械的に入れるのが普通でしたが，それだとあまりに区切りが多くなってしまい，むしろ不自然な音読の習慣がついてしまいます。細かい区切りや修飾関係は「文構造の分析」でやることなので，ここでは英文をもう少し大きく捉える訓練も兼ねるという方針でスラッシュを入れています。

音声の利用法

● ウェブサイトで聞く方法

❶パソコンからインターネットで専用サイトにアクセス
（右のQRコードからもアクセスできます）

https://www.obunsha.co.jp/service/rules/

❷お持ちの書籍をクリック

❸パスワード「rules03n」をすべて半角英数字で入力して，音声ファイルをダウンロード
（またはウェブ上で再生）

注意 ● ダウンロードについて：音声ファイルはMP3形式です。ZIP形式で圧縮されていますので，解凍（展開）して，MP3を再生できるデジタルオーディオプレーヤーなどでご活用ください。解凍（展開）せずに利用されると，ご使用の機器やソフトウェアにファイルが認識されないことがあります。デジタルオーディオプレーヤーなどの機器への音声ファイルの転送方法は，各製品の取り扱い説明書などをご覧ください。● スマートフォンやタブレットでは音声をダウンロードできません。● 音声を再生する際の通信料にご注意ください。● ご使用機器，音声再生ソフトなどに関する技術的なご質問は，ハードメーカーもしくはソフトメーカーにお願いします。● 本サービスは予告なく終了することがあります。

● スマートフォンアプリで聞く方法

音声をスマートフォンアプリ「英語の友」でも聞くことができます。「英語の友」で検索するか，右のQRコードからアクセスしてください。パスワードを求められたら，上記の❸と同じパスワードを入力してください。

Lesson 1 解答・解説

▶問題 別冊 p.3

このLessonで出てくるルール

Rule 14 読解 「具体例」を導く表現に反応する！ ⇒ 問2

Rule 71 構文 〈V *A* as *B*〉は「AをBとみなす」という意味！ ⇒ 問3

Rule 16 読解 「因果表現」を正しく把握する！ ⇒ 問4

Rule 55 解法 「変化・増減」を正しく把握する！ ⇒ 問4

Rule 6 読解 「疑問文」の大事な役割を意識する！ ⇒ 問5

Rule 36 読解 「実験・研究」系での頻出表現をマスターする！ ⇒ 問5

Rule 75 構文 「強調構文」の必殺即断パターン ⇒ 問7

解答

問1 ③ **問2** ④ **問3** ③ **問4** ② **問5** ④ **問6** ①

問7 運動が実際に睡眠の質を妨げ得るのは，実は一流の運動選手レベルでトレーニングをしている場合のみである。

問1 難易度 ★★★

not to mention ～「～は言うまでもなく」という熟語が有名なので，**空所直前のNot toに注目**して，この形にすれば正解してしまいます。大学受験ではそれでもOKですが，厳密には，not to mention ～ には「～は言うまでもなく」という意味の他に，Not to mentionの後ろにSVを伴って「（前文の内容に加えて）さらに～だ」という使い方もあります（辞書にも載っていないことが多いマニアックな用法です）。今回はsleeping pillsの悪い点をnot to mention以下で追加する形なのでこの意味のほうが自然です。

選択肢の訳

① 信じる　② 知っている　**③ 言及する**　④ 期待する

問2 難易度 ★☆☆

》》 *Rule 14* 読解 「具体例」を導く表現に反応する！

A such as *B* は「BのようなA」と訳されますが，実際には「**such asの後ろに具体例がくる**」という発想で，「A，例えばBだ」と考えるのもアリです。こう考えることで「具体例の発見が容易になる」「英文を前から処理できる（返り読みしなくなる）」メリットがあります。

同様に，including も「～を含めて」という訳語だけが有名ですが，これも**具体例の目印**になります。including は，動詞 include が「分詞構文」になったものですが，辞書によっては「前置詞」として扱われています。

「具体例」を導く重要表現

前置詞など	□ such as ～ 例えば～のような	
	□ including ～ ～を含めて	□ like ～ ～のような
名詞	□ incident 出来事	□ experiment 実験

※こういった単語が出てきたら具体例になることがよくある。

今回もいきなり文脈から考えようとしないで，such as ～ の働きに注目してください。

diseasesと（ B ）conditionsは似た意味になるはず！

a key risk factor for diseases and（ B ）conditions such as stroke, heart attack and high blood pressure

diseasesと（ B ）conditionsをsuch as ～ 以下で具体化

andで結ばれている diseases と（ B ）conditions は似た意味（マイナス内容）と予想でき，such as ～ 以下（stroke, heart attack and high blood pressure）がその具体例と考えると，空所に適する語は④unhealthy です（unhealthy conditions「不健康な状態」の意味）。

選択肢の訳

① 有益な　② 望ましい　③ 未知の　**④ 不健康な**

→ ③の「未知かどうか」はプラスにもマイナスにもなりません。また，stroke, heart attack and high blood pressure はそもそも「未知の状態」ではないのでアウトです。

問3 難易度 ★★☆

Shawn Youngstedtの発言としては，16行目にthe potential problems of pharmaceutically induced sleep，17行目に"Sleeping pills are extremely dangerous," Youngstedt said.とあり，「睡眠薬は危険だと考えている」ので，これと合致する③Shawn Youngstedt does not view sleeping pills as being safe.が正解です。③はview *A* as *B*「AをBとみなす」の形で，「睡眠薬を安全だとみなしていない」という意味です（本文は肯定文，選択肢は否定文ですが，表す内容は同じですね）。

>>> Rule 71 構文 〈V *A* as *B*〉は「AをBとみなす」という意味！

知らない動詞でも，**V *A* as *B***の形になっていれば「AをBとみなす」と考えてみてください。大半の動詞で意味がとれてしまいます。例えば，I used the box as a chair.「その箱を椅子として使った」という文で，仮にusedがわからなかったとしましょう。**V *A* as *B***の形に着目して「その箱を椅子とみなした」で意味がとれますね。

この形でよく出る動詞をチェックしておきましょう。参考までにそれぞれの代表的な訳語を横に載せましたが，もちろんすべて**「みなす」**で解決します。

regard型の動詞　V *A* as *B*「AをBとみなす」

文法問題で狙われるもの

- ☐ regard みなす
- ☐ look on みなす
- ☐ think of 考える，みなす

長文でよく出るもの

- ☐ see みなす
- ☐ take 受け入れる
- ☐ view 考える
- ☐ identify 同一視する
- ☐ refer to 呼ぶ
- ☐ describe 説明する
- ☐ recognize 認識する
- ☐ treat 扱う

選択肢の訳

①ケリー・グレーザー・バロンは，不眠症について多くの文献を読んできたが，この病気に関する研究に自身がかかわったことはない。

→ Kelly Glazer Baronの発言として，6行目にIn one study we did, for example, older women suffering from insomnia said ～.とあります。「自分自身でも研究を行った」とわかるのでアウトです。

②クリストファー・クラインによると，比較的しっかりした研究では，運動は，人々が得る睡眠の質に一切影響を与えないことが示された。

→ Christopher Klineの発言として，12行目にThe results show exercise improves both self-reported and objective measures of sleep qualityとあり不適です。

③ショーン・ヤングシュタットは，睡眠薬が安全でないと考えている。

④ヤングシュタットによると，睡眠薬の1つのメリットは，その費用である。
→ Youngstedtの発言として，20行目にIt's less expensive, healthier and just as easy to exerciseとあります。「運動のほうが（睡眠薬より）安い」=「運動のメリットの1つが費用」なので，選択肢とは真逆の内容です。

問4 難易度 ★★☆

Klineが行った研究について，30行目にexercise alone led to a 25% reduction of sleep apnea symptoms over a 12-week periodとあります（このaloneは「ただ〜だけ」という意味の副詞）。これに合致する②In a study that Kline was involved in, exercise alone led to a decline in the number of sleep apnea symptoms.が正解です。a 25% reduction of sleep apnea symptoms 〜が，選択肢ではa decline in the number of sleep apnea symptomsと言い換えられています（inは「範囲」を表し，a decline in 〜 で「〜における減少」→「〜の減少」）。ここではled to（lead toの過去形）に注目してください。

>>> *Rule 16* 読解 「因果表現」を正しく把握する！

「因果関係を示す表現」の理解を試す問題は，高確率で出題されます。しかし，例えばcauseは「〜の原因となる，〜を引き起こす」という日本語訳だけで覚えてしまうと，「原因と結果」を一瞬で判断することができなかったり，難しい英文では混乱してしまいます（特に受動態*be* caused by 〜 の形のときなど）。「因果関係を示す表現」で大事なことは，**原因**と結果をキッチリ把握することです。以下でチェックしてください。

(1) 原因 V 結果 の形をとるもの 「原因によって結果になる」

- □ **原因** cause 結果
- □ **原因** bring about 結果
- □ **原因** lead to 結果 ※**原因** lead up to 結果 の形になることもある。
- □ **原因** contribute to 結果
- □ **原因** result in 結果
- □ **原因** give rise to 結果
- □ **原因** is responsible for 結果
- □ **原因** trigger 結果 ※triggerはもともと「（拳銃の）引き金」という意味。

(2) 結果 V 原因 の形をとるもの 「結果は原因によるものだ」

- □ 結果 result from **原因**
- □ 結果 come from **原因**
- □ 結果 arise from **原因**
- □ 結果 derive［stem］from **原因**
- □ 結果 is attributable to **原因** ※attributable = attributed

(3) V 結果 to 原因 の形をとるもの「結果 を 原因 によるものだと考える」

- □ owe 結果 to 原因
- □ attribute 結果 to 原因
- □ ascribe 結果 to 原因
- □ credit 結果 to 原因

〈応用〉受動態でよく使われるもの　※原因 と 結果 をきっちり把握する！

- □ 結果 is caused by 原因
- □ 結果 is brought about by 原因
- □ 結果 is attributed to 原因

※受動態を無理に「引き起こされる」のように訳すのではなく，原因と結果の位置が変わっただけだと認識することが大切です。

選択肢の訳

①睡眠時無呼吸の人は運動を避けるべきである。

→ sleep apnea について，27行目に Exercise can help with that, too. "For sleep apnea, exercise has always been recommended," とあります。

②クラインがかかわった研究では，運動だけで睡眠時無呼吸の症状発生数減少につながった。

③むずむず脚症候群は，一晩中動き回るのが好きな人々によって引き起こされる病気だ。

→ 33行目に Restless-leg syndrome, a disorder of the nervous system, occurs when the legs — ～ — itch, burn or move involuntarily. とあります。involuntarily「無意識に，不随意に」からもわかるように，本人が動かしたくなくても脚が動いてしまう症状なので，選択肢の caused by people who like to move around は合いません。caused by ～ を使って，本文にない因果関係を利用したひっかけパターンです。このように，因果関係を示す表現は設問にかかわることが非常に多いのです。ちなみに，本文で throughout the night「一晩中」とも言っていませんね。

④バロンによると，多くの研究文献によって，運動すると人々が目覚める頻度が高くなることが示されている。

→ 41行目に，"There is a large amount of literature showing that people who exercise have better sleep," Baron said. "People who exercise reported an increase in deep sleep and <u>a decrease in the number of awakenings</u>. とあります。運動によって「目覚める頻度が減った」と言っているので，選択肢とは真逆の内容です。ここで使われている as a result of ～「～の結果として」も因果関係を示す表現で，さらに「増減」についてもよく問われるので注意しましょう。

>>> *Rule 55* 解法 「変化・増減」を正しく把握する！

「変化・増減」は設問でよく問われるので，しっかりチェックしておきましょう。

「変化を表す名詞」＋ in ～　※inは「範囲（～において）」を表す。
- □ change in ～ ～の変化
- □ increase[rise / growth] in ～ ～の増加
- □ decrease[fall / decline / drop] in ～ ～の減少
- □ improvement in ～ ～の向上，改善
- □ progress[advances] in ～ ～の進歩

※advanceは可算名詞で，複数形で使われる。

本文42行目にan increase in deep sleep「熟睡の増加」，a decrease in the number of awakenings「目覚める数の減少」とあります。正解の選択肢②でも，a decline in ～「～の減少」が使われていました。

問5 難易度★★☆

ブロックⅢの1文目（46行目）は「疑問文」で，ここからの新たな「テーマ」を提示しています。

>>> *Rule 6* 読解 「疑問文」の大事な役割を意識する！

疑問文の役割と位置

(1) **段落の頭**に疑問文がある　→テーマの提示

(2) **文章の最後**に疑問文がある　→反語（まれに予想できない未来に対する疑問の投げかけ）

(3) その他：**英文の途中**など　→「テーマ」か「反語」かは文脈判断

特に「**テーマの提示**」は重要です。その文章全体（もしくは文章の途中まで）の「お題」を提供するからです。テーマを意識することで，今読んでいる内容が「脱線」なのか，「大事なところ」なのかの判断ができるようになります。そもそもテーマに関する内容は間違いなく設問で問われるので，ここを意識するかどうかで，長文全体の理解にかかわってくるとも言えるのです。

今回は，文頭のHow much exercise is needed to get a good night's rest?でテーマを提示し，その直後（46行目）のMost sleep studies have focused on the recommended amount: two and a half hours a week of moderate-intensity aerobic exercise, ～で，テーマに対して答えています。さらに，56行目でOther studies show that people who exercise less than the recommended amount, ～, see moderate benefits. と付け加えており，この英文を言い換えた④Some studies indicate that getting some exercise, but less than the recommended amount, leads to moderate sleep benefits. が正解です（〈**原因** lead to **結果**〉の関係）。疑問文に答えている所が，ズバリ正解の該当箇所になっているわけです。

ちなみに，72行目のIf you're sacrificing sleep for exercise, is that a good idea? は文末で使われ，「反語」になっています。「よい考えだろうか？」→「よい考えではない」と主張しているわけです。

次に，もう1つ重要なルールを確認しておきましょう。「実験・研究」系の文章では，**Other studies show that ～**「他の研究は～と示している」→「他の研究によって～が示されている［わかっている］」のような形が多用されます。

>>> *Rule 36* 読解 「実験・研究」系での頻出表現をマスターする！

研究 show {that} S´V´「研究によってS´V´だとわかっている」

※主語には「研究（者）／実験／結果／データ」がくる。

※show 以外に，reveal「明らかにする」，indicate「示す」，suggest「示唆する」，report「報告する」，prove / demonstrate / confirm「証明する」が頻出です。

今回の英文において，本文ではshow，選択肢ではindicateが使われていますが，このパターンを知っておけば簡単に言い換え可能だと判断できるわけです。

ちなみに，The results show ～（12行目）やResearch suggests ～（22行目）など，何度もこの「実験・研究」に関する表現が使われています。問3の誤りの選択肢②にも使われていました。

選択肢の訳

①よく眠るためには無制限に運動をすべきだと，通常推奨されている。

→ 下線部（58行目）やその次のHigh-level athletes, who may overtrain for a certain event, do have issues with sleep when traveling and under stress「特定の大会のために過度な練習を行うことのあるハイレベルな運動選手は，移動中やストレスを感じているときによく眠れないことがあります」から，「無制限に運動をする」のはよくないとわかります。

②クラインは，早歩きが適度な運動であるとは考えていない。

→ 49行目に，Kline says "brisk walking, light biking ... anything that increases your heart rate so that ～, is considered moderate exercise." とあります。consider OC「OをCとみなす」の受動態〈O is considered C〉で「早歩きは適度な運動とみなされている」を表しており，選択肢とは真逆です。**「本文の正しい内容にnotを入れただけ」**というひ

っかけパターンです（***Rule 43*** ⇒p.58）。

③ヤングシュタットは，晴れた日に屋外で運動すると，体内時計が消えてしまうと考えている。

→ 53行目に，"I think trying to do it outside is also helpful, because bright light can help promote sleep," Youngstedt added. "Light exposure helps regulate the body clock." とあります。選択肢の「体内時計が消える」とは真逆の内容です。

④一部の研究では，推奨されている運動量に満たないけれども，ある程度運動することで，睡眠にそこそこの効果が見られると示されている。

問6 難易度★★☆ 思考力

ブロックⅣでも同じく，文頭の疑問文で「テーマ」を提示しています。それに対してBaronは74行目において，However, one of the benefits of staying with a morning exercise routine, she adds, is that you are less likely to cancel. "Morning exercisers are more consistent," she explained. と言っています。Baronは「朝に運動することのメリット」を述べているので，①Baron discusses a benefit of exercise in the morning. が正解です。選択肢に使われているdiscussは勘違いの多い単語で，日本語の「議論する」から抱くような激しい言い合いとは限らず，今回のように「論じる，扱う」くらいの意味で使われることもあります。

ここが思考力 「大きな視点」が問われることを知っておこう

問いの作り方として，本文の一部をそのまま（もしくは語句を変える程度）使った内容一致問題ではなく，「バロンは〜について論じている」のように**英文または段落の主旨や全体像を大きく捉える**（立場・方針を示す）問いもあります。このように「大きな視点を重視する」傾向は，難関大入試や共通テストの「英文の主旨に対して賛成・反対」を選ぶ問題などに反映されています。

こういった問題は，世間では「思考力を要する」と言われるものですが，「英文または段落全体のテーマ」を把握すれば，実は簡単に解けます。例えば今回は，ブロックⅣ頭（63行目）にWhat's the best time of day to do this sleep-enhancing movement? とあり，テーマが「睡眠促進活動（= 運動）をするのに最適な時間帯」だと示しているので，このテーマ（運動する時間帯）を意識して読んでいけば，「Baronは夜に運動OK，朝の運動にもメリットがあると考えている」という部分に注目できるようになります。「疑問文」→「テーマを意識」というルールを知っていれば，難しくないわけです。

選択肢の訳

①バロンは，朝運動することのメリットについて論じている。

②夜に運動することを推奨する人はいない。

→ ブロックⅣの前半は「昔は朝の運動がベストと言われていたが，その考え方は変わった」という流れです。Youngstedtは68行目で，For most of us, exercise at night, even if it ends just a couple of hours before bedtime, will help with sleep.と言っているので，「夜の運動を推奨する人はいない」という内容はアウトです。nobody「誰も～ない」を見たら,「さすがに0人はないのでは？（1人はいるんじゃないの？）」とツッコミを入れながら本文を探すと見つかりやすくなります。

③バロンによると，睡眠時無呼吸によって睡眠障害が起こりそうもないものになっている。

→ どこにも「睡眠障害が起こりそうもない」とは書かれていません（そもそも，睡眠時無呼吸は睡眠障害の一種です）。

④バロンは，疲れていると運動したい気持ちが高まるかもしれないことをはっきり示している。

→ Baronは82行目で，You will likely feel even less inclined to exercise when you are fatiguedと言っています。〈feel inclined to 原形〉「～したいと思う」という熟語で，今回はless「より～でなく」が使われています。本文は「疲れていると運動したくない」であり，選択肢「疲れていると運動したい」とは真逆です。**比較級**が使われている箇所は設問で狙われやすいので，しっかりチェックしましょう（比較級を利用したひっかけパターンは***Rule 47*** ⇒p.110）。

問7 難易度 ★★☆

「強調構文」がポイントとなる問題です。58行目を見てみましょう。

〈It is only＋副詞＋that ～〉→「強調構文」だと即断！

It's (only when you are training to the level of an elite athlete) that exercise can actually interfere with sleep quality.

「運動が実際に睡眠の質を妨げ得るのは，(実は) 一流の運動選手レベルでトレーニングをしている場合のみである」

>>> *Rule 75* 構文 「強調構文」の必殺即断パターン

強調構文は「見抜けるかどうかがポイント」としか言われず，肝心の「見抜き方」はあまり説明されません（「It isとthatを隠してみて文が成立すれば強調構文」という説明はよくありますが，それは「確認」の方法であって，「見抜き方」ではありませんよね)。強調構文は「他と比べた結果,片方を強調する」働きがあるので,以下のように「対比表現」とセットで使われることが多いのです。以下のパターンを見たら,まずは強調構文だと考えてみてください。

(1) 対比系

- □ It is **not** *A* **but** *B* that ～. ～なのは,決してAではなく,(実は) Bだ
- □ It is **not** *A* that ～, **but** *B*. ～なのは,決してAではなく,(実は) Bだ
- □ It is **not** *A* that ～. *B* (**肯定文**). ～なのは,決してAではない。Bだ
- □ It is **not only** *A* **but also** *B* that ～. ～なのは,実はAだけでなく,Bもだ
  = It is **not only** *A* that ～, **but** *B*.／It is *B* **as well as** *A* that ～.
- □ It is **not so much** *A* **as** *B* that ～. ～なのは,実はAというより,むしろBだ
  = It is **not so much** *A* that ～, **as[but]** *B*. ※asとbutが混同されることもある。
- □ It is *B* **rather than** *A* that ～. ～なのは,実はAというよりむしろBだ
- □ It is [**比較級を含む語句**] that ～. ～なのは,実は[比較級を含む語句]だ

注意 当然ながら,〈It is + [**形容詞**] + that ～〉〈It is p.p. that ～〉の場合,**It は仮S**,**that ～ が真S**の構文です。〈It is not [**形容詞**] that ～〉の形でも強調構文になることはありません。強調構文では,**形容詞を強調することは絶対にない**からです(逆にこの形のときは「仮S・真S構文」と即断できます)。

(2) 限定・強調系

強調のために**only「これだけ!」**などの強い単語を伴います。

- □ It is **only** *B* that ～. ～なのは,実はBだけだ
- □ It is **the very** *B* that ～. ～なのは,まさにBだ
- □ It is **this** *B* that ～. ～なのは,まさにこのBだ
  ※「あれ」じゃなくて「これ!!」と強調。
- □ It is **really[actually / precisely / in fact]** *B* that ～. ～なのは,本当はBだ

(3) 品詞からの即断パターン

It is [**副詞**] that ～ → 強調構文! ※副詞には副詞句・副詞節もOK。
It is [**代名詞**] that ～ → 強調構文!

訳し方 強調構文を訳す問題では,「強調すべきところを日本語で強調する」ことが大事です。It isとthatで挟まれたものを少しオーバーなくらい強調することで,「強調構文がわかっています」と採点者にアピールできるのです。簡単な方法としては**「決して」「実は」「なんと」**などを入れればOKです。

強調構文を訳す際の手順

(1) **推測**　It is not ～ などで強調構文を推測

(2) **確信**　thatを見て，強調構文を確信

(3) **確認**　念のため，It isとthatを取ってみて，文が成立するかを確認

(4) **構造把握**　It isとthatを無視して，文型を把握（その文型に従って訳す）

(5) **強調**　強調すべきところをきちんと強調して和訳

■強調構文だと見抜く

今回の英文は，副詞節（when ～）が，It isとthatに挟まれた形（It is 副詞 that ～）なので瞬時に「強調構文」だと判断できます。この判別法はわりと有名で，今回はそれだけでもわかるのですが，本書を読む皆さんは，It is only ～ の形にも反応できるようにしておくと，今後，圧倒的に強調構文に強くなれますので，ぜひ「即断法」をチェックしておいてください。

全体は「…するのは，実は～のときだけだ」と強調できれば完璧です（この問題は強調構文が最大のポイントなので，ここをきちんと訳出してアピールすることが必要です）。

■総称のyou

when you are training to the level of an elite athlete「一流の運動選手レベルでトレーニングをしているとき」の部分は，to the level of ～「～のレベルまで」という表現の他に，「総称のyou」がポイントです。youには「あなた」だけでなく，「（あなたも私も含んで）人は誰でも，みんな」という意味があります。今回のyouは「一般の人みんな」を表しているため，あえて日本語に訳す必要はありません（「あなた」と訳すのはNG）。

■canは「可能性」

that ～ 以下は，exercise can actually interfere with sleep quality「運動が実際に睡眠の質を妨げ得る」です。canは「あり得る（可能性）」，interfere with ～ は「～を妨げる，～に干渉する」という熟語です。

文構造の分析

1 [1] (If you 're one of the third of all Americans [who suffer from insomnia]) — (roughly) 108 million of us — put away your sleeping pills. [2] Science has a much safer solution. [3] "There has been more and more research (in the last decade) [showing exercise can reduce insomnia]," Rush University clinical psychologist Kelly Glazer Baron said. [4] "(In one study [we did ϕ]), (for example), older women [suffering from insomnia] said 〈their sleep improved (from poor to good) (when they exercised)〉. [5] They had more energy and were less depressed."

the third～Americansの同格

訳 [1]もしあなたが，全アメリカ人の3分の1，つまりおよそ1億800万人のアメリカ人がかかっている不眠症患者の1人なら，睡眠薬を捨てなさい。[2]科学には，はるかに安全な解決策がある。[3]「ここ10年間で，運動によって不眠症が軽減され得ることを示す研究がどんどん出てきました」と，ラッシュ大学の臨床心理学者ケリー・グレーザー・バロンは述べた。[4]「例えば私たちが行ったある研究では，不眠症の高齢女性たちが，運動したらよく眠れるようになったと述べています。[5]活力が増して，落ち込んだ状態が軽減されたのです」

語句 [1]suffer from ～ ～を患う／put away 片付ける，しまう／sleeping pill 睡眠薬／[3]decade 名 10年間／clinical psychologist 臨床心理学者，臨床心理士／[5]depressed 形 落ち込んだ状態の，うつ状態の

文法・構文 [1]the third of all Americans who ～ の直訳は「不眠症に苦しんでいる全アメリカ人の3分の1」です。[2]muchは比較級saferを強調しています。[3]There is ～ 構文が現在完了形（has been）になっています。また，showing exercise can reduce insomniaは分詞のカタマリで，more and more researchを修飾しています。[4]their sleep improved from poor to goodは直訳「彼女ら（高齢女性）の睡眠が悪い状態からよい状態になった」→「高齢女性はよく眠れるようになった」です。[5]andは，had ～ と were ～ を結んでいます。

2 [1] "There are more solid studies (recently) [that looked at people [clinically diagnosed with insomnia disorder], (rather than self-described poor sleepers)]," agreed the University of Pittsburgh's Christopher Kline, [who studies sleep (through the lens of sports medicine)]. [2] "The results show 〈exercise improves both self-reported and objective measures of sleep quality, [such as 〈what's measured (in a clinical sleep lab)〉]〉."

データ表現

具体例の目印

訳 [1]「最近では，自分でよく眠れないと言っている人ではなく，不眠症と臨床的に診断された人を調べた，信頼できる研究が増えています」と，スポーツ医学の視点から睡眠を研究している，ピッツバーグ大学のクリストファー・クラインも同意した。[2]「研究結果によると，運動によって，自己申告でも，臨床睡眠検査室で測られるもののような客観的な計測値でも，睡眠の質が改善されることが証明されています」

語句 [1]solid 形 しっかりした／look at ～ ～を調べる／clinically 副 臨床的に（実際に病人を診察，治療すること）／disorder 名 病気，障害／self-described 形 自称の／through the lens of ～ ～の視点から／sports medicine スポーツ医学／[2]self-reported 形 自己申告の／objective 形 客観的な／measure 名 測定

文法・構文 [1]関係詞節のthat looked at ～ の先行詞は，more solid studiesです。先行詞と関係詞節の間にrecentlyという副詞が割り込んでいます。[2]*A* such as *B*は「A，例えばB」という形で具体例を示すパターンです（***Rule 14*** ⇒p.13）。

3 [1]Exercise is not (quite) as effective as sleeping pills, admits Arizona State University sleep researcher Shawn Youngstedt, but (if you consider the potential problems [of pharmaceutically induced sleep]), one's thinking changes. [2]"Sleeping pills are (extremely) dangerous," Youngstedt said. [3]"They are as bad as smoking a pack of cigarettes a day. [4](Not to mention) they cause infections, falling and dementia [in the elderly], and they lose

因果表現

their effectiveness (after a few weeks). [5]It 's less expensive, healthier and just as easy to exercise," he said, "and there 's an added bonus. [6]Research suggests 〈those [who are physically active] have a lower risk of developing

データ表現

insomnia (in the first place)〉."

訳 [1]アリゾナ州立大学で睡眠を研究しているショーン・ヤングシュタットは，運動に睡眠薬ほどの効果がないことを認めているが，薬によって誘発される睡眠によって起こり得る問題について考えれば，考え方は変わるだろう。[2]「睡眠薬はきわめて危険なのです」とヤングシュタットは述べている。[3]「1日に煙草を1箱吸うのと同じくらい健康に悪いことなのです。[4]さらに，感染症，高齢者における転倒や認知症を引き起こし，2〜3週間で効き目がなくなるのです。[5]運動するほうが安上がりで，健康的で，ちょうど同じくらいお手軽ですよ」と彼は述べた。「それに，おまけ（のメリット）があります。[6]研究によって，よく体を動かす人はそもそも不眠症になるリスクが低いことが示されているのです」

語句 [1]quite 副（否定文で）完全に～というわけではない／induce 動 誘発する／[3]a day 1日につき／[4]not to mention ～（前文の内容を受けて）さらに～／cause 動 引き起こす infection 名 感染症／falling 名 転倒／[5]added bonus おまけ／[6]suggest 動 示唆する develop 動 発症する／in the first place そもそも

文法・構文 [2]Sleeping pillsと無冠詞・複数形になっているので，「睡眠薬というものは全般的に危険」ということです。 [4]1つ目のandは*A*, *B* and *C*の形で，名詞3つ（infections／falling／dementia）を，2つ目のandはthey cause ～とthey lose ～をそれぞれ結んでいます。 [5]1つ目のand以降はjust as easy {as to take sleeping pills} という比較対象が省略されています。このように，比較対象が文脈から明らかな場合は，2つ目のas以下が省略されることがよくあります。

4 [1]There 's more good news (for the 18 million Americans [who struggle with sleep apnea], a dangerous disorder [in which you (temporarily) stop breathing

sleep apneaの同格

(for up to a minute during the night)]). [2]Exercise can help (with that), (too). [3]"(For sleep apnea), exercise has (always) been recommended," Kline said, "(mostly to jump-start weight loss [from dieting]), (because those [with sleep

「人々」を表すthose

apnea] are (normally) overweight or obese). [4]But we did a study [where the participants didn't diet], and exercise alone led to a 25% reduction of sleep

因果関係を示す表現

apnea symptoms (over a 12-week period)."

訳 [1]睡眠時無呼吸という，夜間に最大1分呼吸が一時停止する危険な病気に苦しんでいる1,800万人のアメリカ人にはさらによい知らせがある。[2]運動によってそれも軽減される可能性があるのだ。[3]「睡眠時無呼吸には昔からずっと運動が推奨されてきました」とクラインは述べた。「その主な目的は，食事療法による体重減少の後押しです。なぜなら睡眠時無呼吸の人は通常，標準より太っていたり，肥満だったりするからです。[4]しかし私たちが行ったある研究では，被験者が食事療法をせずに，運動だけで，睡眠時無呼吸の症状が12週間で25パーセント減少したのです」

語句 [1]sleep apnea 睡眠時無呼吸／temporarily 副 一時的に／up to ～ 最大（最長）～／[2]help with ～ ～を助ける／[3]mostly 副 たいていは／jump-start 動 あと押しする，活性化させる／diet 動 食事療法をする／obese 形 肥満の／[4]participant 名 被験者／alone 副 ～だけで／lead to ～ ～につながる／reduction 名 減少／symptom 名 症状

文法・構文 [3](mostly) to jump-start ～ は不定詞の副詞的用法「目的（～するために）」です。和訳では，英文の語順どおりに「その主な目的は，～」と訳してあります。 [4]関係詞節where the participants didn't dietは，a studyにかかっています。このように，関係副詞whereは具体的な「場所」ではなくても，広い意味で「場所（場面）」と考えられる語を先行詞にとることができます。

5 [1]"Exercise has (also) been shown to help (with restless-leg symptoms [across all age groups])," Youngstedt said. [2]Restless-leg syndrome, a disorder

Sの同格

of the nervous system, occurs (when the legs — or other parts of the body [like the arms or face] — itch, burn or move (involuntarily)). [3] The irresistible urge [to move] (often) happens (at night), [which disrupts sleep].

訳 [1]「運動はまた，年齢層を問わずむずむず脚症候群にも効果があることが示されています」とヤングシュタットは述べた。[2]むずむず脚症候群は神経系の病気で，足，あるいは腕や顔など他の身体部位がむずむずしたり，ピリピリしたり，不随意に動いたりしたときに生じる。[3]動きたいという抑え難い衝動が夜間に生じることが多く，それによって睡眠が妨げられるのである。

語句 [1]*be* shown to 原形 ～することが証明されている／restless-leg symptom むずむず脚症候群（脚を中心として不快な症状が現れる病気のこと）／[2]nervous system 神経系／itch 動 むずむずする，かゆい／burn 動 ピリピリする／involuntarily 副 不随意に（体の動きが本人の意思どおりにならないこと）／[3]irresistible 形 抑え難い／urge to 原形 ～したいという衝動／disrupt 動 妨げる

文法・構文 [3]whichは非制限用法の関係代名詞で，先行詞は主節の内容（動きたいという抑え難い衝動が夜間に生じること）です。

6 Finding a safe, healthy type of treatment [for sleep disorders [like insomnia, sleep apnea and restless legs]] is critical, these experts say, (because disturbed sleep is a key risk factor [for diseases and unhealthy conditions [such as stroke, heart attack and high blood pressure]]).

「重要な」を意味する形容詞

訳 睡眠障害は脳卒中，心臓発作，高血圧といった病気および不健康状態の主な危険因子なので，不眠症，睡眠時無呼吸，むずむず脚症候群などの睡眠障害に対する安全で健康的な治療法を発見することは非常に重要だと，上記の専門家たちは述べている。

語句 treatment 名 治療／critical 形 重要な／key 形 主な，重要な／risk factor 危険因子／stroke 名 脳卒中／heart attack 心臓発作／high blood pressure 高血圧

7 [1]"There is a large amount of literature [showing 〈that people [who exercise] have better sleep〉]," Baron said. [2]"People [who exercise] reported an increase [in deep sleep] and a decrease [in the number of awakenings]. [3] (Plus), people felt (less) depressed, and their mood was better."

訳 [1]「運動をする人のほうがよく眠れるということを示している研究文献は数多くあります」とバロンは述べた。[2]「運動をする人は，深い眠りが増えて，（睡眠中の）覚醒が減ったと報告しています。[3]また，落ち込んだ気持ちが軽減され，気分もよくなったとのことです」

語句 [2]report 動 報告する／increase 名 増加／decrease 名 減少／the number of ～ ～の数／awakening 名 覚醒／[3]plus 副 その上／mood 名 気分（日本語では「よいムー

ド（＝雰囲気）のお店」のように使いますが，英語では「気分」という意味です。「雰囲気」には基本的にatmosphereを使います。）

8 [1] How much exercise is needed (to get a good night's rest)? [2] Most sleep studies have focused on the recommended amount: two and a half hours a week of moderate-intensity aerobic exercise, (along with strength or resistance training [that targets every muscle group two days a week]). [3] Kline says "brisk walking, light biking ... anything [that increases your heart rate (so that you can still talk (while exercising) but have to catch your breath every few sentences or so)], is considered moderate exercise."

段落冒頭の疑問文 → テーマの提示

〈S+be動詞〉の省略

can still talk 〜と have to catch your breath 〜を結ぶbut

訳 [1]ぐっすり眠るためには，どれだけの運動が必要なのだろうか。[2]ほとんどの睡眠に関する研究は，次の推奨量に着目している。それは，週2日の全筋肉群を対象とした筋力トレーニング，つまり抵抗トレーニングに加え，週2時間半の中強度の有酸素運動というものである。[3]クラインは「早歩きや軽いサイクリングや，（その他）何であれ運動しながらでも会話できるが，2〜3文おきに息継ぎをしないといけない程度に心拍数が上がるようなものであれば，適度な運動と考えられています」と言う。

語句 [1]get a good night's rest ぐっすり眠る／[2]a week 1週間に／moderate-intensity 形 中強度の（moderate 適度な，中くらいの）／aerobic exercise 有酸素運動／target 動 対象とする／muscle group 筋肉群／[3] brisk walking 早歩き／heart rate 心拍数／catch *one's* breath 息継ぎをする，呼吸を整える／every 基数 複数名詞 〜おきに（今回は 基数 の位置にfewがきています）／〜 or so 〜かそこら

文法・構文 [1]段落冒頭の疑問文は，「テーマ」を表します。第8段落は「ぐっすり眠るために必要な運動量について」がテーマだと判断できます。 [2]後半のthatの先行詞はstrength or resistance trainingです（*A* or *B*が主語になっている場合，動詞は基本的にBに合わせるのでthat targets 〜 と「3単現のs」が付いています）。 [3]〈so that S′ + 助動詞 + V′〉の形は「目的」を表すことが多いですが，今回は「結果」で解釈したほうが自然な意味になります。また，... is considered moderate exercise.は，consider OC「OをCとみなす」が受動態になった形です。so that 〜 の中のbutはcan still talk 〜 とhave to catch your breath 〜 を結んでいます。

9 [1] "I think 〈trying to do it (outside) is also helpful, (because bright light can help promote sleep)〉," Youngstedt added. [2] "Light exposure helps regulate the body clock."

訳 [1]「明るい陽光は睡眠促進に効くことがあるので，屋外でやってみるのもよいと思います」とヤングシュタットは付け加えた。[2]「光に当たることで，体内時計の調節にも効果があります」

語句 [1]help 原形 ～することを助ける，～に役立つ／[2]regulate 動 調節する

10 [1]Other studies show 〈that people [who exercise less than the recommended amount], and those [who go way beyond (in time and intensity)], see moderate benefits〉. [2]It's (only when you are training (to the level of an elite athlete)) that exercise can (actually) interfere (with sleep quality). [3]"High-level athletes, [who may overtrain (for a certain event)], do have issues [with sleep] (when traveling and under stress)," Youngstedt said. [4]"But (for the vast majority of us), that 's not a factor."

it is ... that ～ の強調構文

副詞節中の〈S´+be動詞〉の省略

訳 [1]他の研究によって，推奨量より運動量の少ない人や，推奨の時間や強度をはるかに超えて運動している人にも，そこそこの効果が見られることが示されている。[2]運動が実際に睡眠の質を妨げ得るのは，(実は) 一流の運動選手レベルでトレーニングをしている場合のみである。[3]「特定の大会のために過度な練習を行うことのあるハイレベルな運動選手は，移動中やストレスを感じているときによく眠れないことがあります」とヤングシュタットは述べた。[4]「しかし，私たちの圧倒的多数には当てはまりません」

語句 [1]go way beyond はるかに超える／intensity 名 激しさ／moderate 形 適度な，中くらいの／[2]elite athlete 一流の運動選手／interfere with ～ ～を妨げる／[3]overtrain 動 過度に練習する／certain 形 特定の／issue 名 問題／travel 動 移動する／[4]vast 形 莫大な／majority 名 大多数／factor 名 要因

文法・構文 [1]1つ目のandは，people who ～ と those who ～ を結んでいます。[2]It's only when ～ thatの形から「強調構文」だと判別できます（***Rule 75*** ⇒p.20）。[3]haveの直前のdoは「強調の助動詞」で，動詞haveの意味を強調しています。

11 [1]What 's the best time of day [to do this sleep-enhancing movement]?

段落冒頭の疑問文→テーマの提示

[2]Experts used to say 〈morning was best〉; (in fact), any exercise [within six hours of bedtime] was (strongly) discouraged. [3](On that topic), the science has changed. [4]"One common myth is 〈that exercise should be avoided (at night)〉," Youngstedt said. [5]"There are about 10% of us [for whom exercise at night does disturb sleep], but I (personally) think 〈that 's (because they aren't accustomed to it)〉. [6](For most of us), exercise [at night], (even if it ends (just a couple of hours before bedtime)), will help (with sleep)."

過去を表す語句(現在と対比)

過去との対比(今は違う)

「迷信」

訳 [1]この睡眠促進活動をするのに最適な時間帯はいつなのだろうか。[2]専門家たちはかつて，朝が最適だと言っていた。実際に（それどころか），就寝時刻から6時間以内には一切運動しないよう強く推奨されていた。[3]しかしこのテーマについて，科学は変わったのである。[4]「ある一般に信じられている誤った通説は，運動を夜に行うのは避けるべきだというものです」とヤングシュタットは述べた。[5]「夜に運動すると実際に眠りが妨げられるという人も全体の10パーセント程度はいますが，私個人としては，それは夜の運動に慣れていないからだと思います。[6]私たちの大半にとっては，夜間の運動は，就寝のたった2〜3時間前に終わるものであっても，睡眠を促進してくれるはずです」

語句 [1]enhance 動 促進する，高める／[2]used to 原形 (かつて) 〜したものだった／discourage 動 思いとどまらせる／[3]on 前 〜に関して／[4]common 形 よくある，一般的な／myth 名 神話，誤った通説／avoid 動 避ける／[5]disturb 動 邪魔をする，妨害する／*be* accustomed to 〜 〜に慣れている，〜を習慣としている／[6]a couple of 〜 いくつかの〜／bedtime 名 就寝時間

文法・構文 [1]第8段落同様に，冒頭に疑問文がきています。第11段落は「運動をする適切な時間帯について」がテーマだと判断できます。[2]この文の〈used to 原形〉「(かつて)〜したものだった」で「過去」が表され，次の文の現在完了形has changedで，その変化が対比されています。「過去：朝に運動するのがベスト」→「現在：その考えは変わった」という流れです。[4]多くの受験生はmythを「神話」と暗記していますが，「迷信，誤った通説」の意味が圧倒的に重要です。また，「〜という迷信があるが，実際にはその迷信は間違いだ」のような流れが多いです（今回も，3つあとの文でDestroying that myth is especially helpful 〜「そのような誤った通説が破棄されれば，〜助かる」という流れになっています）。[5]doesは「強調の助動詞」で，動詞disturbを強調しています。また，becauseは副詞節を作る接続詞ですが，今回のようにCのカタマリを作ることもあります。

12 [1]Destroying that myth (S) is (V) (especially) helpful (C) (for those [who tend to stay up later]). [2]"Night owls (S) have (V) problems (O) (getting up in the morning); they (S) (just) can't do (V) it (O)," Baron (S) said (V). [3]"Their mood and ability [to apply effort] (S) (just) isn't there (V). [4]《If you (S') 're sacrificing (V') sleep (O') (for exercise)》, is (V) that (S) a good idea (C)?"

迷信を否定

訳 [1]そのような誤った通説が破棄されれば，特に夜型の人々にとって有益だ。[2]「夜更かしをする人は朝起きるのが苦手なのです。どうしてもできないんです」とバロンは述べた。[3]「気分も乗らないし，努力するだけの力もないのです。[4]運動のために睡眠を犠牲にしているとしたら，それは得策なのでしょうか？」

語句 [1]destroy 動 破壊する／tend to 原形 〜する傾向にある／[2]night owl 夜更かしをする人／have problems -ing 〜するのに苦労する／[3]mood 名 気持ち／apply 動 (心などを) 向ける／[4]sacrifice 動 犠牲にする

文法・構文 [2]justは，否定語の前で「少しも〜ない」となるので，和訳では「どうしても〜ない」と訳してあります。

13 [1] (However), one of the benefits of staying (with a morning exercise routine), she adds, is 〈that you are less likely to cancel〉. [2] "Morning exercisers are more consistent," she explained. [3] "So many of us have competing demands (in our day), so (if we leave it to the evening), we might not follow through."

訳 [1]一方，朝の運動習慣を続けるメリットの１つに，途中でやめる可能性が低いことがあると彼女は付け加える。[2]「朝に運動をする人のほうが継続的に行っているのです」と彼女は説明した。[3]「私たちの非常に多くが，日中はやらなくてはいけないことが色々あるので，運動を夜に残しておくと，実行しない可能性があるのです」

語句 [1] *be* likely to 原形 ～する可能性が高い／cancel 動 止める／[2] consistent 形 一貫した，着実な／[3] competing 形 相反する，競い合うような／demand 名 要望，必要(性)／follow through やり抜く

14 [1] Staying the course is important (to keep sleep benefits in place). [2] "They have to keep it up," Youngstedt said. [3] "I think 〈 it helps to have a consistent schedule〉, so figure out 〈what works best for you〉 and (then) stick to it."

訳 [1]運動の習慣を続けることは，睡眠に関するメリットをきちんと機能させるために重要である。[2]「その習慣は持続させる必要があるのです」とヤングシュタットは述べた。[3]「一貫したスケジュールにするとよいと思うので，どうすれば自分にとって最もうまくいくのかを見極め，それを続けてください」

語句 [1] keep ～ in place ～を持続させる／[2] keep it up 頑張り続ける／[3] figure out 見極める／work best 最もうまくいく／stick to ～ ～に固執する

文法・構文 [1] ここでのstaying the courseは前段落のstaying with a morning exercise routineを受けて，「運動の習慣を続けること」を表しています。[3] 仮主語構文で，helpsは自動詞「役立つ」として使われています。〈help to 原形〉「～するのに役立つ」の形ではありません。

15 [1] "(If you have insomnia or sleep apnea), it 's even more important to exercise," Baron said. [2] "You will (likely) feel (even) less inclined to exercise (when you are fatigued), but keep (with it), (because it can (really) help)."

訳 [1]「不眠症や睡眠時無呼吸があるのなら，運動はいっそう重要です」とバロンは述べた。[2]「疲れているときはなおさら運動する気が起きないでしょうが，本当に有効なので，続けてください」

語句 [2] *be*[feel] inclined to 原形 ～したい気分である／fatigued 形 疲れている／keep with it 頑張り抜く／help 動 役に立つ，助けになる（このhelpは自動詞）

文法・構文 [1と2] evenは「～さえ」ではなく，比較級の強調表現「なおいっそう～」です。

音読をしよう！ 01

If you're one of the third of all Americans / who suffer from insomnia // — roughly 108 million of us — // put away your sleeping pills. // Science has a much safer solution. // "There has been more and more research in the last decade // showing exercise can reduce insomnia," // Rush University clinical psychologist Kelly Glazer Baron said. // "In one study we did, // for example, // older women suffering from insomnia / said their sleep improved from poor to good / when they exercised. // They had more energy and were less depressed." //

"There are more solid studies recently / that looked at people clinically diagnosed with insomnia disorder, // rather than self-described poor sleepers," // agreed the University of Pittsburgh's Christopher Kline, // who studies sleep through the lens of sports medicine. // "The results show / exercise improves both self-reported / and objective measures of sleep quality, // such as what's measured in a clinical sleep lab." //

Exercise is not quite / as effective as sleeping pills, // admits Arizona State University sleep researcher Shawn Youngstedt, // but if you consider the potential problems of pharmaceutically induced sleep, // one's thinking changes. // "Sleeping pills are extremely dangerous," / Youngstedt said. // "They are as bad as smoking a pack of cigarettes a day. // Not to mention they cause infections, // falling // and dementia in the elderly, // and they lose their effectiveness after a few weeks. // It's less expensive, // healthier // and just as easy to exercise," // he said, // "and there's an added bonus. // Research suggests / those who are physically active have a lower risk / of developing insomnia in the first place." //

There's more good news for the 18 million Americans / who struggle with sleep apnea, // a dangerous disorder in which you temporarily stop breathing / for up to a minute during the night. // Exercise can help with that, / too. // "For sleep apnea, exercise has always been recommended," // Kline said, // "mostly to jump-start weight loss from dieting, // because those with sleep apnea are normally overweight or obese. // But we did a study where the participants didn't diet, // and exercise alone led to a 25% reduction of sleep apnea symptoms / over a 12-week period." //

"Exercise has also been shown to help with restless-leg symptoms across all age groups," // Youngstedt said. // Restless-leg syndrome, // a disorder of the nervous system, // occurs when the legs // — or other parts of the body like the arms or face — // itch, // burn // or move involuntarily. // The irresistible urge to move / often happens at night, // which disrupts sleep. //

Finding a safe, // healthy type of treatment / for sleep disorders like insomnia, // sleep apnea // and restless legs is critical, // these experts say, // because disturbed sleep is a key risk factor for diseases and unhealthy conditions // such as stroke, // heart attack // and high blood pressure. //

"There is a large amount of literature showing that people who exercise / have better sleep," // Baron said. // "People who exercise reported an increase in deep sleep // and a decrease in the number of awakenings. // Plus, people felt less depressed, // and their mood was better." //

How much exercise is needed to get a good night's rest? // Most sleep studies have focused on the recommended amount: // two and a half hours a week of moderate-intensity aerobic exercise, // along with strength or resistance training that targets every muscle group / two days a week. // Kline says / "brisk walking, // light biking ... // anything that increases your heart rate / so that you can still talk while exercising / but have to catch your breath every few sentences or so, // is considered moderate exercise." //

"I think trying to do it outside is also helpful, // because bright light can help promote sleep," // Youngstedt added. // "Light exposure helps regulate the body clock." //

Other studies show / that people who exercise less than the recommended amount, // and those who go way beyond in time and intensity, // see moderate benefits. // It's only when you are training to the level of an elite athlete / that exercise can actually interfere with sleep quality. // "High-level athletes, // who may overtrain for a certain event, // do have issues with sleep when traveling and under stress," // Youngstedt said. // "But for the vast majority of us, // that's not a factor." //

What's the best time of day to do this sleep-enhancing movement? // Experts used to say / morning was best; // in fact, // any exercise within six hours of bedtime / was strongly discouraged. // On that topic, // the science has changed. // "One common myth / is that exercise should be avoided at night," // Youngstedt said. // "There are about 10% of us for whom exercise at night does disturb sleep, // but I personally think that's because they aren't accustomed to it. // For most of us, // exercise at night, // even if it ends just a couple of hours before bedtime, // will help with sleep." //

Destroying that myth is especially helpful for those who tend to stay up later. // "Night owls have problems getting up in the morning; // they just can't do it," // Baron said. // "Their mood and ability to apply effort just isn't there. // If you're sacrificing sleep for exercise, // is that a good idea?" //

However, // one of the benefits of staying with a morning exercise routine, // she adds, // is that you are less likely to cancel. // "Morning exercisers are more consistent," // she explained. // "So many of us have competing demands in our day, // so if we leave it to the evening, // we might not follow through." //

Staying the course is important to keep sleep benefits in place. // "They have to keep it up," // Youngstedt said. // "I think it helps to have a consistent schedule, // so figure out what works best for you and then stick to it." //

"If you have insomnia or sleep apnea, // it's even more important to exercise," Baron said. // "You will likely feel even less inclined to exercise when you are fatigued, // but keep with it, // because it can really help." //

Lesson 2 解答・解説

▶問題 別冊 p.9

このLessonで出てくるルール

Rule 20 読解 「感情表現」に注目する！（動詞）⇒問1 (1)
Rule 41 解法 まずは「形」から考える！ ⇒問1 (4)
Rule 2 読解 「重要な」という意味の重要単語に注目！ ⇒問2 (イ)
Rule 72 構文 分詞構文の訳し方のコツ ⇒問3
Rule 46 解法 「過剰」選択肢のパターン（all系）⇒問3
Rule 47 解法 「入れ替え」選択肢のパターン（原因と結果）⇒問3

解答

問1（1） ④　（2） ③　（3） ③　（4） ④　（5） ③
問2（ア） ②　（イ） ③　問3 ②・④

問1

（1） 難易度 ★★☆

空所（1）を含む英文は，The notion that ～「～という考え」が長いSで，has （　1　） and annoyedがVになります。空所部分は**annoyed「イライラさせる，悩ませる」と並ぶもの**です（usを目的語にとる）。ここでannoyという「感情動詞」に注目してください。

>>> Rule 20 読解 「感情表現」に注目する！（動詞）

「感情」を表す動詞は文法問題でばかり注目されますが，長文でも非常に大切です。喜怒哀楽に関することは筆者の主張にかかわりやすく，設問にも絡みやすいからです。

感情動詞

- □ amuse 楽しませる
- □ excite ワクワクさせる
- □ satisfy 満足させる
- □ move / touch 感動させる
- □ interest 興味を与える
- □ please / delight 喜ばせる
- □ relieve 安心させる
- □ fascinate / absorb 夢中にさせる

- □ attract 興味を引く
- □ surprise / amaze / astonish 驚かせる
- □ embarrass 恥ずかしい思いをさせる
- □ bore / tire / exhaust 疲れさせる
- □ depress / disappoint / discourage がっかりさせる
- □ disgust うんざりさせる
- □ trouble / bother / disturb / puzzle 悩ませる［困らせる］
- □ annoy / irritate イライラさせる［悩ませる］
- □ offend 怒らせる
- □ upset ろうばいさせる，むしゃくしゃさせる
- □ dismay ろうばいさせる
- □ shock ショックを与える
- □ scare / frighten / terrify 怖がらせる

選択肢の中でannoyedと自然に並ぶものは，④troubledです。

さらに，後ろにはthis puzzling question「この困惑させる，難解な問題」とあり，これもヒントになります（〈this + 名詞〉については***Rule 4*** ⇒p.71）。

選択肢の訳

① deny「否定する」の過去分詞形　② make「作る」の過去分詞形
③ ignore「無視する」の過去分詞形　**④ trouble「困らせる」の過去分詞形**

（2） **難易度** ★☆☆

空所の後ろにあるroleに注目して，**〈play a 形容詞 role in ～〉「～において形容詞な役割を果たす」**にすればOKです。play only a limited role in ～「～において限られた役割しか果たさない」となります。この形の表現は長文に限らず，英作文でも重宝するので，以下で代表的なものをチェックしておきましょう。inは「分野・範囲（～において）」を表します。

「～な役割を果たす」の頻出表現

- □ play an important [a significant / vital / crucial など] role in ～
  ～において重要な役割を果たす
- □ play a central role in ～ ～において中心的な役割を果たす
- □ play a major role in ～ ～において主要な［重要な］役割を果たす
- □ play a minor role in ～ ～で重要な役割を果たしていない
- □ play a leading[leadership] role in ～ ～において指導的な役割を果たす

選択肢の訳

① 到達する［アクセスする］　② 通知する　**③ 果たす**　④ 叩く

(3) **難易度** ★☆☆

空所前のnot onlyに注目して，**not only *A* but {also} *B*「AだけでなくBも」**を考えます。③butを選んで，Perception derives not only from our five senses but from ～とすればOKです。not only *A* but also *B*は様々な変形パターンがあります。今回のようにalsoが消えるパターンの他に，onlyが**merely/simply/just**になるパターン，**butが消える**パターンがあります（***Rule 1*** ⇒p.107）。

(4) **難易度** ★★☆

>>> *Rule 41* 解法 まずは「形」から考える！

空欄補充問題などでは，多くの受験生が「適切な訳になるもの・自然な意味になるもの」ばかりを考えがちですが，その発想だと訳すのに時間がかかり，知らない単語があれば訳せずに，解けなくなります。

英語は**「形」が大事な言語**です。「品詞・語順・文型・語法」など，「まずは形から考える」発想が入試では求められているのです。例えば「普段から品詞を意識して読んでる？」と言わんばかりに，品詞の問題がよく出ます。どんな問題であれ「**形から入って**，それがダメなときに意味を考える」という姿勢を持つことが難関大攻略のカギになります。

26行目はfrom *A* to *B*「AからBまで」の形で，*A*はour days as hunter-gatherers, *B*はour current existence（ 4 ）on our smartphonesです。（ 4 ）on our smartphonesが後ろからour current existenceという名詞のカタマリを修飾していると考え，現在分詞を使った④paying billsを選べばOKです。our current existence paying bills on our smartphonesとなります。他の選択肢を選ぶと，すべて名詞existenceの直後に名詞がくるのでアウトです。

(5) **難易度** ★☆☆

（ 5 ）us a solutionという形から，〈V 人 物〉の形だと考えます。この形がとれるのは③offersと④takesです。「私たちに解決策を与える」という意味が適切なので，③offersを選びます（**〈offer 人 物〉「人に物を提供する」**）。今回の設問でもまずは「形」に注目して，絞った選択肢で意味を考えることで，処理時間を短縮できます。ちなみに，〈take 人 物〉「人の物(時間)をとる」→「人に時間がかかる」です。他の選択肢は，〈deprive 人 of 物〉「人から物を奪う」，〈help 人 {to} 原形〉「人が～するのを手伝う」／〈help 人 with 物事〉「人の物事を手伝う」の形が大事です。

問2

（ア）**難易度** ★☆☆

in terms of 〜「〜の観点から」という熟語で，意味が近いのは②from the perspective ofです。-spectは「見る」という意味で（inspect「中を見る」→「検査する」），perspectiveは「ものの見方」を表します。

選択肢の訳

① 〜する方法によって　**② 〜の観点から**
③ 〜のために　④（on account of 〜 で）〜が理由で

（イ）**難易度** ★★☆

Perception (イ)matters because 〜 で, mattersが動詞として使われています。**動詞matterは「重要だ」**という意味で，③is importantを選びます。matterは本来「中身が詰まった」という意味で，そこから「(中身が詰まった) もの・こと」（名詞），「(中身が詰まったほど) 重要だ」（動詞）となります。

>>> *Rule 2* 読解 「重要な」という意味の重要単語に注目！

長文の中で「重要だ」という語があれば，当然**大事な内容（つまり設問で聞かれる）**に決まっていますよね。ですから「重要だ」を意味する単語に反応することが大切ですが，importantは有名でもその類義語は意外と知られていません。多くの単語帳では，significantは「意義深い」，fundamentalは「根本的な」，criticalは「批判的な」，vitalは「致命的な」といった訳語を最初に挙げているからです。それらも間違いではありませんが，長文ではまず「**重要な**」という意味を考えることが大切なんです（実際に英英辞典を引いてみると，最初の意味に“important”を載せている辞書がたくさんあるんです）。

「重要な」という意味の重要単語（形容詞編）

□ crucial	□ essential	□ significant	□ fundamental
□ indispensable	□ priceless	□ invaluable	□ principal
□ integral	□ critical	□ vital	□ key
□ grave	□ primary	□ leading	□ foremost
□ capital			

「重要だ」という意味の重要単語（動詞編）
□ matter 名 もの，こと　動 重要だ　※「中身が詰まった」が原義。
□ count 動 数える，重要だ　※「(数に入れるくらい) 重要だ」

ちなみに，36行目・45行目ではessentialが使われています。また，Lesson1の38行目ではcritical，39行目ではkeyが使われていました。本当によく出てきますよ。

選択肢の訳

① はっきりしている　② 難しい　**③ 重要である**　④ 疑わしい

問3 難易度 ★★☆ 思考力

まず正解の選択肢について見てみましょう。

② 私たちが，自分が知覚したものが客観的現実だと思っている時でさえ，感覚過程が私たちの知覚を妨げている。

8行目に，Your brain gives you the impression that your perceptions are objectively real, yet the sensory processes that make perception possible actually separate you from ever accessing that reality directly.とあり，選択肢の内容と合致します。本文のthe sensory processes ～ actually separate you from ever accessing that reality directlyが，選択肢ではThe sensory processes interfere with our perceptionsと表されているわけです。

本文冒頭の疑問文（1行目）**When** you open your eyes, do you see the world as it really is? Do you see reality?で**テーマを提示**しています（***Rule 6*** ⇒p.17）。それに対して6行目The answer is that we don't see reality.で結論を答え，そのあとに「感覚過程が知覚に干渉している，それによって現実をありのまま見ていない」と詳しく説明しています。内容自体は難しいですが，**「疑問文でテーマの提示」→「回答」**という流れで整理できるわけです。

ちなみにこの英文は，他にも疑問文を使ってテーマを提示している文が数か所あります（文構造の分析のページで確認してみてください）。

④ 私たちの知覚は，原始時代から現代に至るまで，私たちが複雑な世界で生き残ることを可能にした。

「知覚によって可能になったこと」を探すと，24行目にClearly our brain's model of perception has served our species well, allowing us to successfully survive in the world and its ever-shifting complexity, from our days as hunter-gatherers to our current existence paying bills on our smartphones. とあり，選択肢と合致します。1つ目のコンマ以降は分詞構文で，分詞構文の訳し方はたくさんあるとされますが，今回のように分詞構文が**後半**にある場合は「**そして〜**」か「**〜しながら**」と訳せばOKです。今回は「そして〜」で十分意味がとれますね。

>>> *Rule 72* 構文 分詞構文の訳し方のコツ

分詞構文は従来，5つの訳し方（時／原因・理由／条件／譲歩／付帯状況）が羅列されてきましたが，それを丸暗記する必要はありません。そもそも分詞構文は2つの文を「**補足的にくっつけたもの**」なので，意味も「軽く（適当に）」つなげればOKなんです。

さらに詳しく説明すると，**分詞構文の意味は「位置」**で決まります。

分詞構文の「意味」

(1) 文頭 [-ing ~], S V. → **適当な意味**

(2) 文中 S, [-ing ~], V. → **適当な意味** ※主語の説明になることが多い。

(3) 文末 S V(,) [-ing ~]. → **「そして〜」「〜しながら」**

「文頭・文中」にある場合は，主節との関係を考えて「適当（適切）」な意味を考えてください。手っ取り早い方法としては「**〜して［〜で］，SVだ**」のように，「て・で」を使うと便利です。

分詞構文が「文末」にある場合は，「そして〜だ／〜しながら」が便利です。「**SVだ。そして〜だ**」か，「**〜しながら，SVする**」の意味がほとんどです。和訳問題では両方を検討して，適切なほうの訳にすればOKです（どちらの意味でも通る場合もあります）。

ここが 思考力 本文の内容が，選択肢で「抽象化」されている

本文の該当箇所と選択肢を見比べてみましょう。下線部がそれぞれ対応しています。

本 文： 〜, allowing us to successfully survive in the world and its ever-shifting complexity, [from] our days as hunter-gatherers [to] our current existence paying bills on our smartphones.

選択肢： Our perception has enabled us to survive in the complex world, [from] primitive ages [to] our modern times.

〈allow 人 to 原形〉「人が～するのを許可する」→ 選択肢では〈enable 人 to 原形〉「人が～するのを可能にする」に言い換えられています。その後は「狩猟採集民としての時代」→**「原始時代」**,「スマホで支払いを行う現在の我々」→**「現代」**と,**「本文の具体的な内容」→「選択肢で抽象的にまとめた内容」**になっています。このパターンは「具体」⇔「抽象」を行き来しないといけないので，思考力を問う問題に分類されます。

しかしこのような場合でも，皆さんはこの本で「from *A* to *B* は対比を表す」などを意識しながら読んでいけば，十分に対応可能となるはずです。

補足 from *A* to *B* が出てきたら，すべて対比となるとは限りませんが,「AからBへと変化する」という意味で，A⇔Bの関係になることが多いと知っておいてください。

今回も本文の from *A* to *B* で「昔⇔現代」という対比関係をつかめていれば，選択肢で言い換えられても「昔⇔現代」という関係は同じだと判断できます。

では，誤りの選択肢について1つずつ確認しましょう。

① 古代の人々は皆，世界のありのままの姿は自分の目でしか見ることができないと考えていた。

選択肢の ancient times「古代」に注目して「過去」の話を探すと，2行目に for thousands of years とあり，この辺りで「数千年前～現在」の話をしているとわかります。そして，3行目に The notion that what we see might not be what is truly there has (1) and annoyed us. Great minds of history have taken up this puzzling question again and again. とあります。昔から「自分の目で見ているものが現実とは限らない」と考える人がいたとわかるので，選択肢の all believed that ～ からアウトだとわかります。all のような「全部」系の語句は誤りの選択肢でよく使われます。

>>> *Rule 46* 解法 「過剰」選択肢のパターン（all系）

内容一致問題でよくある誤りの選択肢に，本文の内容を**「選択肢で過剰に言う（極端に言い過ぎる）」**パターンがあります。例えば本文で「6つのうち，5つはプラス，1つだけマイナス」とあったとして，それを選択肢で「6つ全部がプラス」とする選択肢です（当然アウト）。まずは次ページの「全部」の表現をチェックして，選択肢で反応できるようにしておきましょう。

全部→不正解の可能性「高」

□ all すべての	□ both 両方の（両方とも全部）	
□ every すべての	□ whole 全体の	□ entire 全体の
□ entirely 全体に	□ complete 完全な	□ completely 完全に
□ totally まったく，完全に	□ always いつも	□ necessarily 必ず
□ cannot ～ without ... ～すれば必ず…する（二重否定）		

こういった語句に反応したら,「さすがに全部ではないでしょ？　例外あるんじゃないの？」とツッコミを入れながら, 本文に戻って該当箇所を探してください。また,「全部」の応用として,〈no + 名詞〉や nothing「何もない，まったくない」も同じ発想でチェックしてください。

注意 このテクニックを拡大解釈して,「選択肢にallがあったら必ず不正解」なんて考えないでください。確かに不正解になる確率は高いです（ボクの経験上では7～8割は不正解）が，絶対ではないので，必ず「allに注意しながら本文に戻って確認する」姿勢を忘れずに。

③ 私たちの五感は，単なる機械的な媒体であるという点で，コンピューターのキーボードとは異なる。

10行目にOur five senses are like a keyboard to a computerとあります（likeは前置詞「～のような」)。選択肢は*be* different from ～「～とは異なる」で真逆の内容です。このように,「同じ」or「異なる」に関する内容は設問でよく狙われます。

⑤ 多くの人々は，肉体の死によって知覚の死がもたらされることを望んでいる。

「多くの人が望んでいること」を探すと，37行目にThe death that we all fear is less the death of the body and more the death of perception, as many of us would be quite happy to know that after “bodily death” our ability to engage in perception of the world around us continues. とあります。本文では「私たちは知覚の死を恐れている／「肉体の死」のあとも知覚する能力が続いて欲しい」とあり，選択肢の「肉体の死によって知覚の死がもたらされることを望む」とは真逆の内容です。選択肢で〈結果 is caused by **原因**〉という因果表現が使われていますが，内容一致問題ではこういった表現を利用したひっかけがあるので注意してください。

>>> *Rule 47* 解法 「入れ替え」選択肢のパターン（原因と結果）

因果関係を示す表現はすでに解説しました（***Rule 16*** ⇒p.15）が，内容一致問題でもよく狙われます。選択肢のパターンは以下のものに集約できます。

本文	*A* **cause** *B*. ... *C* **lead to** *D*.
	「Aが **原因** でBが 結果 」「Cが **原因** でDが 結果 」
選択肢	*B* cause *A*. → ✕ 因果関係が「逆」なのでアウト（**超頻出**）
	A cause *D*. → ✕ AとDに因果関係は「ない」のでアウト
	B result from *A*. → ○ 因果関係がバッチリ合ってる

「因果関係はない」という選択肢は判断するのが一番難しいです。「Aが原因・Dが結果」ということ自体はOKなので正解に見えるのですが,「AとDに因果関係はない」ので不正解になるわけです。

⑥ 知覚神経科学は，将来，さまざまな技術革新につながるだろう。

the neuroscience of perceptionについて，45行目にit will lead to future innovations in thought and behaviorとあります。知覚に関する神経科学によって可能になるのは「思考や行動における革新」であり，technological innovation「技術革新」ではありません（両方とも〈**原因** lead to 結果〉の関係）。

さらに，46行目のWhat is the next greatest innovation?に対して，It's not a technology. It's a way of seeing.と述べています（**not *A*. {~~But~~} *B*.**の形は***Rule 1*** ⇒p.107）。ここでも「技術ではなく，ものの見方」と主張しているので，やはりtechnological innovationsはアウトだと判断できます。

文構造の分析

1 [1](When you open your eyes), do you see the world 《as it (really) is》? [2]Do you see reality? [3]Humans have been asking themselves this question (for thousands of years). [4]The notion 《that 〈what we see φ〉 might not be 〈what is (truly) there〉》 has troubled and annoyed us. [5]Great minds of history have taken up this puzzling question (again and again). [6]They all had theories, but (now) neuroscience has an answer.

段落冒頭の疑問文 → テーマの提示
同格のthat
〈this＋名詞〉→ まとめ表現

訳 [1]目を開けたとき，あなたは世界をありのままに見ているだろうか。[2]現実を見ているだろうか。[3]人間は何千年もの間にわたって，この問いを自らに投げかけてきた。[4]私たちに見えているものが実際にそこに存在するものではないかもしれないという考えは，私たちを困らせ，悩ませてきた。[5]歴史上の偉人たちは，この難解な問いを繰り返し取り上げてきた。[6]彼らはみな持論を持っていたが，今では神経科学がその答えを出している。

語句 [1]as it really is ありのままに／[4]notion 名 考え／trouble 動 困らせる／annoy 動 悩ませる／[5]mind 名（特定の分野において）聡明な人／take up 取り上げる／puzzling 形 難解な（puzzleは本来「困らせる」という意味で，puzzlingは直訳「人を困らせるような」→「難解な」となりました）

文法・構文 [1]as it is「そのままで」は様態のasを使った慣用表現としてそのまま押さえておきましょう。直訳「それ（it）がある（is）のと同じように（as）」→「そのままで」となりました。今回は間にreally「実際に」が入り込んでいます。[4]同格のthat以下は，S′とC′どちらにもwhat節が使われています。SのThe notionに対応するV（has ～）を見失わないことが大切です。[5]〈this＋名詞〉は「まとめ表現」の目印です（***Rule 4*** ⇒p.71）。直前の内容がわからなくても，puzzling question「難解な問い」について話しているのだと判断できます。[6]allはSのTheyと同格です。

2 [1]The answer is 〈that we don't see reality〉. [2]The world exists. [3]It's (just) that we don't see it. [4]We do not experience the world (as it is) (because our brain didn't evolve (to do so)). [5]It is a kind of paradox: Your brain gives you the impression 〈that your perceptions are (objectively) real〉, yet the sensory processes [that make perception possible] (actually) separate you (from ever accessing that reality directly). [6]Our five senses are like a keyboard [to a computer] — they provide the means for us [to process

同格のthat
比喩
不定詞の意味上のS

information [from the world]], but they have very little to do with 〈what is then experienced (in perception)〉. [7] They are (in essence) (just) mechanical media, and (therefore) play only a limited role (in 〈what we perceive φ 〉). [8] (In fact), (in terms of the number of connections [that our brain makes φ]), just 10 percent of 〈how we process sight〉 comes (from our eyes). [9] The other 90 percent comes (from other parts of our brains). [10] Perception derives not only (from our five senses) but (from our brain's seemingly infinitely refined network [that makes sense of all the incoming information]). [11] The new findings [of perceptual neuroscience] reveal 〈why we don't perceive reality〉, and 〈why this can lead to creativity and innovation [at work, at home, or at play]〉.

因果表現

データ表現

因果関係を示す表現

訳 [1] その答えとは，私たちは現実を見ていないというものだ。[2] 世界は存在している。[3] 私たちに見えていないだけなのだ。[4] 私たちはありのままの世界を経験していない。なぜなら，そうするように人間の脳が進化しなかったからだ。[5] それは一種のパラドックスになっている。脳は人に，その人が知覚したものが客観的事実であるという印象を与えるが，知覚を生じさせる感覚過程によって実際には，人は決してその現実に直に触れることができないのだ。[6] 私たちの五感は，コンピューターのキーボードのようなものだ。五感は私たちが世界から得た情報を処理する手段を提供してくれるが，そのあと知覚する際に経験されることにはほとんど関係していない。[7] 五感とは，本質的には単なる機械的な媒体にすぎず，したがって私たちが知覚するものにおいて，限られた役割しか果たしていない。[8] 実のところ，私たちの脳が作る接合の数の観点からは，視覚処理の過程のうち，目で行われるのはたったの10パーセントである。[9] 残りの90パーセントは，脳の他の部分で行われるのだ。[10] 知覚は，五感からだけではなく，入ってくるすべての情報を把握する，一見限りなく精密であるように思える脳のネットワークからも生じる。[11] 知覚神経科学における新発見によって，どうして私たちは現実を知覚しないのか，そしてなぜそのことによって，仕事や家庭，遊びにおける創造性や革新が生まれるのかが解明されている。

語句 [2] exist 動 存在する／[3] It's just that S´V´ ただS´V´なだけだ／[4] experience 動 経験する，知覚する／evolve 動 進化する／[5] paradox 名 パラドックス，逆説，矛盾（「パラドックス，逆説」とは，「一見矛盾しているように見えるが，真実を表すもの」です）／impression 名 印象／perception 名 知覚，認識／objectively 副 客観的に／yet 接 しかし／sensory 形 感覚[知覚]上の／process 名 過程，処理／separate *A* from *B*　AをBから引き離す／access 動 到達する，アクセスする／[6] five senses 五感（視覚・聴覚・嗅覚・味覚・触覚のこと）／means 名 手段，方法／process 動 処理する／have little to do with ～ ～とほとんど関係がない／[7] in essence 本質的には／media (mediumの複数形) 名 媒体（情報伝達の仲立ちとなるもののこと）／play a role 役割を演じる／perceive 動 知覚する／[8] in terms of ～ ～の観点から／connection 名 接続，接合／sight 名 視覚／[10] derive from ～ ～に由来する／seemingly 副 一見したところ／infinitely 副 無限に／refined 形精密な，洗練された／make sense of ～ ～を理解する／incoming 形 入ってくる／ [11] reveal 動 明らかにする／lead to ～ ～をもたらす／creativity 名 創造性／innovation 名 革新

文法・構文 [3] It seems that ～やIt's just ～などは仮主語に見えますが，特殊なitで熟語扱いとしています。[4] as it is「ありのままで」は第1段落1文目でも解説しました。また文末のdo soはexperience the world as it is「ありのまま世界を経験する」を指します。[5] この文で使われているyetは「接続詞」で，butとほぼ同じ意味・働きです。[8] just 10 percent ～ our eyesは,「私たちが視覚を処理する過程のたった10パーセントが，目からきている」が直訳です。[10] not only *A* but {also} *B*からalsoが省略されています。後半は形容詞句seemingly infinitely refined「一見限りなく精密であるように見える」がまとめて前からnetworkを修飾し，さらに後ろからも関係詞節（that makes sense of ～）がnetworkを修飾しています。[11] 1つ目のandは，why we don't perceive reality とwhy this can lead to ～ playを結んでいます。

3 [1] (Given this), why does this matter (to you)? [2] Why might you need to depart (from 〈the way [you currently perceive]〉)? [3] (After all), it feels like we see reality (accurately), (at least most of the time). [4] (Clearly) our brain's model of perception has served our species (well), (allowing us to (successfully) survive (in the world and its ever-shifting complexity), (from our days [as hunter-gatherers] to our current existence [paying bills on our smartphones])). [5] We are able to find food and shelter, hold down a job, and build meaningful relationships. [6] We have built cities, launched astronauts (into space), and created the Internet. [7] We must be doing something [right], so who cares 〈that we don't see reality〉?

段落冒頭の疑問文 → テーマの提示

具体例

段落末の疑問文 → 反語

訳 [1] このことを踏まえたうえで，どうしてこれがあなたにとって重要なことなのだろうか。[2] どうして，現在の知覚方法から離れる必要があるかもしれないのだろうか。[3] というのも，少なくともたいていの場合，私たちは現実を正確に見ているように思えるのだ。[4] 私たちの脳の知覚様式は間違いなく私たちの種に役立ってきたし，そのおかげで私たちは，狩猟採集民の時代からスマートフォンで支払いを行う現代の我々にいたるまで，世界とその絶え間なく変化し続ける複雑さの中で生き残ることに成功してきた。[5] 私たちは食糧や住みかを見つけ，安定した仕事に就き，有意義な関係性を築くことができる。[6] 私たちは都市を築き，宇宙飛行士を宇宙に送り出し，インターネットを作り出した。[7] 私たちは正しいことをしているに違いない。だから，私たちに現実が見えていないことなんてどうでもいいのだ。

語句 [1] given 前 ～を考慮すると　※本来分詞構文で，直訳「～を（情報として）与えられると」→

「～を考慮すると」となります。／matter 動 重要である／[2] depart from ～ ～から離れる／the way S´V´ S´V´する方法／currently 副 現在（≒ now）／[3] after all（通例文頭で）何しろ～だから／accurately 副 正確に／[4] serve well 役立つ／successfully 副 うまく～する，～に成功する／shift 動 変化する／complexity 名 複雑さ／hunter-gatherer 名 狩猟採集民／existence 名 存在，生存物／pay a bill 支払いをする／[5] shelter 名 住みか　※「核シェルター」を連想しがちですが，雨をしのぐ程度の簡単なものにも使われます。／hold down a job やめずに仕事をする／meaningful 形 有意義な／[6] launch 動 打ち上げる，送り出す／astronaut 名 宇宙飛行士／space 名 宇宙／[7] Who cares ～？ ～なんてどうでもいい

Lesson 2

文法・構文 [1]段落冒頭の疑問文は「テーマ」を表します。第3段落以降は「なぜ知覚についての正しい認識が重要なのか」「なぜ現在の知覚方法から離れる必要があるのか」がテーマだと判断できます。またmatter「重要である」も押さえておきましょう。[3]after allは，「結局」という意味が有名ですが，文頭に置かれると「だって，というのも」という「理由」を意味することが多いです。またlikeは本来「前置詞」で，〈feel like 名詞〉という形が基本ですが，feel like S´V´のように「接続詞」として用いられることもあります（辞書にも載っています）。[4]from *A* to *B*「AからBまで」は「具体例」を示すときによく使われます。今回も「脳の知覚様式が役に立ってきた」場面の具体例として，「狩猟採集民の時代」「現代の生活」が挙げられています。ちなみに，paying bills ～ は分詞のカタマリで，our current existenceを修飾しています。[5]2つ目のandは，find ～／hold down ～／build ～ の3つを結んでいます。「脳の知的様式が役に立ってきた」ことの「具体例」が羅列されています。[6]前文と同様に，具体例を羅列しています。[7]段落末の疑問文は「反語」を表します（***Rule 6*** ⇒p.17）。直訳「誰が～を気にするだろうか」→「誰も～を気にしない」→「～なんてどうでもいい」となります。

4 [1]Perception matters (because it serves (as the basis of everything [we think φ, know φ, and believe φ] — our hopes and dreams, the clothes [we wear φ], the professions [we choose φ], the thoughts [we have φ], and the people [whom we trust φ ... and don't trust φ])). [2]Perception is the taste [of an apple], the smell [of the ocean], the enchantment [of spring], the glorious noise [of the city], the feeling [of love], and (even) conversations [about the impossibility of love]. [3]Our sense of self, our most essential way [of understanding existence], begins and ends (with perception). [4]The death [that we all fear φ] is less the death [of the body] and more the death [of perception], (as many of us would be quite happy (to know 〈that (after "bodily death") our ability [to engage in perception of the world around us] continues〉)). [5]This is (because perception is 〈what allows us to experience life itself; to see it (as alive)〉). [6]Yet most of us don't know 〈how or why

羅列→具体例

Sの同格

「重要な」を表す形容詞

perceptions work〉, or 〈how or why our brain evolved (to perceive the way [it does])〉.

訳 [1]知覚が重要なのは，私たちが考え，知り，信じるすべての物事，例えば私たちの希望や夢，着る服，選ぶ職業，思考，信頼する人…信頼しない人などの土台としての役割を果たすからだ。[2]知覚とは，リンゴの味，海のにおい，春の魅力，心地よい都市の雑音，愛の感覚であり，さらには愛が叶わないことについての会話でさえある。[3]私たちが存在を理解するうえで最も重要な方法である自己意識は，知覚に始まり知覚で終わる。[4]私たち皆が恐れる死は，肉体の死というよりも，知覚の死なのである。なぜなら私たちの多くは，「肉体の死」が起こってからも身の周りの世界を知覚する能力が持続することを知ったらとても喜ぶであろうからだ。[5]これは，知覚こそが，私たちが人生そのものを味わい，つまり人生を生き生きとしたものとして感じることを可能にするものだからだ。[6]しかし，私たちのほとんどは，知覚がどのように，あるいはどうして機能しているのか，また，脳がどのように，あるいはどうして現在のような知覚の仕組みに進化したのかを知らない。

語句 [1]serve as ～ ～としての役割を果たす／basis 名 土台，基礎／profession 名 職業／trust 動 信頼する／[2]enchantment 名 魅力／glorious 形 すてきな，輝かしい／impossibility 名 不可能性／[3]sense 名 感覚／essential 形 重要な，必要不可欠な／end with ～ ～で終わる／[4]engage in ～ ～を行う／[5]This is because S´V´ これはS´V´だからだ／see *A* as *B* AをBとみなす

文法・構文 [1]3つ目のandは，*A*, *B*, *C*, *D*, and *E*の形で，「知覚が果たす役割」の「具体例」がour hopes ～／the clothes ～／the professions ～／the thoughts ～／the people ～ と羅列されています。[3]essentialは「重要な」を表す表現です。[4]allはweの同格です。[5]becauseは副詞節を作る接続詞ですが，今回のようにCのカタマリを作ることもあります。また，V *A* as *B*の形では，今回のようにBに形容詞がくることもあります。

5 [1](Fortunately), the neuroscience of perception offers us a solution. [2]The answer is essential (because it will lead to future innovations [in thought and behavior [in all aspects of our lives, from love to learning]]). [3]What is the next greatest innovation? [4]It 's not a technology. [5]It 's a way of seeing.

「重要な」を表す形容詞　因果関係を示す表現

訳 [1]幸いにも，知覚神経科学は私たちに解決策を示してくれる。[2]その答えはきわめて重要である。なぜなら，それは愛から学習まで，私たちの生活のあらゆる面における思考や行動の将来の革新につながるであろうからだ。[3]次の大きな革新は何だろうか。[4]それは技術ではない。[5]ものの見方なのである。

語句 [2]innovation 名 革新／aspect 名 側面

文法・構文 [4と5]not *A*, but *B*「AではなくB」から「butが消える」パターンです（***Rule 1*** ⇒p.107）。

When you open your eyes, // do you see the world as it really is? // Do you see reality? // Humans have been asking themselves this question / for thousands of years. // The notion / that what we see / might not be what is truly there / has troubled / and annoyed us. // Great minds of history / have taken up this puzzling question // again / and again. // They all had theories, // but now / neuroscience has an answer. //

The answer is / that we don't see reality. // The world exists. // It's just that we don't see it. // We do not experience the world as it is // because our brain didn't evolve to do so. // It is a kind of paradox: // Your brain gives you the impression / that your perceptions are objectively real, // yet the sensory processes / that make perception possible // actually separate you / from ever accessing that reality directly. // Our five senses are like a keyboard to a computer // — they provide the means for us / to process information from the world, // but they have very little to do / with what is then experienced in perception. // They are in essence just mechanical media, // and therefore / play only a limited role / in what we perceive. // In fact, // in terms of the number of connections / that our brain makes, // just 10 percent / of how we process sight / comes from our eyes. // The other 90 percent / comes from other parts of our brains. // Perception derives not only from our five senses // but from our brain's seemingly infinitely refined network / that makes sense of all the incoming information. // The new findings of perceptual neuroscience // reveal why we don't perceive reality, // and why this can lead to creativity / and innovation / at work, // at home, // or at play. //

Given this, // why does this matter to you? // Why might you need to depart / from the way you currently perceive? // After all, // it feels like we see reality accurately, // at least most of the time. // Clearly / our brain's model of perception / has served our species well, // allowing us to successfully survive / in the world / and its ever-shifting complexity, // from our days as hunter-gatherers / to our current existence / paying bills on our smartphones. // We are able to find food and shelter, // hold down a job, // and build meaningful relationships. // We have built cities, // launched astronauts into space, // and created the Internet. // We must be doing something right, // so who cares / that we don't see reality? //

Perception matters / because it serves as the basis / of everything we think, // know, // and believe // — our hopes and dreams, // the clothes we wear, // the professions we choose, // the thoughts we have, // and the people whom we trust ... // and don't trust. // Perception is the taste of an apple, // the smell of the ocean, // the enchantment of spring, // the glorious noise of the city, // the feeling of love, // and even conversations / about the impossibility of love. // Our sense of self, // our most essential way / of understanding existence, // begins / and ends / with perception. // The death that we all fear / is less the death of the body // and more the death of perception, // as many of us / would be quite happy to know / that after “bodily death” // our ability / to engage in perception of the world around us / continues. // This is because perception / is what allows us / to experience life itself; // to see it as alive. // Yet most of us don't know how // or why perceptions work, // or how or why our brain evolved / to perceive the way it does. //

Fortunately, // the neuroscience of perception / offers us a solution. // The answer is essential // because it will lead to future innovations / in thought and behavior / in all aspects of our lives, // from love to learning. // What is the next greatest innovation? // It's not a technology. // It's a way of seeing. //

Lesson 3 解答・解説

▶問題 別冊 p.13

このLessonで出てくるルール

Rule 79 構文 「動名詞の意味上の主語」の要注意パターン ⇒問1
Rule 22 読解 「対比」を表す表現に反応する！（接続副詞）⇒問2
Rule 69 構文 「同格のthat」をとる名詞 ⇒問3
Rule 12 読解 固有名詞は「具体例」の合図！ ⇒問6
Rule 61 解法 記述問題の心構え ⇒問8
Rule 15 読解 「イコール」関係を作る表現に反応する！ ⇒問9
Rule 43 解法 内容一致でnotを見たら隠してみる！ ⇒問9
Rule 24 読解 過去と現在の「対比」を予測する！ ⇒問9

解答

問1 人々がそれぞれの観点から美に対して異なる見方をしているという考え方は，古代から世界のほとんどの文化に存在してきた　問2 ②

問3 身体的な美，つまり人の外見に基づく美が人それぞれであることには，疑問の余地はほとんどない。　問4 ②

問5 美は対称性と規則性に基づくものであり，数学が本物の美の核にあるという考え。　問6 ④　問7 ②

問8 完成されたものも，完璧なものも，永遠に続くものも何もないのだというメッセージ。(39字)

問9 ① ○　② ×　③ ×　④ ×　⑤ ○

問1 難易度★★☆

まずは全体の構造を把握します。the concept of ～ view が長いS，has beenがVです。

the concept [of people viewing ～ view] (S) has been around (V) (in most cultures of the world) (since ～ times)
「～という考え方は，古代から世界のほとんどの文化に存在してきた」

■「動名詞の意味上のS」を見抜く

the concept of ～「～という概念・考え」の意味でこの**ofは「同格」の働き**ですが，of以下の解釈にミスが出そうです。peopleを分詞viewingが後ろから修飾していると考えると，(✕)「それぞれの観点から美に対して異なる見方をしている人々という考え」という訳になってしまいます。**同格のofは名詞を説明する**ので，「the conceptの内容＝people」になってしまい不自然です。そこで考え方を修正し，viewingは現在分詞ではなく「動名詞」と考えます。

(◯)：viewingは動名詞で，**people**は動名詞の**意味上の主語**

the concept [of 〈people(S´) viewing(V´) beauty(O´) differently (from their own points of view)〉]

the concept of viewing ～「～を見るという考え方」の形で，viewingの前に「意味上の主語」としてpeopleが割り込んでいるわけです。「意味上の主語」なので，主語っぽく「人々が～を見るという考え方」と訳します。

⟫⟫ *Rule 79* 構文「動名詞の意味上の主語」の要注意パターン

〈the 抽象名詞 of〉のあとに**〈意味上の主語＋動名詞〉**がくるパターンは下線部和訳でよく出ますが，正しく理解できる受験生はかなり少ないので，ある程度の頻出パターンをチェックしておくことが有効です。

「動名詞の意味上のS」の注意すべきパターン

□ the concept of 名詞 -ing	名詞が～するという概念，考え
□ the idea of 名詞 -ing	名詞が～するという考え
□ the fact of 名詞 -ing	名詞が～するという事実
□ the prospect of 名詞 -ing	名詞が～する可能性，見込み
□ the possibility of 名詞 -ing	名詞が～する可能性

■ **from ～ points of view「～の観点から」**

from a ～ point of view／from a ～ perspective [viewpoint]「～の観点から」は重要な熟語です。ここでは5行目のsubjectiveを考慮して，from their own points of view「自分自身の観点から」→「主観的に」と訳してもOKです。ちなみにdifferent(ly)は，よく後ろに「相手を表すfrom」がきますが，今回differently from ～「～とは違って」と解釈すると意味が通りません。their own points of viewのtheirはpeopleを表すので，「人々は自分自身の観点とは違うふうに美を見る」と意味不明になってしまうからです。

■ ***be* around「周りにある」→「存在する」**

has been around in most cultures of the worldで「世界のほとんどの文化に存在してきた」となり，これにsince ancient times「古代から」をつければ完成です（timesは「時代」)。このaroundの使い方はあまり強調されませんが，とても重要です。

問2 難易度 ★★★

空所直後のif we consider the fact that everybody has their own favorite piece of music or painting that they consider to be beautifulから，「個人の美の基準は異なる」→「主観的」とわかります。さらに次の文（12行目）は，Nature, on the other hand, consistently comes up with scenes that are universally considered to be beautiful.でon the other handがあるので対立内容と考えられ，反対の内容「美は普遍的だ」になっているはずです。

つまり，空所には「普遍的」に対立する**主観的**な内容が入ります。空所を含む文の前にwhether ～が2つあり，前者は「美は普遍的」，後者は「美は主観的」という内容なので，②を入れて，the latter「後者」とすればOKです。

the former（普遍的）

This definition, however, does not mention whether there is a universal standard for beauty, or whether each individual person views beauty based on a totally different set of standards.

the latter（主観的）

「しかしこの定義は，美に普遍的な基準はあるのか，
それとも個々人がまったく異なる一連の基準に基づいて美を見ているのかということに触れていない」

Some of the arts seem to suggest the latter if we consider the fact that everybody has their own favorite piece of music or painting that they consider to be beautiful.

「誰にでも美しいと思うお気に入りの音楽作品や絵画作品があることを考えれば，
一部の芸術は後者を示唆しているように思える」

⇕

Nature, on the other hand, consistently comes up with scenes that are universally considered to be beautiful.

「一方で自然は常に，世界共通で美しいとみなされる風景を生み出している」

ちなみに，日本語では「A → B，A' → B'」の順番が自然ですが，英語では今回のように「A → B，B' → A'」の順番になることがよくあります（ここでのA'，B'はそれぞれA，Bの補足説明を表しています）。「A → B」と言ったあと，まず近くにあるBを詳しく説明する感覚です。

>>> *Rule 22* 読解 「対比」を表す表現に反応する！（接続副詞）

「対比」表現は設問でもよく狙われます。以下はすべて「副詞」の働きです。品詞もしっかり確認しておきましょう（品詞を問う問題も出るため）。

「対比」を表す接続副詞

- □ however / yet しかしながら
- □ still / all the same / nevertheless / nonetheless それにもかかわらず
- □ on the other hand / by contrast / in contrast 対照的に
- □ on the contrary しかしながら，それどころか
- □ though けれども　※接続詞の用法が有名だが　副詞の用法もある。
- □ even so たとえそうでも

選択肢の訳

① 前者　**② 後者**　③ 逆　④ もう1つ

問3 難易度 ★★☆

There is構文で，主語にあたるdoubtの後ろのthat以下は名詞が欠けていない**完全文**（今回はSVC）なので，thatは「同格」と判断します。直前の名詞を説明して，「～という 名詞 」と訳せばOKです。There is little doubt that ～で「～という疑いはほとんどない」という意味です。

There is little doubt that ～「～という疑いはほとんどない」

There is (V) little doubt (S) 〈that physical beauty, or beauty [based on physical appearance of people], (S') is (V') personal (C')〉.

>>> *Rule 69* 構文 「同格のthat」をとる名詞

同格thatをとる名詞は主に**事実・認識系**です。ムリに覚える必要はありませんが，眺めておくだけで同格のthatに気づきやすくなります。

「同格のthat」をとる主な名詞
fact 事実／evidence 証拠／knowledge 知識／news 知らせ／result 結果／rumor うわさ／sign 証拠，兆候，目印／truth 真実／assumption 仮定／belief 信念／conclusion 結論／hope 希望／idea 考え／thought 考え／fear 心配

■ **physicalとpersonalの訳にこだわろう**

physicalは「身体的な，物質的な」の意味があります（mental「精神的な」の反対）が，今回は直後の文にbeautiful womanとあるので，「身体的な」が適切です。*A*, or *B*は「AまたはB」ではなく，「**AすなわちB**」の意味で，physical beauty, or beauty based on physical appearance of people「身体的な美，つまり人の外見に基づく美」と訳すのが自然です。文末のpersonalは「個人的な」でもよいですが，直後にあるdiffers「異なる」をヒントに「個人によってそれぞれ異なる／人それぞれだ」と訳せば完璧です。

問4 難易度★☆☆

空所を含む文は，**SV although S´V´.** という「**対比**」を表す形です。文末のthis assessment「この評価」は，前半の「ピアスやタトゥーなどのボディアートは美の証と認識されていること」を表しています。〈this + 名詞〉は前の内容を「まとめる」働きがあります（***Rule 4*** ⇒p.71）。

「ピアスやタトゥーなどのボディアートは美の証と認識されているが，この評価（ボディアートは美の証と認識されていること）に（　4　）し続ける人も多い」という文意に合うのは，②disagreeです。disagree with ～「～に反対する」となります。ちなみに，空所直後のwithとつながるのは①copeと②disagreeだけです。こういった「形」もヒントになります。

選択肢の訳

① 対処する　**② 反対する**　③ 出会う　④ 持つ

問5 難易度★★☆

〈This + 名詞〉という形に注目です。This concept「この考え」とあるので，前の内容から「考え」を探すと，前文のbelieved that ～「～と考えていた」やthey were therefore convinced that ～「それゆえ～と確信していた」に気づくはずで

す。2か所ありますが，therefore「それゆえ」でつながっているので，2つとも該当箇所になると判断し，この2か所を訳します（前半だけ，後半だけだと，入試では点数が半分になってしまうでしょう）。

Certain ancient Greek philosophers, including Pythagoras, believed that beauty was based on symmetry and regularity, and they were therefore convinced that mathematics was at the core of true beauty.

「ピタゴラスなど一部の古代ギリシャの哲学者たちは，美は対称性と規則性に基づくと考え，したがって，数学が真の美の中核を成すと確信していた」

This concept was discovered ～

問6 難易度 ★★☆

空所（6）を含む文の次文（27行目）にBritish anthropologist Francis Galtonという「固有名詞」があるので，ここからは前文（つまり空所を含む文）に対する「具体例」になります。実は，**文中の固有名詞は具体例を表す**という超重要ルールがあります。

>>> *Rule 12* 読解 固有名詞は「具体例」の合図！

For exampleなどを使わずに具体例を挙げることがよくあります。そのときの目印の1つが**固有名詞**なんです。「文章中（補足）で固有名詞が出てきたら，その文（固有名詞を含む文）から具体例が始まる」という法則があります。固有名詞を含む文の先頭に「見えないFor exampleがある」と考えてもいいでしょう。

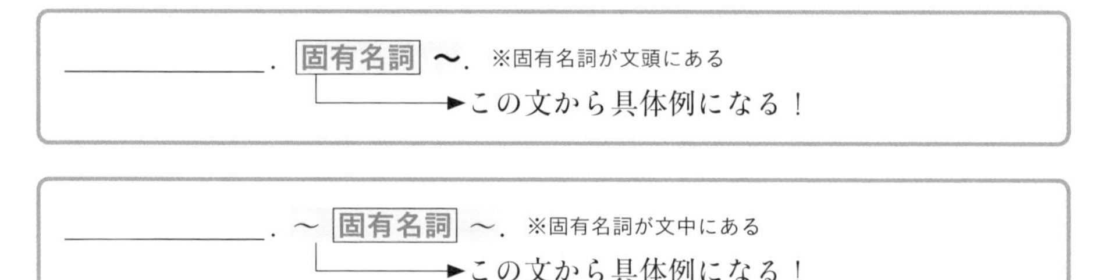

固有名詞自体は英文のどこにあってもかまいません（文頭・文中どこでも，固有名詞を含んだその文からが具体例となります）。

補足 ちなみに，「文章中」とは「第2文目以降」ということです。長文の1文目にいきなり固有名詞があるときはこのルールは使えません（いきなりFor exampleで始まっている英文はほぼあり得ないと考えてください)。

Symmetry and regularity also seem to play a part in (6) beauty.「対称性と規則性はまた, (6) な美においても一役を担っている」という内容に対して, British anthropologist Francis Galton discovered that “averaging” out human faces by mixing them to form one image achieved a level of regularityと,「人の顔」を具体例としているので, ④physicalが正解です。

選択肢の訳

① 感情的な　② 内面的な　③ 後ろ向きの　**④ 身体的な**

問7 難易度 ★☆☆

evolved「進化した, 発展した」に一番近いのは, ②developedです。developは「発展する」という訳語だけでなく, **ブワ〜ッと広がる**イメージを持っておきましょう。developing countries「発展途上国」は, まさに今現在ブワ〜ッと成長している国ですね。さらに, 健康・医療系の話題では「症状が発生し, ブワ〜ッと広がる」→「(病気に) かかる, 発症する」という意味も大事です (例:develop lung cancer「肺がんにかかる」)。

選択肢の訳

① 壊れた　**② 発展した**　③ 飛び込んだ　④ 分かれた

問8 難易度 ★★☆

英文全体はSVCで, Sの部分に下線が引かれています。

the main message [that it includes] (S) is (V) 〈that 〜〉(C).

SVCは“S = C”の関係なので, the main messageの内容は2つ目のthat以下を訳せばよいことになります。

>>> Rule 61 解法 記述問題の心構え

■**「探す」→「きわめて丁寧に訳す」**

記述問題の解答は, 自分の意見を書くわけではありません。求められているのは「英文を正確に読んで, **設問の要求を理解**して, 日本語で表す力」です。そして**内容を丁寧に説明する**姿勢が必要です。例えるなら「校長先生に最新アプリについて説明する」つもりになってみましょう。いきなりアプリの説明を始めるのではなく,「そのアプリとはそもそもスマホで使うものだ」「要するに○○がラクにできるようになるものだ」のように話すべきですよね。記述問題の解答においても,まず前提から説明する心構えを持ってください。

■目指すのは「最大字数」

「60字〜80字で書け」とあるとき,出題者のメッセージは「無駄がない完璧な答案なら60字,多少無駄なこと・冗長な表現を使っても80字が限度」ということなんです。ということは,受験生の答案が60字だった場合,それは完璧な答案か,もしくは何かポイントが欠けた答案なんです。よって,**最大字数を目指す**のが無難です。

■文末は「オウム返し」

「なぜ」と問われたら,「〜だから」と答えることは知っていると思いますが,それ以外は教わりませんよね。ぜひ「文末はオウム返し」という発想を持ってください。例えば「変化について説明せよ」とあれば「〜という変化」,paradoxを説明するなら「〜という矛盾」,「この話はどこがおもしろいのか」なら「〜という点がおもしろい」のように,**説明が求められている言葉をそのままオウム返し**するだけです。

このやり方は,**減点を避けられる**,**見当違いの答案に気づける**ことというメリットがあります。例えば,「この差別を説明せよ」という問題が早稲田大学で出題されたとき,解答を「〜してはいけない」と締めくくってしまった受験生がすごく多かったのです。設問の要求は「差別を説明すること」なので,その答案では0点になりかねません。「文末オウム返し」を意識すれば,答案の最後は「〜という差別」になるはずなので,ミスに気づけるのです。

that以下のnothing is finished, nothing is perfect and nothing lasts foreverは,SVがandによって3つ接続された形です。今回のようにnothingが主語の場合,「〜なものは何もない」と訳すと自然な日本語になります。ちなみに,今回のlastは動詞で「続く」という意味です(「ラスト→最後まで続く」→「続く」と考えてください)。設問は「どのようなメッセージか」なので,答案の文末はオウム返しで「〜というメッセージ」とすれば完璧です。

ちなみに,直後に〈A + 名詞〉(具体例を表す目印として***Rule 8*** ⇒p.89で扱います)の形とfor exampleがあるので,例として入れてもよいですが,字数がキツイため原則不要です。入れるなら「例えば落ち葉のように」くらいで十分です。

問9 難易度 ★★☆

まず，正解の選択肢について解説しましょう。

①「美とは見る者次第」と同じような意味のことわざは，古代より文化を超えて共有されている。

3行目のthe concept of people viewing beauty differently from their own points of view has been around in most cultures of the world since ancient timesと一致します。1行目と選択肢にあるbeauty is in the eye of the beholder「美とは見る者次第」とは，「美の基準は人によって違う」ということです。これが3行目ではpeople viewing beauty differentlyと言い換えられています。さらに，本文のhas been around in most cultures of the worldが，選択肢ではhave been shared across culturesに言い換えられています。

⑤ 美しい芸術で，対称性と規則性に基づいていないものの例には，キュビズムと表現主義が含まれる。

30行目にthere are many forms of art that are considered beautiful, yet are not based on symmetry and regularity. Some examples of this include Cubism, Expressionismとあり，選択肢の内容と合致します。

では，誤りの選択肢を見ていきましょう。

② 古代ギリシャの哲学者たちは，美は簡素さと非対称性に基づいていると考えていた。

21行目にCertain ancient Greek philosophers, including Pythagoras, believed that beauty was based on symmetry and regularityとあります。simplicity「簡潔さ」やasymmetry「非対称性」ではありません。

③「わびさび」の概念は，自然の寂しさと弱さを指しており，一度も変わったことがない。

重要な2つのルールが関係します。このあとで詳しく解説します。

④「わびさび」は日本から中国に伝えられた仏教の概念である。

35行目に*Wabi-sabi* is a Buddhist concept introduced to Japan from Chinaとあります。この選択肢のように，使ってある単語は同じでも「順番が逆」や「主語と目的語が逆」などはひっかけの選択肢としてよく使われるので注意が必要です。

ここからは，選択肢③に関連して2つのルールを見ていきましょう。まず，refer toに注目してください。

>>> Rule 15 読解 「イコール」関係を作る表現に反応する！

多くの人がmeanを見ると「意味する」と捉えますが，そんな日本語はあまり使いませんよね。S mean Oは“S = O”というイコール関係を意識して，**SはOだ**と考えればOKなのです。他にもinvolveの意味は「含む」ですが，この意味を広く「イコールだ」と捉えることができます。例えば，先生が「受験には精神力が含まれるぞ」と言ったら，その先生が言いたいのは「受験＝精神力だ」ということですよね。この「イコール」という発想は長文で大活躍しますよ。

イコール表現を意識する

英単語＼意味	よく示される訳語	重要なイメージ
be	～である	「イコール」を意識
mean	～を意味する	
refer to	～に言及する	
involve	～を含む，巻き込む	広く解釈して「イコール」と考える
include	～を含む	
constitute	～を構成する	
represent	～を代表する	
show	～を示す	
signify	～を示す，意味する	

つまり，選択肢は*wabi-sabi* = the loneliness of nature and weaknessということです。本文36行目にThe word *wabi* originally referred to the loneliness of nature, and *sabi* referred to something that is simplistic.とあり，lonelinessはOKですが，weaknessがアウトだとわかります（ここでもrefer toが使われていますね）。これだけでも十分選択肢が×だとわかるのですが，皆さんは選択肢のneverにも注目してください。

>>> Rule 43 解法 内容一致でnotを見たら隠してみる！

出題者がひっかけ選択肢を作るとき，本文の一部をコピペして，そこにnotをつければ，受験生にひっかかりやすい選択肢が一瞬で作れます。これを踏まえて，内容一致問題の選択肢で**not**（**never**など同意語も）を見たら，指で隠して，「このnotがなければ正解なんじゃないの？」「手抜きで本文にnotをつけただけじゃないの？」とツッコミを入れながら，本文の内容を確認し，not以外が一致していればこのパターンで，×が決定です。ただし，このパターンの選択肢が“×”になる可能性は「半々」です。「notがあるから間違いだ」なんて思いこまないようにしてください。二重否定（cannot ～ without ...）や部分否定（not ～ alwaysなど）は「手抜き選択肢」ではありませんので，隠してみる必要はありません。普通に対処してください。

補足 選択肢にnoがある場合は，notと同じ「not以外本文のコピペでは？」と疑うのも1つの方法です。反対に，「noっていっても，ゼロってことはないんじゃない？　1つくらいあるのでは？」とツッコミを入れてみるのもありです（***Rule 46*** ⇒p.39）。

38行目にThe meaning gradually changed over timeとあり，「意味が変わった」とわかります。選択肢のhas never changedとは真逆ですね。

ちなみに36行目には，originally「もともとは」が使われているので，ここで「過去と現在の対比」を予想しておけば「意味が変わる」ことも記憶に鮮明に残るはずです。そしてそのあとにNowadaysを使って「現在」を説明しています。

>>> *Rule 24* 読解 過去と現在の「対比」を予測する！

「昔は」を表す語句（下の表の左側）を見たら，そのあとには**「しかし今は違う！」**という内容（表の右側）を予想してください。過去と現在の内容が対比される典型的なパターンです。この場合（ほぼ間違いなく）現在の内容が主張になります。しかもButなどが使われるとは限らず，いきなり「現在」の内容がくるのがネイティブの英文の書き方なんです。

「昔は…」のバリエーション	「でも今は…」のバリエーション
□ ～ ago ～前に □ at first ～ 初めは～ □ previously 以前は □ in former times 以前は □ in 過去の西暦 ○○年には □ once かつては □ in the past 昔は □ traditionally 昔から，従来は □ conventionally 昔から，従来は □ originally もとは，初めは □ initially 最初は □ for a long time 長い間	□ now 今は □ today 今日（こんにち）は □ these days / nowadays 最近は

文構造の分析

1 Beauty is in the eye of the beholder.

訳 美とは見る者次第。

語句 beholder 名 見る人

文法・構文 直訳は「美は見る者の目の中にある」ですが,「美しさの基準は人によって異なる」という意味のことわざです。

2 [1] This proverb was (first) recorded (in the English language) (in its current form) (in the 19th century). [2] (However), the concept [of people viewing beauty differently (from their own points of view)] has been around (in most cultures of the world) (since ancient times). [3] But what exactly is beauty, and is it really subjective? [4] The definition [in the Merriam-Webster dictionary] is "the qualities in a person or a thing [that give pleasure to the senses or the mind]." [5] This definition, (however), does not mention 〈whether there is a universal standard (for beauty)〉, or 〈whether each individual person views beauty (based on a totally different set of standards)〉. [6] Some of the arts seem to suggest the latter (if we consider the fact 〈that everybody has their own favorite piece of music or painting [that they consider ϕ to be beautiful]〉). [7] Nature, (on the other hand), (consistently) comes up with scenes [that are (universally) considered to be beautiful].

〈This＋名詞〉→ まとめ表現

動名詞の意味上のS

同格の that

対比表現

訳 [1] このことわざが現在の言い方で最初に英語で記録されたのは,19世紀のことだった。[2] しかし,人々がそれぞれの観点から美に対して異なる見方をしているという考え方は,古代から世界のほとんどの文化に存在してきた。[3] だが美とはそもそも何なのだろうか,そしてそれは本当に主観的なものなのだろうか。[4] メリアム・ウェブスター辞典の定義では「人あるいは物にある,感覚あるいは心に喜びを与える性質」である。[5] しかしこの定義は,美に普遍的な基準はあるのか,それとも個々人がまったく異なる一連の基準に基づいて美を見ているのかということに触れていない。[6] 誰にでも美しいと思うお気に入りの音楽作品や絵画作品があることを考えれば,一部の芸術は後者を示唆しているように思える。[7] 一方で自然は常に,世界共通で美しいとみなされる風景を生み出している。

語句 [1] proverb 名 ことわざ／record 動 記録する／[2] concept 名 概念／point of view 観

点／be around 存在している／[3] subjective 形 主観的な／[4] definition 名 定義／quality 名 性質／sense 名 感覚／[5] mention 動 言及する／standard 名 基準／be based on ～ ～に基づいている／[6] the latter 後者（「前者」はthe former）／[7] consistently 副 常に／come up with ～ ～を生み出す／universally 副 普遍的に（すべての物にあてはまること）

文法・構文 [1]〈This＋名詞〉は「まとめ表現」です。直前の1文を知らなくても，「ことわざ」だと判断できます。[2] viewing ～ points of viewという動名詞のカタマリに，意味上のSとなるpeopleが入った形です。[5] orは2つの節（whether there is ～ とwhether each individual person views ～）を結んでいます。[6] the latter「後者」とは，前文で2番目に例示された「個々人がまったく異なる一連の基準に基づいて美を見る」ことです。ちなみに，the fact that ～は後ろが完全文なので同格のthatですが，music or painting that ～は後ろが不完全文なので関係代名詞です。[7] 関係代名詞thatの節内は，consider O to be C「OをCとみなす」が受動態になった形です。

3 [1] There is little doubt 〈that physical beauty, or beauty [based on physical appearance of people], is personal〉. [2] The ideal "beautiful woman" differs (between cultures), and (in many cases) is based on fashion. [3] Some cultures appreciate fatness, (while others believe 〈that body mutilation represents beauty〉). [4] (For example), body art [in the form of piercings and tattoos] is recognized (as a sign of beauty) (in many countries of the world today), (although there are also many people (in these same countries) [who continue to disagree with this assessment]).

イコール表現

recognize *A* as *B*の受動態

訳 [1] 身体的な美，つまり人の外見に基づく美が人それぞれであることには，疑問の余地はほとんどない。[2] 理想の「美女」は文化によって異なり，多くの場合，流行に基づいている。[3] ふくよかさを尊ぶ文化もあれば，身体切断が美の象徴であると考える文化もある。[4] 例えば，ピアスやタトゥーという形でのボディアートは，今日，世界中の多くの国で美の証と認識されているが，その同じ国々に，この評価に反対し続けている人々も多くいる。

語句 [1] there is little doubt that S´V´ S´V´だということにはほとんど疑問の余地がない／[2] ideal 形 理想の／differ 動 異なる／fashion 名 流行／[3] appreciate 動 尊ぶ，高く評価する／body mutilation 身体切断（ファッションとして身体の形状を改造することで，body modification「身体改造」の批判的な呼称）／[4] piercing 名 ピアスをすること，ピアス穴／tattoo 名 タトゥー／recognize *A* as *B* AをBとして認識する／assessment 名 評価

文法・構文 [2] andは，動詞2つ（differs／is based on）を結んでいます。is based onの前にin many casesという修飾語が割り込んでいるため，少し構造がわかりにくくなっています。[3] some ～, others ～「～するものもあれば，～するものもある」という相関表現です。また，representはオーバーに言えば「イコール表現」と考える動詞でしたね（***Rule 15*** ⇒p.57）。

4 [1] Certain ancient Greek philosophers, (including Pythagoras), believed 〈that beauty was based on symmetry and regularity〉, and they were (therefore) convinced 〈that mathematics was at the core of true beauty〉. [2] This concept was discovered (when they noticed 〈that objects [which matched the golden ratio] appeared to be more attractive (than objects [that were more random in shape])〉). [3] Symmetry and regularity (also) seem to play a part (in physical beauty). [4] (At the end of the 19th century), British anthropologist Francis Galton discovered 〈that "averaging" out human faces (by mixing them) (to form one image) achieved a level of regularity [that was more attractive than each of the individual components]〉.

convince 人 that S´V´ の受動態

〈this ＋ 名詞 → まとめ表現〉

固有名詞 → 具体例

訳 [1] ピタゴラスなど一部の古代ギリシャの哲学者たちは，美は対称性と規則性に基づくと考え，したがって，数学が真の美の中核を成すと確信していた。[2] この考え方が発見されたのは，黄金比に一致する物は，形が不規則な物よりも魅力的に見えることに彼らが気づいたときのことだった。[3] 対称性と規則性はまた，身体的な美においても一役を担っているようである。[4] 19世紀末，イギリスの人類学者フランシス・ゴルトンは，人間の顔をミックスして「平均化」し，1つの像を形成すると，個々の構成要素よりも魅力的なレベルの規則性が達成されることを発見した。

語句 [1] certain 形 特定の，ある／symmetry 名 対称性／regularity 名 規則性／*be* convinced that S´V´ S´V´だと確信している，S´V´だと思い込んでいる／core 名 中核／[2] golden ratio 黄金比／attractive 形 魅力的な／[3] play a part［role］in ～ ～で役割を演じる／[4] anthropologist 名 人類学者／average 動 平均化する／component 名 要素

文法・構文 [1] 文の動詞がbelieved，were convincedと「過去形」なので，that節中の動詞もそれぞれwas based on, wasと「過去形」になっています（時制の一致）。[4] 固有名詞Francis Galtonに注目して，「具体例」だと判断できます。前文の「対称性と規則性が重要である」ということを，Francis Galtonの発見をもとに具体的に説明しています。

5 [1] (Despite this), there are many forms of art [that are considered beautiful, yet are not based on symmetry and regularity]. [2] Some examples of this include Cubism, Expressionism and many other forms of modern art. [3] And, one of the deepest concepts of beauty does not lie (in symmetry, harmony and regularity), but focuses on objects not being perfect, permanent or complete; *wabi-sabi*.

イコール表現

動名詞の意味上のS

訳 [1] それにもかかわらず，美しいとみなされているが，対称性や規則性に基づいていない様式の芸術は多くある。[2] この例にはキュビズム，表現主義，他にも多くの様式の現代

美術などが含まれる。[3]そして，美の最も根底にある概念の1つは，対称性や調和や規則性の中にはなく，物体が完璧でも永続的でも完全でもないことに重点を置く。それが「わびさび」である。

語句 [2]Cubism 名 キュビズム（対象を複数の視点から幾何学的にとらえる技法）／Expressionism 名 表現主義（対象の客観的表現を排して，主観的表現を主張する技法）／[3]lie in ～ ～にある／harmony 名 調和／permanent 形 永続的な

文法・構文 [1]～ are considered beautiful, は，consider OC「OをCとみなす」が受動態になった形です。また，yetは関係詞節中の2つの動詞（are considered／are not based on）を結んでいます。[2]includeはオーバーに言えば「イコール」と考える動詞でした（***Rule 15*** ⇒p.57）。[3]lie in ～ は第1文型として使われているので，「存在・移動」の意味だと判断できます。またobjects以下は，not being ～ completeという動名詞のカタマリに，意味上のS（objects）がくっついた形です。

6 [1]*Wabi-sabi* is a Buddhist concept [introduced to Japan (from China)], [where it evolved (into a distinctly Japanese idea of beauty)]. [2]The word *wabi* (originally) referred to the loneliness of nature, and *sabi* referred to something [that is simplistic]. [3]The meaning (gradually) changed (over time), and (by the 14th century) *wabi* meant "rough simplicity" and *sabi* "beauty" or "calmness." [4](Nowadays) this concept is (usually) described (as "natural simplicity" or "imperfect beauty).")

過去を表す語句（現在と対比）／イコール表現／イコール表現／過去との対比（今は違う）／イコール表現／describe *A* as *B*の受動態

訳 [1]「わびさび」とは，中国から日本に導入された仏教の概念であり，そこで日本独自の美の概念へと発展した。[2]「わび」という言葉はもともと，自然の寂しさを指し，「さび」は簡素なものを指していた。[3]時間の経過とともにその意味はだんだんと変化していき，14世紀には，「わび」は「素朴な単純さ」を，「さび」は「美しさ」や「穏やかさ」を意味するようになっていた。[4]今日では，この概念はたいてい「自然の簡素さ」や「不完全な美」というように表現される。

語句 [1]Buddhist 形 仏教の／evolve into ～ ～に発展する／distinctly 副 はっきりと／[2]originally 副 もともと，初めは／refer to ～ ～を示す／simplistic 形 簡素な／[3]over time 時間の経過とともに／rough 形 素朴な／[4]describe *A* as *B* AをBと表現する／imperfect 形 不完全な

文法・構文 [1]where ～ は関係副詞のカタマリで，先行詞はChinaではなくJapanであることに注意してください。[2]originallyは本来「初めは」という意味で，「初めは～だった。だけど…」という形で，後ろには対比の内容がくることが多いです。今回も2文後ろのNowadays ～ と対比されています。またrefer to ～ という「イコール表現」が2回使われていることも大切です。[3]*wabi* meant "rough simplicity" and *sabi* {meant} "beauty" or "calmness." という動詞の省略が起こっています。今回のように明らかに構文のつじつまが

合わない場合，「重複を避けるための省略」を疑ってみましょう。

7 [1] *Wabi-sabi* is based on the three Buddhist views of existence, [which are impermanence, pain and emptiness]. [2] It was thought 〈that understanding the beauty [contained within emptiness and imperfection] was the first step [to achieving a state of enlightenment]〉. [3] *Wabi-sabi* places the emphasis (on simplicity, economy, modesty, asymmetry and roughness), and the main message [that it includes ϕ] is 〈that nothing is finished, nothing is perfect and nothing lasts forever〉. [4] A fallen autumn leaf, (for example), could be considered to be *wabi-sabi* (because it expresses the beauty of nature (while at the same time emphasizing its imperfection and impermanence)). [5] (In its artistic form), *wabi-sabi* is (best) expressed (in pottery). [6] Asymmetric bowls [with natural base colors], (showing a rough style of imperfection), stimulate the mind (into considering the beauty of the three Buddhist views of existence).

〈(S) + be〉の省略

訳 [1]「わびさび」は仏教の3つの存在観，すなわち無常，苦，空虚さに基づいている。[2]空虚さや不完全さの中にある美を理解することが，悟りの境地に達するための第一歩だと考えられていた。[3]「わびさび」は簡素さ，簡潔さ，慎み深さ，非対称性，粗さを重視しており，それに含まれる主なメッセージは，完成されたものや，完璧なもの，永遠に続くものなど何も存在しないということである。[4]例えば秋の落ち葉は，自然の美を表すと同時にその不完全さや無常を際立たせているので，「わびさび」であるとみなすことができる。[5]芸術様式において「わびさび」が最もよく表現されるのは，陶芸である。[6]自然の色を基調とする非対称な器は素朴な様式の不完全さを表しており，心を刺激して仏教の3つの存在観の美について考えさせる。

語句 [1]impermanence 名 無常／pain 名 痛み，苦しみ／emptiness 名 空虚さ／[2]imperfection 名 不完全／enlightenment 名 悟り／[3]place an emphasis on ～ ～を重視する／[5]pottery 名 陶芸（poetry「詩」とスペルが似ているので注意）／[6]asymmetric 形 非対称の／stimulate 動 刺激する

文法・構文 [1]～, which are ～ はthe three Buddhist views of existenceを先行詞とする関係代名詞（非制限用法）で，the three Buddhist views of existenceが具体的に何を指すのかを説明しています。[2]It was p.p. that ～ を見た時点で「仮主語構文」だと判断できます（it is と thatの間に形容詞，過去分詞が挟まれている場合は必ず「仮主語構文」です）。[4]could be considered to be *wabi-sabi*は，consider O to be C「OをCとみなす」が受動態になった形です。またwhile以下はwhile {it is} emphasizing ～ から〈(S) + be動詞〉が省略されています（at the same timeは挿入）。

8 [1] 〈Whether the true essence of beauty lies (in mathematics, (as believed by the ancient Greeks)), or (in the artistic emptiness of *wabi-sabi*, (as believed by the Japanese))〉, remains open (to question), but one thing is certain. [2]Beauty will (always) remain (in the eye of the beholder).

訳 [1]美の真髄が，古代ギリシャ人が考えたとおり数学にあるのか，あるいは日本人が考えたとおり「わびさび」の芸術的空虚さにあるのかは，疑問の余地を残したままだ。しかし，1つ確かなことがある。[2]美はこれからもずっと見る者次第なのだ。

語句 [1]essence 名 要素／remain open to question 疑問[議論]の余地を残したままである

文法・構文 [1]Whether ～ のカタマリのあとにremainsというVがきていることから，Whether ～ は名詞節「～かどうか」だと判断できます。ちなみに，orはin mathematics, as believed ～ Greeksとin the artistic emptiness of *wabi-sabi*, as believed ～ Japaneseを結んでいます。どちらも「様態」のas「～のように」が使われています。[2]最終文で再び冒頭のことわざを用いて，文章を締めくくっています。

音読をしよう！

🔊 03

Beauty is in the eye of the beholder. //

This proverb was first recorded / in the English language // in its current form / in the 19th century. // However, // the concept of people viewing beauty differently from their own points of view // has been around in most cultures of the world / since ancient times. // But what exactly is beauty, // and is it really subjective? // The definition in the Merriam-Webster dictionary is / "the qualities in a person or a thing / that give pleasure to the senses or the mind." // This definition, // however, // does not mention / whether there is a universal standard for beauty, // or whether each individual person views beauty / based on a totally different set of standards. // Some of the arts seem to suggest the latter / if we consider the fact / that everybody has their own favorite piece of music / or painting / that they consider to be beautiful. // Nature, // on the other hand, // consistently comes up with scenes / that are universally considered to be beautiful. //

There is little doubt that physical beauty, // or beauty based on physical appearance of people, // is personal. // The ideal "beautiful woman" / differs between cultures, // and in many cases / is based on fashion. // Some cultures appreciate fatness, // while others believe / that body mutilation represents beauty. // For example, // body art / in the form of piercings and tattoos / is recognized as a sign of beauty / in many countries of the world today, // although there are also many people in these same countries / who continue to disagree with this assessment. //

Certain ancient Greek philosophers, // including Pythagoras, // believed that beauty was based on symmetry and regularity, // and they were therefore convinced / that mathematics was at the core of true beauty. // This concept was discovered / when they noticed that objects / which matched the golden ratio // appeared to be more attractive / than objects that were more random in shape. // Symmetry and regularity / also seem to play a part in physical beauty. // At the end of the 19th century, // British anthropologist Francis Galton / discovered that "averaging" out human faces / by mixing them to form one image / achieved a level of regularity / that was more attractive / than each of the individual components. //

Despite this, // there are many forms of art / that are considered beautiful, // yet are not based on symmetry and regularity. // Some examples of this include Cubism, // Expressionism // and many other forms of modern art. // And, one of the deepest concepts of beauty / does not lie in symmetry, // harmony // and regularity, // but focuses on objects not being perfect, // permanent // or complete; // *wabi-sabi*. //

Wabi-sabi is a Buddhist concept / introduced to Japan from China, / where it evolved / into a distinctly Japanese idea of beauty. // The word *wabi* / originally referred to the loneliness of nature, // and *sabi* referred to something that is simplistic. // The meaning gradually changed over time, // and by the 14th century // *wabi* meant "rough simplicity" // and *sabi* "beauty" or "calmness." // Nowadays this concept is usually described / as "natural simplicity" // or "imperfect beauty." //

Wabi-sabi is based on the three Buddhist views of existence, // which are impermanence, pain // and emptiness. // It was thought / that understanding the beauty / contained within emptiness / and imperfection / was the first step to achieving a state of enlightenment. // *Wabi-sabi* places the emphasis on simplicity, // economy, // modesty, // asymmetry // and roughness, // and the main message that it includes / is that nothing is finished, // nothing is perfect // and nothing lasts forever. // A fallen autumn leaf, // for example, // could be considered to be *wabi-sabi* // because it expresses the beauty of nature // while at the same time / emphasizing its imperfection / and impermanence. // In its artistic form, // *wabi-sabi* is best expressed in pottery. // Asymmetric bowls with natural base colors, // showing a rough style of imperfection, // stimulate the mind / into considering / the beauty of the three Buddhist views of existence. //

Whether the true essence of beauty lies in mathematics, // as believed by the ancient Greeks, // or in the artistic emptiness of *wabi-sabi*, // as believed by the Japanese, // remains open to question, // but one thing is certain. // Beauty will always remain / in the eye of the beholder. //

Lesson 4 解答・解説

▶問題 別冊 p.17

このLessonで出てくるルール

Rule 50 解法 指示語・代名詞の表す内容を特定する！ ⇒問1
Rule 4 読解 〈this＋名詞〉は「まとめ」を作る！ ⇒問2
Rule 78 構文 第1文型は「存在・移動」と考える！ ⇒問3
Rule 24 読解 過去と現在の「対比」を予測する！(no longer) ⇒問3
Rule 35 読解 長文単語・語句をマスターする！(myth) ⇒問4

解答

問1 (初級者も含めたあらゆるレベルで，ほとんどの学習者は，英語での読み書きに加えて，英語を話せるようになりたがっているが，特に）初級者は，自分の話を相手に難なく理解してもらえるように英語を発音できるようになりたいと強く望んでいること。

問2 (それまでの指導法から）授業中に生徒が英語を話す機会を増やすだけでなく，授業外でも英語を話すよう促す課題を考えたり，英会話の練習ができる地域の施設を教えたりしたという変化。

問3 Vickiが，以前は発音指導に少し自信がなくて授業で教えていなかったが，(英語を話せるようになりたいというフィードバックが続き）生徒の要望は，発音の仕方を明確に教えてもらうことだと気づいて，発音指導を授業に取り入れたから。

問4 発音指導は，すでに英語のさまざまな面で苦労している初級者にとって，嫌なものである［難しすぎる，無理がある］という教師の考えや，自分自身にとっても発音は難しかったり複雑すぎて教えられないという教師の考え。

問1 難易度 ★★★ 思考力

結論としては「直前の文を訳してしまえば正解になる」のですが，その文の主語Theyが何を指すか，が重要です（今回はTheyを「彼ら」としたままでは内容が曖昧になるので減点でしょう)。**一番近くにある主語を第一候補**と見て，2行目の～ and beginners are no exception. They are very keen to learn ～ から，They

= beginnersと考えます。

>>> Rule 50 解法 指示語・代名詞の表す内容を特定する！

代名詞の内容が問われると，訳を基にして考える受験生が大半ですが，それでは英文が難しいときには対応できません。実は英語には，代名詞を使うときの（少しゆるいけれど）ルールがあるのです。

代名詞の解法

（1）同じ格を第一候補にする

→代名詞がSなら，近く（普通は「前文」）の**S**や**S´**を第一候補にする。

注意 **主節の主語とは限らない**：代名詞がSの場合，近くのSではなく「従属節中の主語」や「(不定詞・動名詞などの）意味上の主語（S´)」になることもよくあります（Oの場合も同様)。

代名詞がOなら**O**や**O´**を第一候補にする。

受動態の場合，注意が必要。

（2）数や後ろのヒントも考慮

→「theyは複数」などもヒントに

（3）代入して文脈を確認（もし文意が変なら，そのとき初めて意味から考える）

「同じ格」とは，「主格（つまり主語）なら，近くにある主語」，「目的格（つまり目的語）なら，近くにある目的語」ということです。かなりの確率でこの原則が守られます（ボクの経験値で90%くらい，つまり入試問題の10問中9問はこの発想で解けます)。

受動態の場合：受動態とは「目的語を主語の位置に移動したもの」なので，「受動態の文の主語」＝「能動態（元の文）の目的語」です。つまり，一見「主語」でも実は書き手の中で「目的語」と認識されているときがあるのです。

また，指示語が受けるものは原則その「前」にありますが，指示語の内容を「後ろ」で詳しく説明するので，内容を特定するためのヒントは後ろにあることが多いです。**答えは前，ヒントは後ろ**という発想です。

「指示語」の考え方

〜. **This** is ...

その内容を「後ろ」で詳しく説明する。
→ Thisが表しているものは「後ろ」がヒントになる！

指示語は「前」の内容を受けるのが原則。

よって，解答はThey（= beginners）are very keen to learn ～ を訳せばOKです。チェックポイントは, *be* keen to 原形「～することを熱望している」, in a way that ～「～する方法で，～のように」，make *oneself* understood「自分のことを（人に）理解してもらう」です。以上を「初級者は, 自分の話を相手に容易に理解してもらえるように英語を発音する方法を学びたがっている」とまとめます。

補足「丁寧に」書いたほうがいいので，模範解答は1行目の内容から含めていますが，この直前の内容だけを訳出していれば十分です。

ここが 思考力　指示語を含む設問の解答根拠

この問題は「Thisが直前の文を指す」という単純なものに見えますし，普通はこれ以上の解説もないでしょう。ところが受験生の中には「Theyは, 文章の冒頭Most learners at every levelを指すのでは？」と疑問に思う人も多いはずです。そういった質問に対して「文脈上から考えてbeginnersが自然」と言っても納得できませんよね。そこで，完璧な根拠を考えてみましょう。

Thisは指示語なので，**答えは前，ヒントは後ろ**から，後ろをチェックします（***Rule 50*** ⇒p.69）。This became very clear to Vickiなので, Thisは「（それまではハッキリしなかったが）Vickiにとってclearになったこと」, つまり「clearになった変化」を意識することがポイントとなります。その観点で読むと，5行目のAt the time, Vicki was working with a class of beginning-level learnersから，Vickiは「初級者」に授業をしているとわかります）。さらに16行目Vicki gradually came to understand that ～ explicit instruction in pronunciation. から「（当時，Vickiが教えていた）初級クラスの生徒が発音指導を望んでいることをVickiが理解した（= Vickiに明らかになった）」とわかります（came to 原形「～するようになった」が変化を表し, became very clear to ～ に対応しているわけです）。

以上から, 下線部のThis（つまりclearになったこと）は「初級レベルの生徒は発音の指導を望んでいる」という内容だと判断できます。これはまさに下線部Thisの直前の内容と一致するので，ここが該当箇所だという決定的な証拠になるのです。

問2 難易度 ★★★

these changesは〈this[these] + 名詞〉の形なので, 前の内容をまとめて「～する変化」と書くと考えます。

>>> Rule 4 読解 〈this + 名詞〉は「まとめ」を作る！

英文中に〈this + 名詞〉がきたら，その直前の内容を「まとめる」働きがあります。筆者が何かしらを説明して，そこまでの内容を整理する目的で，〈this + 名詞〉でまとめるわけです。thisの後ろの「名詞」は，そこまでの内容を1語にギュっと凝縮した単語が使われます。ということは，英文を読んでいて〈this + 名詞〉が出てきたら，次のようなことがわかります。

(1) 難しい内容のあとに〈this + 名詞〉が出てくる場合

例えば難しい内容のあとにthis experiment「この実験」があれば，その前の長々とした内容はexperiment「実験」のことなんだとわかる。

(2) thisのあとの名詞を知らない場合

どうせ**「前に述べたことのまとめ」**なので,「今言ったこのこと」と考えれば，文意をつかむことができる。

入試の設問で超頻出事項ですから〈this + 名詞〉に注目することはものすごく大事です。また，〈these + 名詞〉もまったく同じ発想です。

下線部より前でchanges「変化」に類する内容を探すと，10行目にshe responded to these requests by ～ が見つかります。「～することで要望に応じた」＝「何かを変えた」と考え，このby以下（具体的に変えた内容）を該当箇所だと判断します。by以下は複雑なので，ここを訳出できるかがポイントです。

the opportunity for 人 to 原形「人が～する機会」

～ by not only increasing the opportunity for her students [to speak in class],

encourage 人 to 原形「人に～するよう促す」

but also { devising assignments [that encouraged them to speak outside the

advise 人 of ～「人に～を知らせる」

class] and advising them of community-based facilities [where they could practice]. }

「生徒たちが授業中に（英語を）話す機会を増やすだけでなく，授業外でも（英語を）話すよう促す課題を考案したり，（英会話の）練習ができる地域の施設を教えてあげたりすることによって（要望に応えた）」

■ **not only *A* but also *B*全体をきっちり訳す**

全体が**not only *A* but also *B***「AだけでなくBも」の形なので，AもBもしっかり訳す必要があります。これが「丁寧に書く」ということです（***Rule 61*** ⇒p.55）。

Aに相当するのは〈increasing the opportunity for 人 to 原形〉「人が～する機会を増やすこと」です。Bは，「andが結んでいるもの」に注意して，not only *A* but also ***B₁* and *B₂***「AだけでなくB₁とB₂も」の形で，devising ～ and advising ... という構造を把握します。B₁は〈encourage 人 to 原形〉「人に～するよう促す」，B₂は〈advise 人 of ～〉「人に～を知らせる」の形に注意してください（このadviseの語法は，〈tell［inform/notify］人 of ～〉「人に～を知らせる」などと同じ形です）。文末はオウム返しで「～という変化」と締めくくれば完成です。自分の解答にA・B₁・B₂の3点が含まれているかをチェックしてください。

問3 難易度 ★★★

下線部の「理由」が問われていますが，まずは下線部自体を考えてみましょう。全体が，Once S′V′, SV.「いったんS′V′するとSVだ」の形になっています。

> (Once ～), (however), the need [to learn to speak]$_S$ no longer featured$_V$ (in the feedback [from students]).
>
> 「しかし，**いったん～すると**，話せるようになりたいという要望は生徒からのフィードバックで目立たなくなった」

feature「主要な部分を占める」という意味を知っている受験生はまずいないですよね（「特集する」という意味なら知っている人もいるでしょうが）。こんなときは「**第1文型（SVM）の動詞は"存在・移動の意味"になる**」を使いましょう。

>>> *Rule 78* 構文 第1文型は「存在・移動」と考える！

> それぞれの文型ごとに（大体ではありますが）動詞の意味が決まっており，第1文型（SVM）の場合は「**存在・移動」の意味が基本**です。つまり，意味を知らない動詞であっても第1文型であれば，「**いる・動く**」と考えればOKなのです。
>
> 例えばWe **got** to Tokyo. という英文は，Weが**S**，gotが**V**，to Tokyoが**M**のSVMですね。よって，「私たちは東京に**移動した**」と考えれば意味がとれてしまいます（今回は「方向・到達」を表す前置詞toがあるので，「存在」よ

り「移動」が自然です)。get to ～「～に着く」という熟語として教わりますが，実は「文型」に注目することで解決するのです。これからは，動詞の意味がわからなくても「第1文型(SVM)」であれば「いる・動く」と考えてみてください。もちろん例外はありますが，この考え方で意味がとれることは驚くほど多いのです。

no longer ～「もはや～ない」を加味して，「もはや要望はフィードバックに**なくなった**」で意味がとれます。

さらに，no longer 自体の特徴も利用したいところです。

>>> *Rule 24* 読解 過去と現在の「対比」を予測する！(no longer)

no longer ～「もはや～ない」の「意味」は有名ですが，「働き」を意識できる受験生はほとんどいません。no longer は「**昔は○○だったけれど，もはや［今では］そうではない**」というニュアンスを含み，「**過去と現在の対比／変化**」を表すことが多いのです。

この問いは「話せるようになりたいという要望が(もはや)なくなった理由」を書くわけですが，設問指示に「以前のフィードバックの内容を踏まえて」とあることからも，no longer を見て**過去と現在の対比・変化**を意識することで，「以前は～だったが，…に変更したから」といった答案の型を作ることができます。

came to 原形「～するようになった」で変化を表す

Vicki gradually **came to** understand that what the students really wanted was not an increased opportunity to speak, but explicit instruction on how to speak, that is, explicit instruction in pronunciation.

答案：「生徒の要望は，話す機会を増やすのではなく，発音の仕方を明確に教えてもらうことだと理解した」－①

過去完了進行形で「教え方を変える前」の説明

She realized she **had been avoiding** actually teaching pronunciation because she was a little unsure how to go about it.

答案：「発音指導に少し自信がなかったため，(以前は)発音指導を避けていた」－②

started to [原形]「～し始めた」で変化を表す　incorporate *A* into *B*「AをBに取り入れる」

Once she **started to** incorporate pronunciation instruction into her classes, however, (3) the need to learn to speak no longer featured in the feedback from students.

答案：「発音指導を授業に取り入れた」－③

第2段落1文目（16行目）にはcame to [原形]「～するようになった」という「変化」や，not *A* but *B*「AではなくBだ」という「対比」があります。そして，2文目（18行目）では過去完了進行形で「教え方を変える前」について説明し，3文目（20行目）で「どう変えたか？」という変更内容を述べています。

補足 話の基準が「過去形」の場合，それよりも前には「過去完了形」が使われます（今回はVickiの経験したことを述べているので，「過去」が基準となります）。この過去完了形の使い方は物語文やエッセイで多用されます。

2文目は「教え方を変える前」のことなので，これを最初に持ってきて「②→①→③」の順番でまとめるときれいになります。答案の型「以前は～だったが，…に変更したから」を意識して，「以前は発音指導に少し自信がなくて教えていなかったが（②），生徒の要望は発音の仕方を明確に教えてもらうことだと理解し（①），発音指導を授業に取り入れた（③）から」とまとめればOKです。

皆さんは自分の答案に①②③の要素を入れたかを確認してください。解答文末は，問いの「なぜか」に合わせて，「～から，～ため」で締めくくりましょう。

問4 難易度 ★★☆

Such views「そういった考え」は〈**such＋[名詞]**〉の形で〈this＋[名詞]〉のように**「前に述べられている内容を受ける」**ので，この前の部分を見て「考え」を述べている箇所を探します（厳密には少し違うのですが，〈such＋[名詞]〉も〈**this＋[名詞]**〉（***Rule 4*** ⇒p.71）と同じ発想をしても問題はありません）。さらに，Such viewsの後ろにare based on misconceptions of ～「～に対する誤解に基づいている」とあることから，「誤解に基づく考え方」を探せばいいとわかります。

以上を踏まえて，「（誤解に基づく）考え」を念頭に探すと，35行目にhave the **idea** that ～「～という考え」が見つかります。Other teachers may have the **idea** that ～は，その前のSome teachers may even **feel** that ～とペアになっていて，feel that ～以下に「考え」が含まれると判断できます。Some teachers ～. Other teachers ... .「～する教師もいれば，…する教師もいる」を「～という教師の考えや，…という教師の考え」とまとめればOKです。

生徒目線

Some teachers may (even) feel 〈that instruction [in pronunciation] is too threatening or challenging (for beginners [who are already struggling (with so many different aspects of English)])〉.

答案：「英語のさまざまな面で苦労している初学者にとって，発音指導はやっかい」―①

Other teachers may have the idea 〈that pronunciation is too difficult or complicated for them to teach〉.

教師目線

答案：「発音はあまりに難しかったり複雑すぎて教師は教えられない」―②

Lesson 4

1つ目は「生徒目線」，2つ目は「教師目線」になっています。「初学者に発音を指導するのは無理がある／教師にとっても発音指導は難しい」ということです。ただし，いずれも教師の考えであり，**SomeとOtherを使って並列**されているので，答案にはどちらか一方ではなく，きちんと**2つの考え**を入れてください。

補足 34行目threateningは「脅迫的な」，challengingは「骨の折れる」で，まとめて「やっかいな，嫌な」と意味をとるか，34行目who are already strugglingから考えて「苦労するような」としてもよいです。

設問とは関係ありませんが，最後に重要なルールを加えておきます。入試問題に取り組む際，英文を読む前に**出典を見る**ことをオススメします。出典を明示するかどうかは大学によるのですが，もしあれば，それが大きなヒントになることもあります。

今回の場合が究極の例と言えるのですが，出典にあるタイトル“Pronunciation instruction is not appropriate for beginning-level learners,” *Pronunciation Myths*の最後にmythという重要単語があるのです。

>>> Rule 35 読解 長文単語・語句をマスターする！（myth）

多くの受験生はmythを「神話」と暗記していますが，ギリシャ神話などが入試に出ることはほとんどありません。

実際には，「神話」より「迷信」の意味が圧倒的に重要です。日本語でも「学歴神話」＝「学歴があれば一生安泰という迷信」，「安全神話」＝「安全だという迷信」と言いますが，これと同じように，**mythは「迷信，作り話」**の意味を優先してください。そして，長文では「～という迷信があるが，実際にはその迷信は間違いだ」のような流れが多いです。

まさに今回も「迷信」なので，出典のタイトルで「発音に関する誤解」がテーマだと予想できてしまうのです。もちろんいつもこんなラッキーなことが起きるわけではありませんが，タイトルを見る時間などほんの数秒ですから，必ず先にチェックするようにしましょう。ちなみに，Lesson 1の66行目と70行目にもmythが出ており，共に「迷信」の意味です。

文構造の分析

1 [1] Most learners [at every level] are keen to learn how to speak as well as how to read and write (in English), and beginners are no exception. [2] They are very keen to learn how to pronounce English (in a way [that makes themselves understood easily]). [3] This became very clear (to Vicki), a colleague of ours [with considerable experience [teaching adult learners]]. [4] (At the time), Vicki was working (with a class of beginning-level learners [from very diverse backgrounds]). [5] (Because she is always conscientious (about meeting the needs of her students)), she decided to collect feedback [about different aspects of her classes] (on a regular basis). [6] This feedback (consistently) indicated 〈that her students were pleased with her teaching but they wanted to learn how to speak (in their daily lives)〉. [7] (At first), she responded (to these requests) (by not only increasing the opportunity for her students [to speak in class], but also devising assignments [that encouraged them to speak outside the class] and advising them of community-based facilities [where they could practice]). [8] (However), (even after these changes), the students (still) reported 〈that they wanted to learn to speak (in their daily lives)〉.

構文反復

Vickiの同格

Butを予想

不定詞の意味上のS

〈these＋名詞〉→ まとめ表現

訳 [1] あらゆるレベルの大半の学習者は，英語での読み書きに加えて，英語を話すこともできるようになりたがっており，初学者も例外ではない。[2] 彼らは，自分の話を相手に難なく理解してもらえるように英語を発音できるようになりたいと強く思っている。[3] 私たちの同僚で，成人学習者への指導経験が豊富なヴィッキーは，このことをとてもよく理解するようになった。[4] 当時ヴィッキーは，さまざまな環境で育った初級レベルの学習者のクラスを受け持っていた。[5] 彼女は常に生徒の要望に応えようと気を遣っているので，自分の授業に関するさまざまな角度からのフィードバックを定期的に集めることにした。[6] このフィードバックが一貫して示していたのは，生徒たちは彼女の授業に満足しているが，日常生活において話す方法を学びたいと思っているということだった。[7] 最初，こういった要望に対して，彼女は，生徒たちが授業中に話す機会を増やすだけでなく，授業外でも英語を話すように促す課題を考案したり，練習ができる地域の施設を教えてあげたりすることによって応えた。[8] しかし，このように変更を行ってからも，生徒たちは依然として，日常生活で英語を話せるようになりたいと訴えた。

語句 [1] *be* keen to 原形 ～したがっている／*A* as well as *B*　BだけでなくAも／

Lesson 4

beginner 名 初級者，初心者／exception 名 例外／[2] pronounce 動 発音する／way 名 方法／make *oneself* understood 人の考えを理解してもらう（直訳「人（の言っていること）を理解される状態にする」→「人の考えを理解してもらう，話が通じる」となります）／[3] considerable 形 たくさんの／[4] diverse 形 さまざまな, 多様な／background 名 背景，環境／[5] conscientious 形 誠実な，真面目な／meet a need ニーズを満たす，要求に応える／feedback 名 反応，（参考）意見／aspect 名 観点／on a regular basis 定期的に／[6] consistently 副 一貫して／indicate 動 示す／*be* pleased with ～ ～に満足している／[7] devise 動 考案する／assignment 名 課題／encourage 人 to 原形 人に～するように促す, 推奨する／advise 人 of ～ 人に～を伝達する／community-based 形 地域密着型の／facility 名 施設，設備／[8] report 動 報告する

文法・構文 [2] *be* keen to 原形／how to 原形という直前の文と同じ形が使われており，どちらも「英語を話せるようになりたいと思っている」という内容です。このように同じ形の反復は同じ意味になります（***Rule 25*** ⇒p.103）。 [3] a colleague of oursは，a friend of mine「友人のうちの1人」と同じ構造で，「私たちの同僚のうちの1人」という意味です（文章で初出の場合は，まだ特定されていないのでmy colleagueやmy friendとは言わない場合が多いです）。 [7] At first「初めは」は，「初めは～だった。だけど…」という形で，後ろにbutやhoweverが続くことが多いです。今回も次の文の冒頭でHoweverが使われていますね。ちなみに，後半のandは動名詞のカタマリ2つ（devising ～ とadvising ～）を結んでいます。 [8]〈these + 名詞〉は「まとめ表現」です。直前の内容がわからなくても，「授業に変化を加えた」のだと推測できます。

2 [1] Vicki (gradually) came to understand 《that 〈what the students (really) wanted φ〉 was not an increased opportunity [to speak], but explicit instruction [on how to speak], (that is), explicit instruction [in pronunciation]》. [2] She realized 〈 she had been avoiding (actually) teaching pronunciation (because she was (a little) unsure how to go about it)〉. [3] ((Once she started to incorporate pronunciation instruction (into her classes)), (however), the need [to learn to speak] no longer featured (in the feedback [from students]). [4] (In addition), former students [who had moved (to higher levels)] came back (to attend her beginner classes), ((so much so that), (at times), her classes would be overflowing (with past students as well as current class members)). [5] They (obviously) felt 〈 they were learning to speak〉!

Once S´V´, SV. の形

so ～ that S´V´ 構文

訳 [1] ヴィッキーはだんだんと，生徒たちが本当に望んでいるのは，英語を話す機会を増やすことではなく，話し方に関する明確な指導，つまり発音の明確な指導だと理解するようになっていった。[2] 彼女は, 発音指導をどうやってやればよいのか少し自信がなかったので, 実際に発音を教えることを避けていたことに気づいた。[3] しかし，いったん彼女が授

業に発音指導を取り入れ始めると，話せるようになりたいという要望は生徒からのフィードバックで目立たなくなった。[4]さらに，上のレベルに移っていた前の生徒たちも戻ってきて彼女の初級クラスに出るようになり，そういった人があまりに多かったので，彼女のクラスはときに，現在の受講生と前の生徒であふれてしまうのだった。[5]彼らは，英語を話せるようになりつつあるとはっきり感じていたのだった！

語句 [1]gradually 副 だんだんと／come to 原形 ～するようになる／explicit 形 明確な instruction 名 指導／on 前 ～に関する／that is {to say} すなわち／pronunciation 名 発音／[2]go about ～ ～に取り組む／[3]once S´V´ いったんS´V´すると（「副詞」のonce「一度，かつて」と区別してください）／incorporate *A* into *B* AをBに取り入れる／no longer ～ もはや～ない／feature in ～ ～に登場する，～の中で大きな特徴となる／[4]former 形 かつての／attend 動 参加する／so much so that ～ 非常にそうなので～／overflow 動 あふれかえる

文法・構文 [2]*be* unsure of[about] ～「～について不安だ，自信がない」の形でよく使われますが，後ろにwhat節・how節などが続く場合は前置詞が省略されます。[3]文頭のonceは「接続詞」で，Once S´V´, SV.「いったんS´V´すると，SVだ」の形で使われます。[4]so much so that ～は「非常にそうなので～」という意味です。1つ目のsoとthatでso ～ that S´V´構文「とても～なのでS´V´だ」を作っており，2つ目のsoは「そのように，そのようで」という意味（I think so.のsoと同じ）です。この文では，2番目のsoは「上のレベルに移っていた前の生徒たちが戻って初級クラスに出るようになった」ことを表しているため，和訳では「そういった人があまりにも多かったので」と訳しています。[5]they were learning to speakは「過去進行形」なので，あくまで「話せるようになりつつあった」という意味です（「(実際に）話せるようになった」ではないので注意してください)。

3 [1](When teaching beginner adult learners of English), we are faced with a (seemingly) daunting task. [2]There are so many things [they need to learn φ]. [3]They need to learn how to speak, listen, read, and write (in English), and proficiency [in each of these skills] requires the mastery of many different sub-skills. [4]It can (therefore) be difficult to establish priorities (when deciding what to teach (in a beginning-level classroom)). [5](Unfortunately), pronunciation is (often) overlooked (as a teaching priority at this level) (because other aspects of English are deemed to be more important). [6]Some teachers may (even) feel 〈that instruction [in pronunciation] is too threatening or challenging (for beginners [who are already struggling (with so many different aspects of English)])〉. [7]Other teachers may have the idea 〈that pronunciation is too difficult or complicated for them to teach〉. [8]We

〈S´＋be動詞〉の省略

〈S´＋be動詞〉の省略

不定詞の意味上のS

disagree! [9] Such views are based on misconceptions of pronunciation and its role [in 〈how we learn to speak a language〉].

〈such + 名詞〉→ まとめ表現

訳 [1] 初級者の成人英語学習者に指導をするとき，私たちは一見困難な課題に直面する。[2] 学ばないといけないことがあまりにも多いのだ。[3] 英語で話す，聞く，読む，書く方法を学ぶ必要があり，これらの各技能の習熟には，多くのさまざまな副次的技能の習得が求められる。[4] そのため，初級レベルのクラスで何を教えるかを決める際に優先順位を定めるのは難しいことがある。[5] 残念ながら発音は，英語の他の側面のほうが重要だとみなされるために，このレベルにおける指導の優先事項としては見落とされることが多い。[6] 指導者の中には，すでに英語のとてもさまざまな面で苦労している初学者にとって，発音指導はあまりにも脅迫的だったり，骨が折れるものだったりすると思ってさえいる人がいるかもしれない。[7] また，発音はあまりに難しかったり複雑だったりして教えられないという考えを持つ指導者もいるかもしれない。[8] 私たちはそうは思わない！ [9] そういった考えは，発音と，言語が話せるようになる過程における発音の役割に対する誤解から来ているのだ。

語句 [1] *be* faced with ～ ～に直面する／seemingly 副 一見／daunting 形 おじけづかせる，ひるませる／[3] proficiency 名 上達，習熟／mastery 名 習得／sub-名詞 ～の下の，下の～，副～／[4] establish 動 決める，確立する／priority 名 優先順位／[5] overlook 動 見落とす／deem O to be C OをCとみなす／[6] threatening 形 厳しい，脅迫的な／challenging 形 困難な／[9] *be* based on ～ ～に基づいている／misconception 名 誤解

文法・構文 [1] *be* faced with ～ の face は他動詞で 人 を目的語にとって「(困難が人に) 面と向かわせる」。ここでその受け身で直訳「～に直面させられる」→「～に直面する」となります。 [3]「学ばなければいけないこと」の具体例が speak／listen／read／write と羅列されています。 [4] when deciding ～ は，分詞構文の冒頭に接続詞を加えた形です（意味を明確にするために，分詞構文の -ing の前に接続詞を明示することがあります）。 [5] because 以下は deem other aspects of English to be more important が受動態になった形です。 [7] 前文と共に，Some ～. Other ～.「～する人がいる。～する人もいる」という相関表現になっています。また同格の that 以下は，〈too ～ to 原形〉「～すぎて…できない」に意味上の S (for them) が加わった形です。 [9] and は pronunciation と its role in ～ language を結んでおり，どちらも misconceptions にかかっています。its は pronunciation を指します。

音読をしよう！ 🔈 04

Most learners at every level / are keen to learn how to speak // as well as how to read and write in English, // and beginners are no exception. // They are very keen to learn / how to pronounce English / in a way that makes themselves understood easily. // This became very clear to Vicki, // a colleague of ours / with considerable experience teaching adult learners. // At the time, // Vicki was working with a class of beginning-level learners / from very diverse backgrounds. // Because she is always conscientious / about meeting the needs of her students, // she decided to collect feedback / about different aspects of her classes / on a regular basis. // This feedback consistently indicated / that her students were pleased with her teaching / but they wanted to learn how to speak / in their daily lives. // At first, she responded to these requests / by not only increasing the opportunity / for her students to speak in class, // but also devising assignments / that encouraged them to speak outside the class // and advising them of community-based facilities / where they could practice. // However, // even after these changes, // the students still reported / that they wanted to learn to speak / in their daily lives. //

Vicki gradually came to understand / that what the students really wanted / was not an increased opportunity to speak, // but explicit instruction on how to speak, // that is, // explicit instruction in pronunciation. // She realized / she had been avoiding actually teaching pronunciation // because she was a little unsure / how to go about it. // Once she started to incorporate pronunciation instruction into her classes, // however, // the need to learn to speak / no longer featured in the feedback from students. // In addition, // former students who had moved to higher levels // came back to attend her beginner classes, // so much so that, // at times, // her classes would be overflowing with past students // as well as current class members. // They obviously felt / they were learning to speak! //

When teaching beginner adult learners of English, // we are faced with a seemingly daunting task. // There are so many things they need to learn. // They need to learn how to speak, // listen, // read, // and write in English, // and proficiency in each of these skills / requires the mastery of many different sub-skills. // It can therefore be difficult / to establish priorities / when deciding what to teach / in a beginning-level classroom. // Unfortunately, // pronunciation is often overlooked as a teaching priority / at this level // because other aspects of English / are deemed to be more important. // Some teachers may even feel / that instruction in pronunciation / is too threatening or challenging for beginners // who are already struggling / with so many different aspects of English. // Other teachers may have the idea / that pronunciation is too difficult or complicated for them to teach. // We disagree! // Such views are based on misconceptions of pronunciation // and its role in how we learn to speak a language. //

Lesson 5 解答・解説

▶問題 別冊 p.21

このLessonで出てくるルール

Rule 80 構文 SVOCになる形に注意！（使役動詞と知覚動詞）⇒ 問1

Rule 19 読解 「総称のyou」の意味に注意！ ⇒ 問2

Rule 49 解法 印象の強い単語・同じ単語を使ったひっかけパターン ⇒ 問3

Rule 59 解法 空所補充問題の解法 ⇒ 問6

Rule 8 読解 〈A＋名詞〉を見たら「具体例」と考える！ ⇒ 問6

解答

問1 (A) ⑥　(C) ②　(F) ⑤

問2 革新を可能にするためには，壮大なアイディアを思いつくだけでは足りない。それをはっきりと伝えるために懸命に努力することも必要なのである。

問3 ②

問4 彼（ファラデー）の科学的才能は，皆が理解できないような実験結果を生み出すことだけでなく，それら（その実験結果）を説明することにもあった。

問5 ③　**問6** (あ) ②　(い) ④　(う) ①　(え) ③

問7 実は私たちは，自分が人に伝えられないことはどんなことであれ，あまり理解していないのだ。　**問8** ②

問1 難易度 ★★☆

整序問題は**まずは動詞に注目する**のが鉄則です。語群にはmadeとwasがありますが，まずはmadeに注目して，**make OC「OをCにする」**の形を予想します。使役動詞と知覚動詞は，最優先で考えてほしい超頻出事項です。Oにhim，Cにso effectiveを当てはめてmade him so effectiveとします。whatが（madeの主語になり）名詞節を作ると考えると，what made him so effective「彼をあれほど印象的にしたもの」がthat節中の主語で，動詞wasにつながります。whatとmakeはよくセットになります（例：What makes you think so?「あなたはどうしてそんな風に考えるのですか？」)。すぐ前の文what I remember best was how the talk endedという同じwhatのSVCの文もヒントになります。

ちなみに，空所を含む箇所は未来を表す仮定法〈if S′ were to 原形, S should 原形.〉の形になっています。

>>> Rule 80 構文 SVOCになる形に注意！（使役動詞と知覚動詞）

SVOCを作る動詞の中でも，「使役動詞と知覚動詞」は特に重要です。以下の動詞を見たら「SVOCがくるんじゃないか？」と考えるようにしてください。

使役動詞	知覚動詞	
□ make（強制・必然）	□ see 見える	□ hear 聞こえる
□ have（利害）	□ feel 感じる	□ consider 思う
□ let（許可）	□ find 思う	□ catch 目撃する
の3つだけ！	□ smell においがする　など	

■ SVOCの考え方と訳し方

SVOCは「**Sによって，OがCする・Cになる**」と訳すときれいになることが多いです。例えば，The news made me happy. は「そのニュースは私を嬉しくさせた」より，「そのニュースによって［を聞いて］，私は嬉しくなった」のほうが自然ですね。

構文	S	V	O	C
	↓	↓	↓	↓
実際	M′（原因・理由）	×（無視 or 助動詞や副詞）	S′（主語）	V′（動詞）
訳	「Sによって」	（基本的に訳さない）	「Oが」	「Cする・Cになる」

SをM′（原因・理由），Vは無視して，Oを「主語」，Cを「動詞」っぽく考えます（Vのニュアンスを加えられれば完璧ですが，意味がわからなければ無視してOKです⇒p.106）。

問2 難易度 ★★☆

make OC「OをCにする」

(In order to make innovation possible), it（仮S） 's（V） not enough（C） to just come up with big ideas.（真S）

■ make OC

make innovation possibleはmake OCの形です。ここでは直訳「革新を可能にする」でもOKですし（in order to 原形「～するために」の直後の場合，直訳でも自然なことが多い），せっかく今学んだばかりなので，「革新［イノベーション］が起こるには」としてもOKです。

■ 主節は仮主語構文

〈it's not enough to just 原形〉「～するだけでは十分でない」は仮主語構文です（toの直後は「動詞の原形」が原則ですが，実際にはjustのような副詞が割り込むことがよくあります）。come up with ～「～を思いつく」, big ideasは「大きなアイディア」よりも，文脈を考えて「立派な［すごい，壮大な］アイディア」などと訳したほうが自然ですね。2文目も見ておきましょう。

work hard to 原形「～するよう懸命に努力する」

You (S) also need to work hard (V) (to communicate them clearly).

総称用法

■ 総称のyou

文頭のYouは「あなた」ではなく**「人は誰でも」**という**総称のyou**という用法です。

>>> *Rule 19* 読解 「総称のyou」の意味に注意！

youには「あなたも私も，人は誰でも，みんな」という意味があります（辞書にも「総称」という見出しで載っています）。多くの人が見落としている用法ですが，実際には大学受験・日常会話・広告のキャッチコピー・ことわざなどさまざまな場面で使われるメジャーな用法です。

「みんな，誰でも」と訳したり，または（みんなに当てはまることなので）**あえて日本語では表さない**ことも多いです。「あなた」と訳してしまうと不自然になることがあるので注意が必要です。例えば，次の文はとある有名国立大学で出た英文です：You can't buy friendship.

これを「あなたは友情を買うことはできない」とすると，まるで「（あなた以外の）他の人なら買える」のように聞こえてしまいます。これは総称のyouで，「（みんな誰もが）友情を買うことはできない」という意味なんです。

■ work と communicate を丁寧に訳す

〈need to 原形〉「～する必要がある」の後ろは，〈work hard to 原形〉「～するよう［～するために］懸命に努力する」という表現です。ここで「仕事する」は不自然です。communicate them clearly は「それら（big ideas）をはっきり伝える」と訳せばOKです。「彼らとコミュニケーションをとる」なんて訳してはいけません。「～とコミュニケーションをとる」は communicate with ～と，with が必要です。them は big ideas を指しますが，「説明問題」ではなく，単なる「和訳問題」なので，「代名詞が指すもの」を明らかにせず「それら」としても OK です。

ちなみに，1文目では not と just，2文目では also が使われ，not only ［just］ *A* but {also} *B*「AだけでなくてBも」から **but が消えた形**になっています（***Rule 1*** ⇒p.107）。

問3 難易度 ★★☆

take ～ for granted「～を当たり前だと思う」という熟語で，「私たちは電気を当たり前のものだと思っている」という意味です。次の文にある without a second thought「よく考えることなく」もヒントになります。これに意味が近いのは，② we fail to fully appreciate electricity です。〈fail to 原形〉「～しない，～できない」，appreciate「よさ，価値がわかる」がポイントです。ちなみに，ここでも to と動詞の原形の間に副詞 fully が割り込んだ形です（問2の解説参照）。

> **多義語 appreciate の核心：「よ～くわかる」**
>
> **(1) 正しく理解する**　　**(2) 正しく評価する，よさがわかる**
>
> **(3) 鑑賞する**　　**(4) 感謝する**

appreciate の "preciate" は「値段をつける」という意味です（つづりが price と似ていますね）。「(値段をつけて) 正しく理解する／正しく評価する，よさがわかる」から，「人の作品を正しく評価する」→ (3)「鑑賞する」，「人の行為を正しく評価する」→ (4)「感謝する」となりました。今回の選択肢では，「よさ，価値がわかる」くらいの意味で使われています。

さて今回は，誤り選択肢③にも重要なルールが含まれています。③は，本文と同じ単語（grant）を使ったひっかけです。本文では take ～ for granted「～を当たり前だと思う」という熟語ですが，選択肢では単純に「(電気の使用を) 認める」という動詞として使われています。こういった「本文と同じ単語を使ったひっかけ」はよくあるパターンです。

»» Rule 49 解法 印象の強い単語・同じ単語を使ったひっかけパターン

本文の中で「印象の強い単語」や，受験生が勘違いしやすい「多義語」を**誤りの選択肢**で使ってひっかけるパターンがよく使われます。
同じ単語が使われていても,「本文での意味」と「選択肢での意味」が違えば当然アウトです。**選択肢に本文と同じ単語がある**ときほど，すぐには飛びつかず，本文と選択肢をよく見比べるようにしてください。また,「熟語」や「多義語」をしっかり覚えていくと, この手のひっかけに対処できるようになります。

選択肢の訳

① 私たちは，電気は常に使えるわけではないと考えている
→ 本文で「使えるor使えない」という話はしていません。
② 私たちは，電気の価値を十分には理解できていない
③ 私たちは皆に電気の使用を認める
④ 私たちは，電気は便利なものであると認識している

問4 難易度 ★★★ 思考力

SVをつかんで, 第1文型だと把握してください。

His scientific genius (S) lay (V) not simply (in producing experimental results [that were beyond everyone's understanding]) but (in explaining them) too.

自動詞lieの過去形　not simply *A* but *B*「AだけでなくBも」

■ **lie in ～「～にある」は頻出表現**
layは自動詞lie「ある」の過去形です。他動詞layと区別してください。

lie 自動詞	**lay** 他動詞 ※目的語が必要
「いる，ある，横になる」 （活用）lie – lay - lain	「置く，横にする」 （活用）lay – laid - laid

lie「横たわる」，lay「横たえる」と習いますが，実際は，lieは「ある」，layは「置く」と訳すことが非常に多いのです。

そもそも今回は**SVM（第1文型）**なので，layは自動詞だとわかります（他動詞の直後には目的語が必要です）。なお，**SVMのとき動詞の意味は「存在，移動」が基本**です（***Rule 78*** ⇒p.72）。さらにここではinがあるので，lieは「～にいる，ある」だと推測できます。His scientific genius lay in ～「彼の科学的才能は～の中にあった」と訳せます。

■ **not only *A* but {also} *B*のバリエーション**

not simply *A* but {also} *B*「Aだけでなく Bも」が使われています。onlyが**simply**に変わって，also（今回は省略されていますが）が**too**になっています。lay not simply in *A* but in *B* too「Aだけでなく Bにもあった」という形です。

Aに当たる部分は，producing experimental results that were beyond everyone's understanding「皆が理解できないような実験結果を生み出すこと」です（thatは関係代名詞）。beyondは本来「超越（～を超えて）」で，beyond everyone's understandingは「皆の理解を超えた」でOKですが，「皆が理解できないような」と，否定で訳すと完璧です。Bに相当するところはexplaining them「それらを説明すること」です。このthemはexperimental results「（皆が理解できないような）実験結果」を指します。

ここが 思考力 前文の言い換えに気づけるか?

下線部は，実は前にある Yet Faraday was more than just a talented scientist. {But} He was also a very effective communicator.の言い換えなんです。more than justはnot onlyと同じ意味で（more thanの意味は***Rule 31*** ⇒p.150），**more than just *A*. {~~But~~} also *B*.「単にAだけでない。Bもだ」**です。これが，下線部（4）ではnot simply *A* but *B*に言い換えられています。それぞれAとBの内容も対応しているので，理想を言えばその内容を吟味して下線部を読むべき深い問題なのです（実際には下線部だけしっかり読めばできてしまうのですが，皆さんにはここまで考えられるようになってほしいと思います）。

問5 難易度 ★★☆

The effort paid off.は「その努力は報われた」という意味で，**pay off**は「うまくいく，報われる」という熟語です。これに近い意味の③を選べばOKです。

その後のHis regular lectures at the Royal Institution made him, and the Institution itself, well-known in the scientific world. に「科学界で有名になった」とあり,「努力が報われた」と確認できます。The effortは前文のhe worked hard at itを受けており，itはその前のThisと同じ，つまりさらに前の「皆が理解できないような実験結果を生み出し，それを説明する」ことを指しています。

選択肢の訳

① その努力によって多額の金が得られた。
② その努力は借金がなかった。
→ ①・②共にpayを「(お金を) 払う」と勘違いした人をひっかける選択肢です。
③ その努力は成功を収めた。
④ その努力には価値がなかった。
→ ④は本文と真逆の内容です。

問6 難易度 ★★☆

>>> Rule 59 解法 空所補充問題の解法

空所補充問題はいきなり文脈を考えるのではなく，以下の3ステップで考えてください。

(1) 選択肢を品詞ごとに分ける

選択肢の品詞がバラバラなときはラッキーです。**空所の前後から入るべき品詞を絞る**ことで，速く確実に解けるようになります。「意味は通るけど，品詞が違うからNG」というのが典型的なひっかけパターンです。

補足 難関大になるほど，異なる品詞を選択肢にする問題は出なくなりますが（つまり，選択肢は全部同じ品詞），まずは選択肢をチェックする習慣をつけておいてください。

また，**品詞分けを「やりすぎない」**ことも大事です。例えばhaveは一般動詞「持つ」と助動詞（完了形を作るhave)，besidesは前置詞「〜の他に」と副詞「加えて」があります。やっかいな例ではcanが助動詞ではなく名詞「缶」だった問題もあります。本番では「別の品詞の可能性」も念頭に入れておきましょう。

(2) ペアを疑ってみる

「空所が，前後の単語とペアになるのでは？」と考えてみてください。特によくセットになるのは，以下の2パターンです。

1. 後ろの前置詞とセットになる

(a) 直後の前置詞と⇒「熟語」 例）(look) for 〜 〜を探す

(b) 離れた前置詞と⇒「語法」　例）(provide) *A* with *B* AにBを与える

2. 直後の名詞とセットになる　例）(waste) time 時間を無駄にする

(3) 文脈で解く

「形から」考えても解けない場合に初めて文脈を考えます。ただし，なんとなく解くのではなく，本書の他のルールを駆使できないか考えてみてください。

今回は，選択肢の品詞はすべて同じ（動詞）ですが，「形から考える」という鉄則は忘れないようにしましょう。

Lesson 5

(あ)

まずこの空所（**あ**）を含む第5段落が本文のなかでどのような役割になっているかを確認しましょう。第5段落はA more recent geniusと始まっています。〈A＋名詞〉の形に注目して，「具体例」だと考えてください。

>>> *Rule 8* 読解 〈A＋名詞〉を見たら「具体例」と考える！

文章中で〈A＋名詞〉で始まる文を見つけたら，そこから**具体例が始まる**と考えます（Aは先頭にくることがほとんどなので大文字で示しています。ときに，〈副詞, a 名詞 〜〉の形の場合もあります）。

主張. A＋名詞 〜.
└──▶この文から具体例になる！

筆者が主張を述べたあとで「例えば1つ，とある名詞があるとして，それは…」といった感じで，**主張した内容について具体的な説明**をするのです。たまたま熟語（A littleやA lot ofなど）で始まるときは具体例にならないケースもありますが，まずは「例えば」と考えてみてください。英文の意味がハッキリわかるケースがほとんどですよ。

A more recent genius was Richard Feynman.では，〈A＋名詞〉に加えて，**固有名詞**（ここでは人名）もあります（***Rule 12*** ⇒p.54）。さらにmoreとあるので前述の何かと比較していることがわかります。つまりこの段落では「才能だけでなく，コミュニケーション力も大切」という主張の具体例として（前述のファラデーとは）別の人物（ファインマン）が紹介されていると予想できるのです。さらに，空所（**あ**）を含む文のlike Faraday「ファラデーと同じように」からも，ファラデーの例と同じ流れになると考えられます（***Rule 14*** ⇒p.13）。よって，②

hideを選んで，Yet like Faraday, Feynman was not content to hide his tricks.「だがファラデー同様，ファインマンも自分の秘術を隠して満足することはなかった」とすればOKです。この文で「才能だけではない」，次の文で「コミュニケーションも重視」と予想どおりの内容が続きます（“not *A*. {~~But~~} *B*.”のパターン）。

(い)

空所直後（knowledge and communication as two separate spheres）の，前置詞asに注目して，④treatを選び，**treat *A* as *B***「AをBとして扱う」とします（***Rule 71*** ⇒p.14）。We tend to treat knowledge and communication as two separate spheres.「私たちは知識とコミュニケーションを2つの別々の分野として扱いがちである」となり，文意も通りますね。

(う)

空所直後は名詞が2つ並んでいます（communicationとlittle or no attention）。**V *A B***の形をとるのは，①giveで，give *A B*「AにBを与える」の形です。give communication little or no attention「コミュニケーションに，ほとんどあるいは一切注意を与えない」→「注意を払わない」となります。

(え)

空所直後の前置詞inから，空所には「自動詞」が入ると考え，③liveを選びます。we live in a communication age「私たちはコミュニケーションの時代に生きている」となります。

選択肢の訳

①与える　②隠す　③生きる　④扱う

問7 難易度★★☆

構文は難しくないのですが，anythingのあとにある関係代名詞thatに注意してください。**anything that** we **can't** communicateは「私たちが伝え**られないことはどんなことでも**」となります。communicateは他動詞「伝える」ですね。

(In truth), we(S) can't (really) know(V) anything [that we can't communicate ϕ](O).

■ **not really ～「あまり～でない」**

in truth「実のところ，実際には」，not really ～「あまり～ではない」です。we

can't really know 〜は「あまり〜を理解していない」と訳せばOKです。

補足 ちなみに，語順が逆（really not 〜）なら，「本当に〜でない，まったく〜でない」となります。

問8 難易度★★☆ 思考力

11行目のYou also need to work hard to communicate them clearly.などで「考えを伝えることが大事」と主張し，その後は具体例を通してその主張を裏付けています。本文の最後もThe fact is that although it may be fashionable to say that our present era is an information age, we live in a communication age and it's time we start taking it seriously.と締めくくっています。これらの主張に合致する②It is important to convey our understanding in a clear way.が正解です。

Lesson 5

ここが思考力 全体の「主張」を把握する問題

今回は「才能だけでなく，コミュニケーション力も大事」という本文の主張を把握しておけば，簡単に正解を選べます。こういった「筆者の主張を選ぶ」問題は当然どんな英文でも問われますが，解答方法として「主張を見つけ出そう」としかアドバイスされないことが多いのではないでしょうか。

しかし皆さんは，本書で学んだ「主張・具体例の発見方法」を使いこなすことで，確実に主張を見つけ出してください（今回の英文で言えば"not only *A*, but {also} *B*."のバリエーション／"not *A*. {~~But~~} *B*."のパターン／固有名詞や〈A＋名詞〉は「具体例」の合図など）。

選択肢の訳

① 十分な知識を持っていれば，他の人に理解してもらうことができる。

→ 本文の「知識だけでなく，伝える力が大事」という主張とは真逆の内容です。47行目にはっきり，To assert that we can possess knowledge, but are unable to explain what it is, makes no sense.と書かれています。

② 自分の意見を明確な方法で伝えることは重要である。

③ 自分の領域で黙々と勉強することによって，コミュニケーションが取れるようになる。

→ 42行目にWe act as if having the skills of an expert was a private matter, earned through quiet study.とありますが，「黙々と勉強することでコミュニケーションが取れるようになる」とは書かれていません。

④ 私たちは知識とコミュニケーションを同時に追い求めることはできない。

→ 本文で「同時に追い求めることが可能or不可能」には言及していません。また，41

行目にWe tend to treat knowledge and communication as two separate spheres. とあり，44行目のYet, as Wittgenstein argued decades ago, that position is logically unsound because it assumes that we are able to communicate to ourselves in a private language. でこの考えを否定しています。(tend to 原形「～しがち」で一般論を表し，Yetから主張になっています)。つまり，「知識とコミュニケーションを別々に扱うべきでない」=「同時に求めることは可能」とも考えられます。ただし，実際にはこの辺りの判断は難しいので，今回は「②が確実に正解」という解き方がラクでしょう。

文構造の分析

1 [1] (When I was in high school), a man came (to speak about Winston Churchill). [2] (Mostly), it was the usual mix of historical events and anecdotes, but 〈what I remember φ best〉 was 〈how the talk ended〉. [3] The speaker concluded (by saying 〈that (if we were to remember one thing [about Churchill]), it should be 〈that what made him so effective was his power to communicate〉〉). [4] I didn't understand that (at the time). [5] (Growing up), I had always heard about the importance of hard work, honesty and other things, but (never) communication.

未来を表す仮定法

訳 [1] 私が高校生のとき，ある男性がウィンストン・チャーチルについて話すためにやってきた。[2] ほとんどは，歴史上の出来事と逸話をありきたりに寄せ集めたものだったが，私が一番よく覚えているのは，話の終わり方だった。[3] その講演者は，私たちがチャーチルについて1つ覚えておくとしたら，それは彼をあれほど印象的にしたのは彼のコミュニケーション能力だったことですと言って話を締めくくったのであった。[4] 当時，私にはその意味がわからなかった。[5] 生きていく中で，勤勉や誠実さなどの重要性についてはいつも聞いてきていたが，コミュニケーションの重要性について聞いたことは一切なかったのである。

語句 [2] event 名 出来事／anecdote 名 逸話／[3] conclude 動 締めくくる／were to 原形 もし仮に～するなら／effective 形 注意を引く，印象に残る，効果的な／[5] honesty 名 誠実さ

文法・構文 [1] ここでのcame to 原形は，〈come to 原形〉「～するようになる」ではなく，「～しに来る」という意味です（to 原形は副詞的用法で「目的」です）。[2] itは前文の「ウィンストン・チャーチルについての話の内容」を指しています。[3] it should be that以下は，what made him so effective「彼をあれほど印象的にしたもの」というwhatのカタマリが(S)になっています。it = one thing (about Churchill)。[5] Growing upは分詞構文「～して，～しながら」です。but never communicationが難しいですが，but {I had} never {heard about the importance of} communicationから，反復による省略が起きた形です。

2 [1] Yet (now), (thirty years later), I 've begun to understand 〈what he meant φ〉. [2] (As Walter Isaacson argues), the ability [to work together effectively] is decisive. [3] (In order to make innovation possible), it 's not enough to just come up with big ideas. [4] You also need to work hard (to communicate them clearly).

「重要な」を表す形容詞

訳 [1] しかし，あれから30年経った今，彼が言っていたことの意味がわかり始めてきた。

Lesson 5

²ウォルター・アイザックソンが主張するように，うまく協働する能力は決定的に重要なものである。³革新を可能にするためには，壮大なアイディアを思いつくだけでは足りない。⁴それをはっきりと伝えるために懸命に努力することも必要なのである。

語句 ²decisive 形 決定的に重要な／³innovation 名 革新／come up with ～ ～を思いつく

文法・構文 ³~⁴仮S構文が使われてつながりが見えにくいですが，これも not just *A* but also *B*「AだけでなくBも」の形で，「butが消える」パターンです。

3 ¹(Today), we take electricity (for granted). ²We switch on lights, watch TV and enjoy connected devices (without a second thought). ³It 's hard 〈to imagine an earlier age [in which we had to use smoky, smelly candles (in order to see at night) and didn't have the benefit and convenience of basic household appliances]〉.

訳 ¹今日，私たちは電気があることを当然だと思っている。²私たちはよく考えることなく電気をつけ，テレビを見て，電源（やネットワーク）に接続された機器を享受している。³夜に物を見るためには煙たくて臭いロウソクを使わなくてはならず，基本的な家電の恩恵と便利さがなかった昔の時代は想像し難い。

語句 ¹take ～ for granted ～を当然だと思っている／²without a second thought よく考えずに／³benefit 名 恩恵／convenience 名 便利（な状態）／household appliance 家電

文法・構文 ²「電気が当然だと思っている」ということを，switch on ～，watch ～，enjoy ～ という「具体例」を羅列して説明しています。³1つ目のandは，had to use ～ と didn't have ～ を結び，2つ目のandはbenefitとconvenienceを結んでいます。

4 ¹Michael Faraday, (probably more than anyone else), transformed electricity (from an interesting curiosity into the workhorse [of the modern age]). ²Yet Faraday was more than (just) a talented scientist. ³He was (also) a very effective communicator. ⁴(As Nancy Forbes and Basil Mahon write), "His scientific genius lay not simply (in producing experimental results [that were beyond everyone's understanding]) but (in explaining them) too." ⁵This wasn't a natural talent; he worked hard (at it), (taking plentiful notes [on his own lectures and those of others]). ⁶The effort paid off. ⁷His regular lectures [at the Royal Institution] made him, and the Institution itself, well-known (in the scientific world).

訳 ¹マイケル・ファラデーはおそらく他の誰よりも，電気を興味深く珍しいものから現代の主力製品に変えた。²だがファラデーは，単なる才能ある科学者ではなかった。³彼はまた，非常に効果的なコミュニケーションができる人だったのだ。⁴ナンシー・フォーブスとバジル・マホンが記しているように，「彼の科学の才能は，皆が理解できないような実験結果を生み出すことだけでなく，それらを説明することにもあった」のである。[5]これは生まれ持った才能ではなかった。彼は懸命にそれに取り組み，自分の講義と他の人たちの講義についてたくさんメモを取った。[6]その努力は報われた。[7]彼が王立研究所で行った定期講義によって，彼も研究所自体も科学界で有名になった。

語句 [1]transform *A* from *B* into *C*　AをBからCに変える／curiosity 名 珍しいもの／workhorse 名 主力製品，役に立つ機械／[2]more than ～ ～ではない，～だけでない／talented 形 才能のある／[4]genius 名 非凡な才能／lie in ～ ～にある／experimental 形 実験に関する／beyond *one's* understanding ～の理解を超えている／[5]natural talent 生まれ持った才能／take notes メモを取る／plentiful 形 たくさんの／[6]pay off　報われる，成果が出る／[7]regular 形 定期的な／institution 名 機関，組織／well-known 形 よく知られていた，有名な

文法・構文 [2]more than ～ には「～以上」という意味の他に「～ではない（= not）」という意味があり，more than justはnot onlyを表しています。次の文と合わせてmore than just *A*. {But} also *B*.「AだけでなくBも」から「Butが消える」パターンです。[4]not only *A* but {also} *B*のonlyがsimplyに変わったイメージです（意味はnot only *A* but {also} *B*と同じと考えてOKです）。[5]taking ～ はheを意味上のSとする分詞構文です。[7]make OCの形で，Oにhim, and the Institution itselfがきています。

5 [1]A more recent genius was Richard Feynman. [2]He won the Nobel Prize for Physics (in 1965), but also made important discoveries (in biology) and was an early pioneer of parallel and quantum computing. [3]His talent, (in fact), was so remarkable that even other elite scientists considered him to be a magician. [4]Yet (like Faraday), Feynman was not content to hide his tricks. [5]He insisted on teaching an introductory class [for undergraduates] — exceedingly rare (for top academics). [6](With his Brooklyn accent, ironic sense of humor and talent [for explaining things (in practical, everyday terms)]), he was a student favorite.

〈A＋名詞〉→ 具体例

so ～ that S´V´構文

訳 [1]もっと最近の例では，リチャード・ファインマンという天才がいた。[2]彼は1965年にノーベル物理学賞を受賞したが，生物学でも重要な発見を成し遂げ，並列計算および量子計算の初期の先駆者でもあった。[3]実際，彼の才能はあまりに卓越しており，他の一流科学者たちでさえも彼のことをマジシャンだと思っていたほどだった。[4]だがファラデー同様，ファインマンも自分の秘術を隠して満足していることはなかった。[5]彼は学部生向けの入門クラスを教えることにこだわっていたのだが，これは一流の学者にしては非常に珍しいことであった。[6]ブルックリンなまり，皮肉っぽいユーモアのセンス，そして物事を実用的な普段使いの言葉で説明する才能のあった彼は，学生たちから大人気だった。

語句 [1] recent 形 最近の／[2] biology 名 生物学／pioneer 名 先駆者／parallel computing 並列計算（複数の計算装置が協力して1つの処理を行うこと）／quantum computing 量子計算／[3] in fact 事実，実際／remarkable 形 非凡な，目立った／consider OC OをCとみなす，考える／magician 名 魔術師／[4] *be* content to 原形 ～することに満足している／hide 動 隠す／trick 名 秘訣（ひけつ），優れた技術／[5] insist on -ing ～するといって譲らない／introductory class 入門クラス／undergraduate 名 学部生／exceedingly 副 非常に／rare for ～ ～では[としては]珍しい／academic 名 学者／[6] ironic 形 皮肉っぽい／sense of humor ユーモアのセンス／practical 形 実際に役立つ，実践的な／everyday 形 日常の，普通の／term 名 専門用語，言葉／favorite 名 人気者

文法・構文 [1]〈A + 名詞〉は具体例の目印です（***Rule 8*** ⇒p.89）。今回も，「才能だけでなく，コミュニケーション力も大切」という主張の具体例としてRichard Feynmanが挙げられています。[2] 1つ目のandは，過去形の動詞2つ（madeとwas）を結んでいます。[5] 前文と合わせてnot *A*. {But} *B*.「AでなくB」から「Butが消える」パターンです。

6 [1] (Perhaps) the best example of 〈how Feynman combined brilliance with exceptional communication skills〉 was a talk [he gave ϕ a few days (after Christmas) (in 1959)]. [2] (Starting from a basic question [about 〈what it would take to shrink the Encyclopedia Britannica (to fit on the head of a pin)〉]), he moved (step by step) (until, (in less than an hour), he had invented the field of nanotechnology).

限定の副詞　仮S´　真S´

訳 [1] ファインマンがどのように優れた才能と並外れたコミュニケーション能力を組み合わせたかを示すのに最もよい例はおそらく，1959年のクリスマス数日後に彼が行った講演だろう。[2] ブリタニカ百科事典を圧縮して針の先端程度の面積に収めるにはどうする必要があるだろうかという基本的な問題から始まって，彼は段階を追って話を進め，1時間もしないうちにナノテクノロジーという領域を発案してしまったのである。

語句 [1] combine *A* with *B* AとBを組み合わせる／brilliance 名 抜群の才能，才気／exceptional 形 並外れた／[2] shrink 動 圧縮する／Encyclopedia Britannica ブリタニカ百科事典／fit 動 ぴたりと収まる／step by step 段階を追って／invent 動 発明する，考え出す／nanotechnology 名 ナノテクノロジー

文法・構文 [1] a few daysはafter Christmas「クリスマスのあと」の範囲を限定していて，「クリスマスの数日後」という意味になります。[2] what it would take to ～ は，本来〈it would take 名詞 to 原形〉「～するには名詞が必要である」で，名詞がwhatになり前に出た形です（間接疑問）。

7 [1] Schopenhauer (once) said 〈that, "talent hits a target [no one else can hit ϕ]; Genius hits a target [no one else can see ϕ]〉." [2] Feynman was a genius [who wanted us to see it too].

訳 [1]かつてショーペンハウアーは「才人は他の誰も命中させられない的に命中させる。天才は他の誰にも見えない的に命中させる」と言った。[2]ファインマンは天才だったが, 私たちにも的を見てほしいと望んでいた。

語句 [1]talent 名 (単数・複数扱い) 才能のある人々／[2]want 人 to 原形 人に～してほしいと思う

文法・構文 [2]it は前文の a target no one else can see を受ける代名詞です。

8 [1]We tend to treat knowledge and communication (as two separate spheres). [2]We act (as if having the skills of an expert was a private matter, (earned through quiet study)). [3]Communication, (on the other hand), is often reduced to the realm of the social, a tool [we use ϕ (to interact with others of our species)]. [4]Yet, (as Wittgenstein argued decades ago), that position is (logically) unsound (because it assumes 〈that we are able to communicate (to ourselves) (in a private language)〉). [5](In truth), we can't (really) know anything [that we can't communicate ϕ]. [6]〈To assert 〈that we can possess knowledge, but are unable to explain what it is〉〉, makes no sense.

仮定法過去

the realm of the social の同格

訳 [1]私たちは知識とコミュニケーションを2つの別々の分野として扱いがちである。[2]私たちは, 専門的なスキルを身に付けるのは個人の問題で, 黙々と勉強することで得られるものであるかのように振る舞う。[3]一方でコミュニケーションは社交の領域, つまり他の人間と交流するために使うツールとして片づけられることが多い。[4]しかし, ウィトゲンシュタインが何十年か前に主張したように, その立場は私たちが私的言語で自分自身とコミュニケーションをとることができると仮定したものであるため, 論理的な根拠がない。[5]実は私たちは, 自分が人に伝えられないことはどんなことであれ, あまり理解していないのだ。[6]知識を持つことはできるが, それが何かは説明できないと主張したところで意味をなさないのである。

語句 [1]tend to 原形 ～する傾向にある／treat *A* as *B* AをBとして扱う／sphere 名 領域／[2]act as if S´V´ S´V´であるかのように振る舞う／private 形 個人的な／earn 動 得る, 手に入れる／[3]*be* reduced to ～ ～で片付けられる／realm 名 領域／interact with ～ ～と交流する／our species 人類／[4]unsound 形 信用できない／assume 動 仮定する／private language 私的言語（本人にのみ通じ, 他人に伝達不可能な言語のこと）／[6]assert 動 主張する／possess 動 持っている, 備えている／make sense 意味をなす

文法・構文 [2]as if S´V´の後ろに仮定法過去が続く形です。仮定法過去の be 動詞は人称に関係なく were を用いるのが原則ですが, 今回のように was が用いられることも多くあります。 [3]our species は直訳「私たちの（生物）種」→「人類」という意味です。定冠詞のついた the species の形でも「人類」の意味になることがあります。 [6]but は can possess ～ と

are unable to explain ～ を結んでいます。explain の O には what it is という what のカタマリができています。

9 [1] And (so) it is curious 〈that we give communication little or no attention〉. [2] Schools don't teach communication. [3] They teach math, some science and history, but provide very little guidance [on 〈how to express ideas (clearly)〉]. [4] (When we enter professional life), we (rarely) put serious effort (toward expressing ourselves (in a language [that can be understood by those outside our own group])). [5] (When our efforts and achievements fail to receive a sympathetic response), we are left wondering why. [6] The fact is 〈that (although it may be fashionable to say 〈that our present era is an information age〉), we live (in a communication age) and it 's time [we start taking it (seriously)]〉.

訳 [1] そのため，私たちがコミュニケーションに，ほとんどあるいは一切注意を払わないのは妙である。[2] 学校はコミュニケーションの指導をしてくれない。[3] 数学や多少の科学と，歴史は教えるが，考えをはっきりと表現する方法についてはほとんど指導してくれないのだ。[4] 私たちは職業人生を始めると，自分の属する集団以外の人たちにも理解してもらえる言葉で自分の考えを表現しようと真剣に努力することはめったにない。[5] 自分の努力や業績に好意的な反応が得られないとき，私たちはその理由を不思議に思ったままになる。[6] 実際は，現代は情報の時代だと言うのが流行かもしれないが，私たちはコミュニケーションの時代に生きているのであり，それに真剣に取り組むべき頃合いなのである。

語句 [1] curious 形 奇妙な，不可解な／little 形 (a を伴わないで) ほとんど～ない／[3] guidance 名 指導／on 前 ～について／[4] rarely 副 めったに～ない／toward{s} ～ ～に対して／[5] fail to 原形 ～できない／sympathetic 形 共感の／[6] fashionable 形 流行している／it is time S´V´ S´V´ してもよい頃だ

文法・構文 [3] 前文と合わせて not *A*. {But} *B*.「A ではなく B」から「But が消える」パターンです。[4] those は後ろに関係詞の続く those who ～「～な人々」の形が有名ですが，過去分詞句（ex. those involved in the accident「事故に巻き込まれた人々」）や，今回のように形容詞句が続くこともあります。[5] we are left wondering why は，S leave us wondering why の O（us）を S にした受動態の形です（leave O –ing「O を～するままにしておく」）。また，why の後ろには why {our efforts and achievements fail to receive a sympathetic response}. が省略されています。[6] it is time S´V´ は仮定法過去が続く形が有名ですが，今回のように原形（現在形）が続くこともあります。

音読をしよう！ 05

When I was in high school, // a man came to speak / about Winston Churchill. // Mostly, // it was the usual mix / of historical events and anecdotes, // but what I remember best / was how the talk ended. // The speaker concluded by saying / that if we were to remember one thing about Churchill, // it should be that what made him so effective / was his power to communicate. // I didn't understand that at the time. // Growing up, // I had always heard about the importance of hard work, // honesty // and other things, // but never communication. //

Yet now, // thirty years later, // I've begun to understand what he meant. // As Walter Isaacson argues, // the ability to work together effectively is decisive. // In order to make innovation possible, // it's not enough / to just come up with big ideas. // You also need to work hard / to communicate them clearly. //

Today, // we take electricity for granted. // We switch on lights, // watch TV // and enjoy connected devices / without a second thought. // It's hard to imagine an earlier age / in which we had to use smoky, // smelly candles / in order to see at night // and didn't have the benefit and convenience / of basic household appliances. //

Michael Faraday, // probably more than anyone else, // transformed electricity from an interesting curiosity / into the workhorse of the modern age. // Yet Faraday was more than just a talented scientist. // He was also a very effective communicator. // As Nancy Forbes and Basil Mahon write, // " His scientific genius / lay not simply in producing experimental results / that were beyond everyone's understanding // but in explaining them too." // This wasn't a natural talent; // he worked hard at it, / taking plentiful notes on his own lectures / and those of others. // The effort paid off. // His regular lectures at the Royal Institution / made him, // and the Institution itself, // well-known in the scientific world. //

A more recent genius was Richard Feynman. // He won the Nobel Prize for Physics in 1965, // but also made important discoveries in biology / and was an early pioneer / of parallel and quantum computing. // His talent, // in fact, // was so remarkable / that even other elite scientists / considered him to be a magician. // Yet like Faraday, // Feynman was not content to hide his tricks. // He insisted on teaching an introductory class for undergraduates // — exceedingly rare for top academics. // With his Brooklyn accent, // ironic sense of humor // and talent for explaining things in practical, // everyday terms, // he was a student favorite. //

Perhaps the best example / of how Feynman combined brilliance / with exceptional communication skills // was a talk he gave a few days after Christmas in 1959. // Starting from a basic question / about what it would take to shrink the Encyclopedia Britannica / to fit on the head of a pin, // he moved step by step until, // in less than an hour, // he had invented the field of nanotechnology. //

Schopenhauer once said that, // "talent hits a target no one else can hit; // Genius hits a target no one else can see." // Feynman was a genius / who wanted us to see it too. //

We tend to treat knowledge and communication / as two separate spheres. // We act as if having the skills of an expert / was a private matter, // earned through quiet study. // Communication, // on the other hand, // is often reduced to the realm of the social, // a tool we use to interact with others of our species. // Yet, / as Wittgenstein argued decades ago, // that position is logically unsound / because it assumes that we are able to communicate to ourselves / in a private language. // In truth, we can't really know anything / that we can't communicate. // To assert that we can possess knowledge, // but are unable to explain what it is, // makes no sense. //

And so it is curious that we give communication / little or no attention. // Schools don't teach communication. // They teach math, // some science // and history, // but provide very little guidance / on how to express ideas clearly. // When we enter professional life, // we rarely put serious effort / toward expressing ourselves in a language / that can be understood / by those outside our own group. // When our efforts and achievements / fail to receive a sympathetic response, // we are left wondering why. // The fact is / that although it may be fashionable to say / that our present era is an information age, // we live in a communication age / and it's time we start taking it seriously. //

Lesson 6 解答・解説

▶問題 別冊 p.25

このLessonで出てくるルール

Rule 25 読解 「同じ形」なら「同じ意味」だと考える！ ⇒ 問3
Rule 17 読解 「前後関係」の表現に注目！（follow）⇒ 問5
Rule 80 構文 SVOCになる形に注意！（SV 人 to 原形）⇒ 問6
Rule 1 読解 消えたbutに気づいて「主張」を発見する！ ⇒ 問7
Rule 13 読解 数字を見たら「具体例」だと考える！ ⇒ 問8
Rule 47 解法 「入れ替え」選択肢のパターン（比較級）⇒ 問9
Rule 24 読解 過去と現在の「対比」を予測する！（new）⇒ 問9

解答

問1 ④　問2 ④　問3 ③　問4 ②　問5 ①
問6 （私たちは気持ちが）焦っていると，食事の準備にかける時間が短くなる。（24字）
問7 ①　問8 ①　問9 ④・⑦

問1 難易度 ★★☆

前半はWith the chairs gone「椅子が無くなったので」という意味です（これは「付帯状況」のwithで，**with OC「OがCの状態で／OがCなので」**の形）。後半はthere was no risk of -ing「～する危険性がなかった」，〈spend 時間 over ～〉「～に時間をかける」という形です（over lunch「ランチを食べながら」という熟語もありますが，今回はそれではありません）。最も意味が近い選択肢は④ Removing the chairs kept the students from taking too long a lunch break.で，本文With the chairs gone → 選択肢Removing the chairsに相当します。全体は〈keep 人 from –ing〉「人が～するのを妨げる」の形です（〈prevent 人 from –ing〉「人が～するのを妨げる」と同じ形・同じ意味）。

選択肢の訳

① 椅子を提供することは，生徒たちが十分に長い時間の昼休憩をとるのに役立たなかった。

② 椅子を提供することは，生徒たちが十分に長い時間の昼休憩をとるのに役立った。
→ 文頭のProviding「提供すること」が本文と真逆です。ちなみに，後ろは〈help 人 原形〉「人が〜するのに役立つ」の形になっています。
③ 椅子を取り除いても，生徒たちが昼休憩を長くとり過ぎるのを防ぐことにはならなかった。
→ did not keepと否定文なのでアウトです。「**正しい内容にnotを加えただけ**」という典型的なひっかけパターンです（***Rule 43*** ⇒p.58）。
④ 椅子を取り除くことが，生徒たちが昼休憩を長くとり過ぎるのを防いだ。

問2 難易度 ★★☆

sacrifice *A* for *B*「BのためにAを犠牲にする」という意味です。「生徒の健康が×，成績が○」を表す，④worsens the students' health in order to improve their academic scoresが正解です。本文のsacrifice「犠牲にする」が**worsen**「悪化させる」に，for「〜のために」が〈**in order to 原形**〉「〜するために」に言い換えられています。

選択肢の訳

① 生徒たちの健康にも学業成績にも貢献しない
→〈原因 contribute to 結果〉の形です。neither *A* nor *B*「AでもBでもない」で，「健康，成績共に×」となりアウトです。
② 生徒たちの健康を保ち，同時に，彼らの学業成績を向上させる
→ 前半はkeep OC「OをCに保つ」です。「健康，成績共に○」でアウトです。
③ 健康状態を改善するために生徒たちの学業成績を悪化させる
→「成績は×，健康は○」で，本文と真逆の関係です。「健康」と「成績」を入れ替えたひっかけパターンです。
④ 学業成績の向上のために生徒たちの健康を悪化させる

問3 難易度 ★★★

直後の文（17行目）はIs the student in China quickly eating a 10-minute lunch so different from the office worker who lunches on a protein bar because there are too many emails and not enough hours in the day? で，**段落末の疑問文**なので，**反語**の可能性があります（***Rule 6*** ⇒p.17）。「〜な生徒は…とそれほど変わるのだろうか？→いや，それほど変わらない」と，実質「否定文」で解釈すると，直前の空所（**3**）を含む文も否定文であることからこれと「同じ内容」だと考えられます。空所（**3**）にふさわしいのは，この直後の文「時間がないのでプロテ

インバーを食べる」につながる，③the hurried manner in which ～「～する急いだやり方」です。このmannerは「方法」の意味で，mannerの直後のin whichは，in the hurried manner「急いだ方法で」→「急いで」ということです。

> 多義語mannerの核心：「振る舞う方法」
> **(1) 方法　(2) 態度　(3) 行儀 (manners)　(4) 風習 (manners)**

ちなみに，今回は直後の文と形がそっくりなので，**形が同じ→意味も同じ**と考えることができます。下の図解を見てください。

> Yet the disturbing thing about dining arrangements at the Chinese high school is that they are not so different from (3) millions of other children and adults now consume meals around the world.
>
> ② こちらも「時間がないので急いで食べる」という内容になるはず
>
> Is the student in China quickly eating a 10-minute lunch so different from the office worker who lunches on a protein bar because there are too many emails and not enough hours in the day?
>
> 段落末の疑問文 →「反語」
> ①「時間がないのでプロテインバーを食べる」

>>> Rule 25 読解「同じ形」なら「同じ意味」だと考える！

> 英文では「同じ"形"を繰り返す」ことによって，**同じような内容を列挙する，同じような内容を別の表現で言い換える**手法があります。同じ形が続く限り，内容も同じだということです。途中で知らない語句が出てきても（もっと言えば一文丸ごとわからなくても），「形が同じだから意味も同じ」と判断できるのです。
>
> 補足 一見単純に思えるのですが，きちんと紹介されることは少なく，決まった呼び方も存在しないので，本書では「構文反復」と呼びたいと思います。
> 「構文反復」のやっかいな点として，「どの程度同じ形を取るのかは，その都度変わる」ということがあります。そのため明確にパターン化はできないのですが，意識して確認すれば，必ず自力で気づけるようになります（これはボクが何万人も教えてきて，最後にはみんな習得できているので自信を持って言えます。時間はかかりますが，同じ形が出てくるたびにしっかり読み込んでいきましょう）。

選択肢の訳

① ～という幸運な事実
→「幸運・不運」は関係ありません。
② ～という残念な事実
③ Sが慌ただしくVするやり方
④ SがゆっくりVするやり方
→「否定」を表すun-がついて，unhurried「急がない，ゆっくりした」です。「否定語をつけるだけ」という問1の選択肢③と同様の典型的なひっかけです。

問4 難易度 ★★★

下線部は，compromises {which} we never quite intendedで，compromises「妥協」がwe never quite intended「決して意図しなかった（＝不本意）」ということです。前にforces us intoとあるので，「マイナスだけど妥協して取り入れざるを得ないもの」と考えて，②a protein bar for lunch「昼食用のプロテインバー」を選べばOKです。

ちなみに18行目にthe office worker who lunches on a protein bar because there are too many emails and not enough hours in the dayとあり，「プロテインバー」が時間の不足のせいで急いでとる食事の例だと確認できます。

選択肢の訳

① ちゃんとした朝食
② 昼食用のプロテインバー
③ 時間不足
→ 下線部（4）を含む文の主語Itは直前の文の主語A lack of time「時間の不足」を指すので，③を選ぶと「時間の不足によって，時間の不足を強いられる」と意味不明な文になります。
④ あまりにも多くのEメール
→ 19行目にthere are too many emailsとあり，マイナスのものに思うかもしれませんが，これは「急いで食事する理由」であって「妥協すること」ではありません。

問5 難易度 ★★☆

下線部は直訳「スライスしたパンは始まりに過ぎなかった」です。直後に（38行目）Everywhere you look, there are products promising to save you time, from two-minute rice to quick-cook pasta.とあり，「時間を節約する食品」の例として最初にsliced bread，そのあとにtwo-minute riceやquick-cook pastaなどの例が

続いています。よって，この内容を表した①Many other examples followed sliced bread.が正解です。この①ではfollowの使い方がポイントになります。

>>> Rule 17 読解 「前後関係」の表現に注目！（follow）

followは「追いかける」という訳語だけでは，結局「どっちが先で，どっちが後か」を瞬時につかめないことがあるので，〈後 **follow** 前〉と考えることが必要です。例えば Wine followed the food. は「ワイン ← 食事」，ワインは食事のあとに出てきた，ということです。

また，followは受動態で〈前 **is followed by** 後〉も重要です。The food was followed by wine. は「食事 → ワイン」，「食事のあとにワインが出てきた」ということです。さらに，*be* followed by ～ は分詞構文でも使われます（SV, followed by ～「SVだ。そのあとに～がくる」）。もちろんこれも受動態なので〈前 **is followed by** 後〉という順番は同じです。

followの理解のしかた

(**1**) *A* follows *B*.	(**2**) *A* is followed by *B*.	(**3**) SV, followed by ～
後 ← 前	前 → 後	前 → 後

正解の選択肢①Many other examples followed sliced bread.も「たくさんの他の例←スライスしたパン」という順番だとわかります。「パンが最初の例，そのあとに多くの他の例が続く」ということです。

選択肢の訳

① **多くの他の例が，スライスされたパンに続いた。**
② スライスされたパンは市場に出たばかりだった。
③ そのパンは，最初からスライスされていた。
④ 最初にすべきことは，パンをスライスすることだった。

問6 難易度 ★★☆

下線部（6）は〈SV 人 to 原形〉の形で，この形は非常に重要です。

>>> Rule 80 構文 SVOCになる形に注意！（SV 人 to 原形）

〈SV 人 to 原形〉をとる動詞

☐ allow / permit 許可する　　☐ enable 可能にする

- expect 期待する
- ask 頼む
- encourage 勧める
- determine 決心させる
- require / request 要求する
- oblige 義務としてさせる
- cause 引き起こす
- want / would like 望む
- advise 勧める，忠告する
- incline する気にさせる
- urge 説得する，強く迫る
- force / compel 強制する
- order 命令する

補足 inclineやdetermineなど，実際にはほぼ，受動態〈*be* p.p. to 原形〉の形でしか使わないものあります。

〈SV 人 to 原形〉は第5文型（SVOC）になります。SVOCは「**Sによって，OがCする**」と訳すときれいになるのでしたね（***Rule 80*** ⇒p.83）。ということは〈SV 人 to 原形〉でVの意味がわからなくても（どのみちVを訳さなくてよい），英文の意味がわかってしまうのです。

■ SV 人 to 原形 → SVOC →「SによってOがCする」という意味になる！

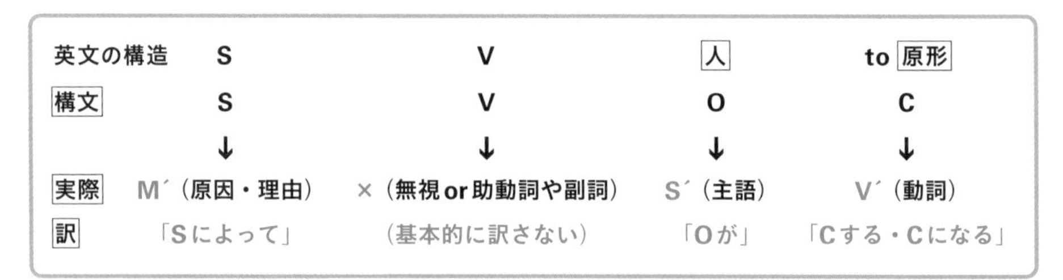

英文の構造	S	V	人	to 原形
構文	S	V	O	C
	↓	↓	↓	↓
実際	M´（原因・理由）	×（無視 or 助動詞や副詞）	S´（主語）	V´（動詞）
訳	「Sによって」	（基本的に訳さない）	「Oが」	「Cする・Cになる」

■ V部分の詳述　可能な限りV本来のニュアンスを和訳に盛り込む

知らない動詞 ⇒訳出不要（時制は当然考慮する：-edであれば過去形で訳す）
知っている動詞⇒V´に，V本来の意味を元にして，助動詞や副詞のニュアンスを加える

例えばenable「可能にする」の場合，助動詞canのニュアンスを付け加えればOKです。

Her help (S / M´) enabled (V / 助) me (O / S´) to do the job. (C / V´)

彼女の助けは私がその仕事をするのを可能にした。

⇒**彼女が手伝ってくれたので**（M´），**私は**（S´）**その仕事をする**（V´）**ことができた**（助）**。**

下線部（6）は〈SV 人 to 原形〉なので,「Sによって人が〜する」と考えます。Feeling rushedは「急かされているように感じること」→「慌ただしく感じる，気持ちが焦ること」なので,「(私たちは気持ちが）焦ることによって」とします（causeを「引き起こす」なんて訳すと，解答欄にある「私たちは気持ちが」とうまくつながりません。この問題では明らかに〈SV 人 to 原形〉の考え方が試されているわけです)。

to以下は〈spend 時間 -ing〉「〜することに時間を費やす」で, spend less time preparing our meals「私たちの食事を準備するのにより短い時間を費やす」→「食事を準備する時間がより短くなる」とします。

暫定和訳 （私たちは気持ちが）焦ることによって, 食事を準備する時間がより短くなる。(26字)

これを，25文字以内に収めるために，少し整えれば完成です。

和訳 （私たちは気持ちが）焦っていると, 食事の準備にかける時間が短くなる。(24字)

※（私たちは気持ちが）は最初から提示されているため解答としては不要です。

問7 難易度 ★★★

44行目の we are not making a simple statement of fact. We are talking about cultural values and (7)the way our society tells us that our days should be divided. では,「消えたbutに気づく」ことで，対比関係が見えてきます。

>>> Rule 1 読解 消えたbutに気づいて「主張」を発見する！

主張を伝えるとき，not *A* but *B*「AでなくBだ」の形が基本なので,「butのあとには主張がくる」とよく言われます。しかし実際にはこの形がそのまま使われるとは限りません。not *A*で文が切られ,（文が切れた以上は直後にある接続詞butは不要になるので）not *A*. {~~But~~} *B*. という形がよく使われます。ですから，**notがあれば，そのあとに肯定文**がくることが多いわけです。その肯定文の前にButを補って意味が通れば，その肯定文は**筆者の主張**と言えます。

消えたbutを見つけ出す

基本の形　not *A*（一般論）but *B*（主張）

Butが消滅する

not *A*. ~~But~~ *B*.（Aのあとにピリオドがあれば，接続詞Butは不要）

Butのバリエーション（消えるだけでなく，But以外の単語が使われることも多い）

not *A*.	**Instead**, *B*.	Aではない。(Aではない) その代わりにBだ。
	Indeed, *B*.	Aではない。(Aではなくて) 実際はBだ。
	In fact, *B*.	Aではない。(Aではなくて) 実際はBだ。
	Rather, *B*.	Aではない。(Aではなくて) むしろBだ。

not only *A* but also *B*「AだけでなくBも」もbutが消えることがよくあります。今回も，we are not making a simple statement of fact. {But} We are talking about ～ で〈not *A* {But} *B*.〉の形です（厳密に言えば，not ～ simpleとあり，not simply *A* but also *B*「(単に) AだけでなくBも」を表しているのですが，いずれにせよ「AとBの対比」に気づけば勝負アリです)。つまり「事実 (fact)」vs.「価値観 (values) と下線部分」なので，下線部は**「事実と対立し，『価値観』に似た内容」**だとわかります。その視点で選択肢を見ると，①people's ideas about how a person should spend his or her timeが適切だと判断できるのです。本文のthe way S′V′「S′V′する方法」が選択肢ではhow S′V′に，our days should be dividedがa person should spend his or her timeに対応していると確認できますね。

このような問題を大半の受験生は「直訳して考える」のでミスをしやすいのです。皆さんは「消えたbutを補う」という発想から解くようにしてください。

選択肢の訳

① 人がどのようにして自分の時間を使うべきかについての人々の考え

② 頻繁にカレンダーをチェックしなくてはいけないという人々の感覚

→ people's senseは「価値観」に近い点では問題なさそうですが，最後のcheck their calendarがアウトです。

③ カレンダー上でどのように行事を予定に入れるべきかという政府の計画

④ 人が自分の時間をどのように使うべきかについての政府の提言

→ ③のgovernment's plan，④のgovernment's recommendationは「人々・個人の価値観」とはまったく異なり，下線部のour societyからの連想を利用したひっかけです。

問8 難易度★★☆ 思考力

have ～ on *one's* handsは「自分の手元に～を持っている」→「～がある，～を抱える」という熟語です。ただしこの熟語を知らなくても，本文のso much time

をplenty of ～ timeと言い換えているだけなので①と予想がつくかもしれませんし，次のように考えることもできます。まず，48行目By objective standards, most of us in wealthy countries have far more free time on average than workers **did** a hundred years **ago**で，**「過去と現在の対比」**があります（***Rule 24*** ⇒p.59）。「過去：自由な時間が少ない」⇔「現在：自由な時間が多い」ということです。そして，このあとに続く3文は「数字」を使って，「過去：労働時間が長い」⇔「現在：労働時間が短い」という対比を具体的に説明しているだけなのです。

>>> *Rule 13* 読解 数字を見たら「具体例」だと考える！

文章中で数字を用いた文を見つけたら，そこから「具体例」が始まると考えてください。

主張. ～ 数字 ～.
→この文から具体例になる！

何かを主張したあとで「例えば2021年には」のように，具体的な数字を挙げることはよくありますよね（数字そのものは文頭とは限りません。固有名詞のパターンと同じで，文中でもOKです）。Compared with many of the workers of the past, the average worker today (8) has so much time on their hands. とあるので，下線部は「現在の労働者」について，「労働時間が短い」→「余暇が多い」と考えて，①has plenty of leisure timeを選ぶことができます。

ここが 思考力 意味を推測する問題も，形とルールで

この問は「受験生にとって難しい表現を，文脈から推測する」問題で，思考力重視の風潮から今後ますます増えていくでしょう。しかしながら普通は「文脈に合う意味を考える」「思考力が必要」のように言われるだけのことが多いでしょう。皆さんは対比を把握するルールなどを習得することで，選択肢を絞っていく発想をマスターしてください。漠然と「どの選択肢が文脈に合うか？」だけで解こうとするのは非効率的です。

選択肢の訳

① **余暇時間がたくさんある**
② やらなくてはいけない仕事がたくさんある
③ たいていフルタイムで働く

→ フルタイムを長いと捉えると，「昔は労働時間が長く，現在は短い」と逆になってしまいます。本文にworkがあるからといって，何となく選ばないようにしましょう。
④ たいてい手を使って働く
→ workを使い，さらに下線部にあるtheir handsをそのまま利用したひっかけです。実際に「手を使って働く」わけではありません。

問9 難易度 ★★☆

まず，正解の選択肢2つを見ていきましょう。

④ 時間に追われていると感じているときには，リラックスしているときよりも食べる量が増えることが知られている。

36行目に，There is evidence that when someone feels lacking in time, he or she will cook less, enjoy meals less and yet end up eating more food.とあり，ここが④と合致します（end up -ing「結局〜する」に注意してください。これを「〜するのをやめる」なんて勘違いしてしまうミスが多いです）。

本文のfeels lacking in time「時間が足りないと感じる」が，選択肢ではfeeling pressed for time「時間に追われていると感じる」に言い換えられています。*be* pressed for timeは「時間を求めて（for time）押されている（*be* pressed）」→「時間に追われている」です。

⑦ 私たちの社会は，食事よりも時間が重要だとみなされている社会である。

55行目にwe live in a world that places a higher value on time than it does on foodとあり，選択肢の内容と合致します。本文はplace a higher value on 〜 than ...「…より〜に高い価値を置く［重要視する］」の形で，「食事よりも時間を重視する」という比較関係を表しています（本当に「比較」はよく出ますね）。選択肢はconsider *A* to be *B*「AをBとみなす」の受動態***A* is considered to be *B***で，同じく「食事よりも時間が重視されている」を表しているわけです。

>>> Rule 47 解法 「入れ替え」選択肢のパターン（比較級）

内容一致問題では，**比較級**がよく使われます。選択肢に比較表現が出てきたらチェックして，きっちりと大小関係（「A＞B」「A＜B」「A＝B」）を把握してください。ひっかけパターンとしては，**「大小関係を入れ替える」**ものが多いです。また，難関大では「そもそも比較なんかしていない」パターンもよく出ます（選択肢⑤参照）。

本文	A＞B，C＞D	
選択肢	A＜B → ×	大小関係が逆
	A＞D → ×	AとDを比べているわけではない
	A＞B → ○	大小関係がバッチリOK

続いて，誤りの選択肢の理由を確認しましょう。

① ある医師は，立ったまま食事をとることは身体によく，病気の予防に役立つと述べている。

11行目にA medical doctor said that this practice would be very bad for the digestion and could set children up for a lifetime of illnesses.とあります。this practice「この習慣，やり方」は，その前の「生徒を立ったまま食べさせること」を表し（〈**this＋名詞**〉については***Rule 4*** ⇒p.71），それが「消化に悪い」「生涯にわたる病気を招きかねない」と述べています。選択肢とは真逆の内容です。

② 何十年にもわたって，私たちはしっかりと食事をとる時間が足りないと感じてきた。

23行目にFor decades, people have complained that modern life does not leave enough time to cook.とあり，「ここ数十年は料理する時間がない」です。②の「食べる時間がない」とは合いません。本文は「ここ数十年間：料理する時間がない」→「新しい悩み（The new worry）：食べる時間すらない」という流れで，このnewに注目しておくと，記憶に残ってこの問題に対処しやすくなるはずです。

>>> *Rule 24* 読解 過去と現在の「対比」を予測する！（new）

newは基本語なので，注目する受験生はほぼいないでしょうが，newは**今までとは違う**ことを強調する，**「過去と現在」の対比**の目印となります。大事な内容なので，設問でも狙われます。ちなみにリスニングでも，newに反応することで，設問が1つ解けることがよくありますよ。

23行目For decadesと，そのあとのThe new worry「新たな悩み」が「過去と現在の対比」なのです。次ページで対比関係を確認しましょう。

For decades／現在完了形で「ここ数十年間」を表す

For decades, people have complained that modern life does not leave enough time to cook.

「何十年にもわたって，人々は，現代生活では料理をする時間が十分にとれないと不満を漏らしてきた」

ここ数十年：料理する時間の不足 vs. 新しい悩み：食べる時間の不足

new／現在形で「現在の新たな悩み」を表す

The new worry is that we often feel we do not even have the time to eat.

「新たな心配事は，私たちが食事をとる時間さえもないと頻繁に感じることである」

③ 英国のますます多くの人々が，時間的制約のために朝食用シリアルを買うようになっている。

32行目にSales of breakfast cereal in Britain fell by 3.6 million kilograms.とあります（byは「差（～の分だけ）」）。シリアルの販売量は「減少した」ので，選択肢とは真逆です。「増減」を入れ替えた，典型的なひっかけパターンですね。

⑤ 人々は，インターネットの閲覧に時間を使うよりも料理に時間を使うほうがよいと考える傾向にある［人々は，インターネットの閲覧よりも料理のほうが，時間の使い方としてよいと考える傾向にある］。

40行目にit can convince us that there is no point even trying to cook anything that takes longer than 20 minutes — even though those same 20 minutes feel like nothing when we are browsing online shoppingとあります。「20分以上料理に時間を使いたくない／オンラインショッピングだと20分使っても何とも思わない」というだけで，筆者は「どちらがよいか」という比較はしていません。これが「そもそも本文では比較なんかしていない」パターンの例です。

⑥ 今日の平均的なアメリカ人は，先祖よりもはるかに長い時間働いている。

50行目にIn 1900, the average American worked 2,700 hours a year. By 2015 the average American worked just 1,790 hours a year.とあります。「現在のほうが，労働時間が短い」ので，選択肢は比較関係が逆です。

文構造の分析

1 [1] There are no chairs (in the cafeteria [at one high school in central China]). [2] They disappeared (during the summer) (so that students could store up a few precious extra minutes of study time). [3] (With the chairs gone), there was no risk of spending too much time (over lunch). [4] Students eat (standing at tables) (before rushing back to class). [5] "We learnt this (from other places)," an official said (in a Chinese newspaper), (adding 〈that it should be possible to shorten the time [students spent ϕ on eating their lunch] (down to just 10 minutes)〉).

付帯状況のwith

訳 [1] 中国中部のある高校では，食堂に椅子がない。[2] 生徒たちが貴重な勉強時間を数分でも長く確保できるようにと，椅子は夏のうちに姿を消したのだ。[3] 椅子がなくなったので，昼食に時間をかけすぎる危険性がなくなった。[4] 生徒たちはテーブルで立って食べ，食べ終えると急いで教室に戻る。[5]「このやり方は他のところから学んだのです」と，1人の職員が中国の新聞で述べ，生徒たちが昼食をとるのに費やす時間をわずか10分まで短縮できるはずだと付け加えた。

語句 [1] cafeteria 名 食堂／[2] disappear 動 消える／so that S´ 助動詞 V´ S´V´するために／store up 蓄積する／precious 形 貴重な／[4] rush to ～ 急いで～に向かう／[5] learnt 動（主にイギリス英語で）learnの過去形・過去分詞（=learned）／official 名 職員／spend 時間 {on / in} -ing ～することに時間を費やす

文法・構文 [4] 直訳は「教室に急いで戻る前に生徒たちはテーブルで立って食べる」です。
[5] the time students spent on eating ～ は，本来students spent the time on eating ～「生徒たちは～を食べることに時間を費やす」で，the timeが先行詞として前に出た形です。

2 [1] (After the story [of this chairless cafeteria] became known), the school's policy was (widely) criticized. [2] "It 's a terrible idea to make students eat (while standing)," stated an editorial [in the same newspaper]. [3] "It sacrifices the students' health (for academic scores). [4] It 's unacceptable." [5] A medical doctor said 〈that this practice would be very bad (for the digestion) and could set children up for a lifetime of illnesses〉.

〈this＋名詞〉→ まとめ表現

〈S´＋be動詞の省略〉

〈A＋名詞〉→ 具体例の合図

訳 [1] この椅子のない食堂の話が世に知られるようになると，その学校の方針は広く非

Lesson 6

難された。[2]同新聞の社説には，「生徒たちに立ったまま食べさせるなんて，とんでもない考えだ」と述べられていた。[3]「学業成績のために生徒たちの健康を犠牲にしている。[4]とても受け入れられない」[5]ある医師は，このようなやり方はとても消化に悪く，子どもたちが生涯にわたる病気を抱えかねないと述べた。

語句 [1]名詞-less ～のない／policy 名 やり方，方針／criticize 動 批判する，非難する／[2]terrible 形 ひどい／make 人 原形 人に～させる／state 動 述べる／[3]sacrifice 動 犠牲にする／academic 形 学業の／score 名 成績，得点／[4]unacceptable 形 受け入れられない／[5]practice 名 やり方，行為／digestion 名 消化／set 人 up for ～ 人に～の状況を作る（for以下にはプラス・マイナスどちらの内容もきます）

文法・構文 [1]〈this + 名詞〉はまとめ表現です。第1段落の内容がわからなくても，「食堂に椅子がない」という話だと判断できます。[2]while以下は，while {they are} standingから〈S´ + be動詞〉が省略された形です。[5]〈A + 名詞〉で始まる文は「具体例が始まる」合図です。前文の「生徒たちの健康を犠牲にしている」ことを，医師の発言を持ちだして具体的に説明しています。ちなみに文の動詞が過去形のsaidなので，that以下の助動詞もそれに応じてwould/couldと過去形になっています（時制の一致）。

3 [1]Most of us dislike the notion of a chairless cafeteria [that makes children eat faster]. [2]Yet the disturbing thing [about dining arrangements at the Chinese high school] is 〈that they are not so different (from the hurried manner [in which millions of other children and adults now consume meals around the world])〉. [3]Is the student [in China] [quickly eating a 10-minute lunch] so different from (the office worker [who lunches on a protein bar (because there are too many emails and not enough hours in the day)])?

一般論 → 対比を予想

ここから主張

段落末の疑問文 → 反語

ここから主張

訳 [1]私たちのほとんどは，子どもたちに速く食べさせる，椅子のない食堂という考えを快く思わない。[2]しかし，その中国の高校の食堂のシステムについて憂慮すべきことは，それが，現在世界中の何百万人もの他の子どもや大人が慌ただしく食事をかき込んでいる様子とあまり変わらないということだ。[3]10分間で急いで昼食をとる中国の生徒は，あまりにもEメールが多くて，その日のうちに十分な時間がないという理由でプロテインバーを昼食にする会社員と，それほどの差があるのだろうか。

語句 [1]dislike 動 嫌いだ／notion 名 考え／[2]disturbing 形 憂慮すべき，気がかりな／arrangement 名 取り決め／manner 名 方法（「マナー，礼儀」という意味ではないので注意しましょう。「マナー，礼儀」という意味の場合は，mannersと複数形になります）／consume 動 消費する，飲食する／[3]lunch on ～ 昼食に～をとる文法・構文 [1]Most of us「私たちのほとんどは」から，ここは「一般論」だと判断し，後ろに筆者の主張がくると予想します。[3]Is the student (S) eating (V) という進行形の文と見間違えないように注意しましょう（進行形ととるとso different以下の説明がつかなくなります）。quickly eating ～ lunchは分詞のカタマリで，the studentを修飾しています。

4 [1]〈What makes the chairless cafeteria at the school seem shocking〉 is 〈that the lack of time for eating is so deliberate and calculated〉. [2](In the rest of the world), (by contrast), many of us do not (quite) understand 〈why we are eating (in such an irritated state) (so often)〉. [3](For decades), people have complained 〈that modern life does not leave enough time to cook〉. [4]The new worry is 《that we (often) feel 〈 we do not (even) have the time to eat〉》.

対比表現

過去を表す語句（現在と対比）

過去との対比（今は違う）

訳 [1]その学校の椅子のない食堂が衝撃的に思えるのは，食べる時間の不足があまりにも意図的で入念に計画されたものだからだ。[2]一方で，世界の他の場所では，私たちの大半が，どうしてこうもイライラした状態で食べてばかりなのか，よくわからずにいる。[3]何十年にもわたって，人々は，現代生活では料理をする時間が十分にとれないと不満を漏らしてきた。[4]新たな心配事は，私たちが食事をとる時間さえもないと頻繁に感じることである。

語句 [1]deliberate 形 意図的な／calculated 形 入念に計画された／[2]irritated 形 イライラした／state 名 状態／[3]decade 名 10年間（decadesで「数十年」になります）／complain 動 不満を漏らす

具体例の合図

5 [1]How else can we explain the successful marketing of products [such as liquidized breakfast cereal [to drink]]? [2]A bowl of cornflakes [with milk] used to be 〈what you ate φ (when you lacked the time [to cook a proper breakfast])〉. [3]But (now), even sales of breakfast cereals have become a victim of time pressure.

過去の表現（現在との対比）

今は違う

訳 [1]飲み込めるように液化された朝食用シリアルのような商品のマーケティングが成功していることを，他にどう説明できるだろうか。[2]かつては，ボウルに盛ったコーンフレークに牛乳をかけたものが，ちゃんとした朝食を作る時間のないときに食べるものだった。[3]しかし今では，朝食用シリアルの売上さえも，時間的制約の犠牲になっている。

語句 [1]cereal 名 シリアル（コーンフレークなどの穀物の加工食品）／[2]cornflakes 名 コーンフレーク／proper 形 ちゃんとした／[3]victim 名 犠牲者，被害者／pressure 名 圧力，プレッシャー

文法・構文 [1]段落冒頭の疑問文は「テーマ」の提示を考えるのが原則（***Rule 6*** ⇒p.17）で

すが，今回は「テーマ」の提示では文脈が通らないので，elseやcanから「反語」(「どうして～できるだろうか？いや，できるはずがない」)だと判断しましょう（段落の冒頭に「反語」がくるという珍しいパターンです)。[2]過去の表現〈used to 原形〉「(かつて)～したものだった」に注目して，「現在との対比」だと予想します。次の文のBut now, ～で「現在」が表されており，変化が対比されています。「過去：シリアルは作る時間がないときに食べるもの」→「現在：そのシリアルを食べる時間さえ惜しい」という流れです（第4段落3～4文目の対比に対応しています)。[3]「シリアルの売上でさえ時間のプレッシャーの犠牲になっている」とは，「シリアルを食べる時間さえ惜しいと思われて，売上が落ちている」ということです。

6 [1] (According to research [in 2015]), 40 per cent of people surveyed said 〈that cereal was an inconvenient breakfast (because it takes time to clean up the bowl (after eating))〉. [2] Sales of breakfast cereal [in Britain] fell (by 3.6 million kilograms).

数字 → 具体例

数字 → 具体例

訳 [1]2015年の研究によると，調査対象者の40パーセントが，シリアルは食べたあとにボウルを洗うのに時間がかかるため面倒な朝食だと回答した。[2]英国における朝食用シリアルの販売量は，360万キログラムも減った。

語句 [1]survey 動（人に）調査を行う／inconvenient 形 不便な／[2]fall 動 減少する／by ～（差を表して）～分だけ

文法・構文 [1]2015／40という「数字」に注目して，「具体例」だと判断できます。「シリアルを食べる時間さえ惜しい」ということを具体的に説明しています。形容詞と分詞は，1語で名詞を修飾するときは名詞の前に置くのが原則ですが，今回の40 per cent of people surveyedのように，名詞の後ろに置く場合もあります。[2]byは「差」を表すので，360万キログラム分減ったという意味です。「360万キログラムにまで減った」を表すならtoが使われます。

7 [1] A lack of time — or what we think is a lack — is one of the main reasons [why modern food habits differ (from those of previous generations)]. [2] It makes it impossible for us to pursue our desires and forces us (into compromises [we never quite intended φ]). [3] There is evidence 〈that (when someone feels lacking in time), he or she will cook (less), enjoy meals (less) and (yet) end up eating more food〉.

不定詞の意味上のS

同格のthat

訳 [1]時間がないこと――あるいは，時間がないと思っていること――は，現代の食習慣が前の世代の食習慣と異なる主な理由の1つである。[2]そのせいで私たちは，自分の希望を追い求めることができず，意図していなかった妥協を強いられている。[3] 人は時間がないと感じているとき，料理をすることが減り，食事が楽しくなくなり，それなのに食べる量は増えてしまうということが証明されている。

語句 [1] habit 名 習慣／previous 形 前の／[2] pursue 動 追い求める／force 人 into ～ 人 を無理やり～に追いやる／compromise 名 妥協／intend 動 意図する／[3] end up -ing 結局～する

文法・構文 [1] what we think is a lackは，we think {that} 名詞 is a lackの名詞が関係代名詞whatに変わり文頭に出た形で，直訳は「私たちが（時間の）不足だと思っているもの・こと」です。[2] 文頭のItは前文のSであるA lack of time「時間がないこと」を指しています。andは動詞2つ（makesとforces）を結んでいます。

8 [1] Sliced bread was only the start. [2] (Everywhere you look), there are products [promising to save you time], (from two-minute rice to quick-cook pasta). [3] All this talk [about time] is a clever marketing device (too), (because it can convince us 〈that there is no point even trying to cook anything [that takes longer than 20 minutes]〉) — (even though those same 20 minutes feel like nothing (when we are browsing online shopping)). [4] Feeling rushed causes us to spend less time preparing our meals. [5] (When we say 〈we lack time [to cook] — or even time [to eat] —〉) we are not making a simple statement of fact. [6] We are talking (about cultural values and the way [our society tells us 〈that our days should be divided〉]).

具体例

訳 [1] スライスされたパンは始まりに過ぎなかった。[2] 見渡す限りどこを見ても，2分チンしたらできるご飯から早ゆでパスタまで，時間の節約をうたう商品がある。[3] 時間に関するこのような話すべてが，巧みなマーケティングの手法にもなっている。なぜなら，それによって私たちは，調理に20分以上かかるものを作ろうとすることさえ無駄だと思い込まされるからだ――オンラインショッピングのサイトを見ているときには，同じ20分でも何とも思わないのに，である。[4] 焦っていると，食事の支度にかける時間が短くなってしまう。[5] 料理する時間がない――あるいは食事をとる時間さえない――と言うとき，私たちは単に事実を語っているのではない。[6] 文化的価値観や，社会が私たちに時間配分を求めている様子についても語っているのだ。

語句 [3] clever 形 巧みな／device 名 手段，仕掛け／convince 人 that S´V´ 人 にS´V´であると納得させる，説得する／there is no point -ing ～しても意味がない／browse 動（インターネットを）閲覧する／[4] rushed 形 慌ただしい，急かされた／cause 人 to 原形 人 に～させる／[5] statement 名 発言，供述／[6] value 名（通例複数形で）価値観／the way S´V´ S´V´する方法／divide 動 分割する

文法・構文 [2] everywhereが接続詞のように働いており，everywhere S´V´, SV「S´V´する

場所ならどこでも，SVだ」の形になっています（everytime S´V´, SV「S´V´するときはいつでも，SVだ」のtimeがwhereに変わったイメージです)。また，from *A* to *B*「AからBまで」は具体例を示すときによく使われます。[5]a simple statement of factはsimpleがM（simply），statementがV（state），factがOというイメージで読むと「単に事実を語る」となり，理解しやすくなります。[6]前文と合わせてnot simply *A*. {But also} *B*「AだけではなくB（も）」の形で，後半のBut alsoが省略された形です。simplyが名詞構文の中でsimpleに変わっているため，つながりが見えにくくなっています。

9 [1]There is something paradoxical, (however), (in the way [we think 〈that we have too little time to eat properly〉]). [2](By objective standards), most of us [in wealthy countries] have far more free time (on average) (than workers did a hundred years ago): nearly 1,000 more hours a year, (in fact). [3](In 1900), the average American worked (2,700 hours a year). [4](By 2015) the average American worked (just 1,790 hours a year). [5](Compared with many of the workers of the past), the average worker today has so much time (on their hands). [6](Except, it seems, for time [to eat]). [7]Many of us are trapped (in a lifestyle [in which eating well seems all but impossible]). [8]Yet this is partly (because we live (in a world [that places a higher value on time (than it does on food)])).

対比表現　数字 → 具体例　数字 → 具体例　数字 → 具体例　対比表現

訳 [1]しかし，しっかり食事をとる時間があまりにも少ないと私たちが考えるのには，何か逆説的なものがある。[2]客観的に見ると，裕福な国に住む私たちのほとんどは，100年前の労働者と比べて，平均してはるかに多くの自由時間がある。実は，年間1,000時間近くも増えているのだ。[3]1900年には，平均的なアメリカ人は年間で2,700時間働いていた。[4]それが2015年までには，平均的なアメリカ人は年間たったの1,790時間しか働かなくなった。[5]過去の多くの労働者と比べると，今日の平均的な労働者にはこれほど多くの自由時間があるのだ。[6]ただし，食事時間を除いて，であるようだが。[7]私たちの多くは，しっかりと食事をとることが不可能も同然であるようなライフスタイルにとらわれている。[8]しかしこれは，1つには，食事よりも時間を重要視する世界に私たちが生きているためである。

語句 [1]paradoxical 形 逆説的な／properly 副 しっかり／[2]objective 形 客観的な／standard 名 尺度／a year 1年につき／[5]compared with ～ ～と比較すると／have time on *one's* hands 時間を持て余している／[6]except for ～ ～を除いて／[7]*be* trapped in ～ ～にとらわれている／all but ～ ～も同然の，ほとんど／[8]partly because ～ 1つには～が理由で／place a high value on ～ ～に高い価値を置く，～を重要視する

文法・構文 [1]paradoxical「逆説的な」から，後ろには「対比」がくると判断できます。「主観的な考えと客観的な数値」が対比されています。[2]farは比較級を強調する副詞です。ま

た，than workers didは直前のhave free timeを受けており，繰り返しを避けるために代動詞didを用いています。 [3]1900／2,700という「数字」に注目して，「具体例」だと判断できます。次の文と合わせて「過去と現在の労働者の労働時間（自由時間）」を具体的に説明しています。 [4]By objective standardsからここまでの文で，1,000 more hours／In 1900／2,700 hours／By 2015／1,790 hoursと数字が使われていることから，「具体例」だと判断できます。「何か逆説的なもの」を具体的に説明しています。 [8]becauseのカタマリが補語の働きをしています。また，～ than it does on foodは，～ than it places ～ value on foodのことで，繰り返しを避けるために代動詞doesが使われています。

音読をしよう！ 🔈06

There are no chairs in the cafeteria / at one high school in central China. // They disappeared during the summer // so that students could store up / a few precious extra minutes of study time. // With the chairs gone, // there was no risk of spending too much time over lunch. // Students eat standing at tables / before rushing back to class. // "We learnt this from other places," // an official said in a Chinese newspaper, // adding that it should be possible / to shorten the time students spent on eating their lunch / down to just 10 minutes. //

After the story of this chairless cafeteria became known, // the school's policy was widely criticized. // "It's a terrible idea / to make students eat while standing," // stated an editorial in the same newspaper. // "It sacrifices the students' health / for academic scores. // It's unacceptable." // A medical doctor said / that this practice would be very bad for the digestion // and could set children up for a lifetime of illnesses. //

Most of us dislike the notion of a chairless cafeteria / that makes children eat faster. // Yet the disturbing thing about dining arrangements / at the Chinese high school / is that they are not so different / from the hurried manner in which millions of other children and adults / now consume meals around the world. // Is the student in China quickly eating a 10-minute lunch / so different from the office worker / who lunches on a protein bar / because there are too many emails / and not enough hours in the day? //

What makes the chairless cafeteria at the school seem shocking / is that the lack of time for eating / is so deliberate and calculated. // In the rest of the world, // by contrast, // many of us do not quite understand / why we are eating in such an irritated state so often. // For decades, people have complained / that modern life does not leave enough time to cook. // The new worry is that we often feel / we do not even have the time to eat. //

How else can we explain the successful marketing / of products such as liquidized breakfast cereal to drink? // A bowl of cornflakes with milk / used to be what you ate / when you lacked the time to cook a proper breakfast. // But now, // even sales of breakfast cereals / have become a victim of time pressure. //

According to research in 2015, // 40 per cent of people surveyed said that cereal was an inconvenient breakfast // because it takes time to clean up the bowl after eating. // Sales of breakfast cereal in Britain / fell by 3.6 million kilograms. //

A lack of time // — or what we think is a lack — // is one of the main reasons / why modern food habits / differ from those of previous generations. // It makes it impossible for us to pursue our desires // and forces us into compromises / we never quite intended. // There is evidence / that when someone feels lacking in time, // he or she will cook less, // enjoy meals less // and yet end up eating more food. //

Sliced bread was only the start. // Everywhere you look, // there are products promising to save you time, // from two-minute rice / to quick-cook pasta. // All this talk about time / is a clever marketing device too, // because it can convince us / that there is no point even trying to cook anything / that takes longer than 20 minutes // — even though those same 20 minutes / feel like nothing when we are browsing online shopping. // Feeling rushed / causes us to spend less time preparing our meals. // When we say we lack time to cook // — or even time to eat

— // we are not making a simple statement of fact. // We are talking about cultural values / and the way our society tells us / that our days should be divided. //

There is something paradoxical, // however, // in the way we think that we have too little time to eat properly. // By objective standards, // most of us in wealthy countries / have far more free time on average / than workers did a hundred years ago: // nearly 1,000 more hours a year, // in fact. // In 1900, // the average American worked 2,700 hours a year. // By 2015 // the average American worked just 1,790 hours a year. // Compared with many of the workers of the past, // the average worker today has so much time on their hands. // Except, // it seems, // for time to eat. // Many of us are trapped in a lifestyle / in which eating well seems all but impossible. // Yet this is partly because we live in a world / that places a higher value on time / than it does on food. //

Lesson 7 解答・解説

▶問題 別冊 p.31

このLessonで出てくるルール

Rule 5 読解 「まとめ単語」による言い換えを見抜く！ ⇒問3

Rule 38 読解 「自然・災害」関係の語彙をマスターする！ ⇒問3

解答

問1 invisible　　問2 ②／If there

問3 ① ○　② ×　③ ○　④ ×　⑤ ×　⑥ ○

問1 難易度 ★★★

invisible「目に見えない」が正解です。invisibleもtransparent「透明な」も受験では必須単語なので語彙力で解くのも1つの手ですが，少しだけ「探し方」にも触れておきます。この手の問題は，**同じ内容の箇所かまったく反対内容の箇所**にその単語があるものです。下線部を含む文にあるdust and debrisやa cloud forms in the funnelから，10行目のA cloud of debrisやa funnel is invisibleを含む文と「似た内容」だとわかります。よって，ここを集中的に探すことで，invisibleを効率よく見つけ出すことができるわけです。

問2 難易度 ★★★

設問文に「地下室の無い一軒家」とあるので，表のIn a structure「建造物の中にいる場合」の欄にある，38行目のIf there is no basement, ～「地下室がない場合は～」を参照します（structureは「構成，構造」→「建物の構造」→「建物（そのもの）」となります）。go to the center of an interior room on the lowest level (e.g. closet, interior hallway) away from corners, windows, doors, and outside wallsとあるので，図を見て「角，窓，ドア，外壁から離れた場所」を探すと，② Bathが適切だと判断できます。また，この文そのものが「根拠となる一文」となります。

①・③・④はWindowがあるので×，⑤はOutsideやDoorwayと書かれているので×，⑥は「屋内スペース」ではないので×です。

問3 難易度★★☆ 思考力

① ときには，警報が出される前に竜巻が襲来することもある。

8行目にOccasionally, tornadoes develop so rapidly that little, if any, advance warning is possible., 15行目にThey may strike quickly, with little or no warning. とあり，選択肢の内容と合致します。ちなみに，選択肢では重要多義語issueが「(警報を）出す」の意味で使われています。

> **多義語issueの核心：「ポンッと出てくる」**
> **(1) 問題，論争　(2)（雑誌の）号　(3) 発行する，出す**

「ポンッと出てくる」→「問題，論争」,「雑誌がポンッと（書店に）出てくる」→「(雑誌の）号」,「本や雑誌などをポンッと出す」→「発行する，出す」と考えてください。

② ほとんどの竜巻は，他の自然災害と何の関係もない。

22行目にTornadoes can accompany tropical storms and hurricanes as they move onto land. とあり，「他の自然災害と関係がある」ことを表しています。選択肢は真逆で，**本文の内容にnoを入れただけ**のひっかけパターンです（***Rule 43*** ⇒p.58)。また，**accompany**は***Rule 17***（⇒p.174）で扱います。

③ 竜巻がどのような進路をたどるのかを，正確に知ることは不可能だ。

18行目にThe average tornado moves Southwest to Northeast, but tornadoes have been known to move in any direction. とあります。「あらゆる方角に進む」→「進路を正確に知るのは不可能」なので，この選択肢は○です。

④ 竜巻は早朝に発生することが最も多い。

29行目にTornadoes are most likely to occur between 3 p.m. and 9 p.m. とあります。

⑤ 都心部では，車が竜巻から逃げるのに，役立つかもしれない。

54行目にNever try to outrun a tornado in urban or congested areas in a car or truck. Instead, leave the vehicle immediately for safe place. とあります。**Never *A*. Instead, *B*.**「決してAではない。(Aではなくて）その代わりにBだ」のパターンです（***Rule 1*** ⇒p.107)。選択肢の「車が役立つ」は真逆の内容です。

ちなみに，その該当箇所でcar or truckが，直後ではvehicle「乗り物」で表されています。こういった**総称的にまとめて表す単語**は，世間ではほぼ注目されないのですが，実はとても重要です。

>>> Rule 5 読解 「まとめ単語」による言い換えを見抜く！

ある単語を「より広い範囲を表す単語」で「まとめる［言い換える］」ことがよくあります。例えばguitar→**instrument**「楽器」や，smartphone→**device**「装置」となって，「総称的にまとめた単語」がよく使われます。こういう単語に慣れておくと「単語の言い換え」に気づきやすくなりますし，何より設問でよくキーになるので必ず意味をチェックしておきましょう（リスニングでもよく使われます）。

重要な「まとめ単語」

- ☐ artwork 芸術品
- ☐ vehicle 乗り物
- ☐ equipment 装置，機器
- ☐ tool 道具
- ☐ produce 農作物
- ☐ document 資料
- ☐ supplies 備品
- ☐ furniture 家具
- ☐ instrument 道具，楽器
- ☐ machine / machinery 機械
- ☐ device 機械，機器
- ☐ facility 施設，設備
- ☐ product 製品
- ☐ item / goods / merchandise 商品
- ☐ appliance 家電製品

⑥ 竜巻に巻き上げられた壊れた物が，けがの原因になることがある。

59行目にFlying debris from tornadoes causes most fatalities and injuries.とあるので，選択肢と合致します。

ここが 思考力

本文の内容が選択肢にすべて反映されるとは限らない！

今回の本文の該当箇所と選択肢⑥をよ～く比べてみてください。

本文　Flying debris from tornadoes causes most fatalities and injuries.

選択肢　Broken objects caught in tornadoes can cause injuries.

3種類の下線それぞれが対応する部分ですが，本文のfatalitiesは選択肢の文にはありません。しかし，選択肢自体の内容は100%正しい（**本文に書かれていることだけ**）ので，これは○になります。こういう「片手落ちの選択肢」は入試で頻繁にあるということを知っておくと，本番でも変に迷ったり，慌てたりせずに対応できるようになるでしょう。

>>> Rule 38 読解 「自然・災害」関係の語彙をマスターする！

「自然・災害」関係の語彙は，今回のような新傾向の問題や，リスニングや英作文でも頻出です。特有表現を知らないとかなりキツいでしょうし，一気にチェックする機会もなかなかないと思うので，ここでしっかり押さえておきましょう（英作文対策をする人は日本語→英語に練習するリストとしても使ってください）。

災害一般

- □ disaster 災害
- □ a disaster-stricken area 被災地
- □ victim / casualty 被災者，被害者（死者とは限らず　けが人も含む）
- □ fatality（通例 fatalities で）死亡者，災難
- □ devastating / catastrophic 破壊的な
- □ hazard 危険，災害
- □ debris がれき，破片，ごみ
- □ hit / strike（台風・地震などが）起こる
  ※ 災害 hit [strike] 場所　災害 が 場所 を襲う
- □ break out（火事，戦争，疫病などが）起こる
- □ occur（災害，事故などが）起こる
- □ sign 前兆，兆し

台風・嵐・雷

- □ typhoon 台風
- □ hurricane ハリケーン
- □ cyclone サイクロン
- □ tornado トルネード，竜巻
- □ storm 嵐
- □ stormy 嵐のように荒れた
- □ snowstorm 吹雪
- □ tropical storm 熱帯(性)低気圧，熱帯暴風雨
- □ thunder 雷
- □ thunderstorm 雷雨
- □ make landfall in [at] 場所 ／land in [at] 場所 （台風が）場所 に上陸する
- □ die down（風などが）徐々にやむ，弱まる

地震・火山

- □ earthquake 地震
- □ tsunami 津波
- □ volcano 火山
- □ an active [a dormant] volcano 活火山［休火山］
- □ erupt 噴火する
- □ eruption 噴火

干ばつ・洪水など

- □ a dry spell 日照り続き
- □ drought 干ばつ（dry spellより深刻な状態）
- □ have a water shortage 水不足に陥る
- □ forest fire 山火事，森林火災
- □ a good harvest 豊作
- □ a poor harvest／crop［harvest］failure 不作
- □ heat wave 熱波
- □ cold wave 寒波
- □ flood 名 洪水　動 川が氾濫する
  - 例 The river flooded. 川があふれた。
  - 例 My house was flooded. 家が水浸しになった。

災害への対処

- □ get［hide］under the desk 机の下にもぐる
- □ evacuation 避難
- □ fire drill 消火訓練
- □ escape from the building / evacuate the building 建物から避難する

補足 evacuateは本来「空にする」で，evacuate the building「建物を空にする」→「建物から避難する」，evacuate to the building「（今いる場所を）空にして建物へ行く」→「建物へ避難する」となる。

- □ {an evacuation} shelter 避難所
- □ structure 建物，建造物
- □ high-rise building 高層ビル
- □ basement 地階，地下室
- □ in an emergency 緊急の際は
- □ emergency supplies 緊急物資
- □ stay［keep］calm 冷静でいる
- □ minimize damage 被害を最小限に抑える

「天気予報」でよく使われる表現

- □ weather forecast / weather report 天気予報
  - 例 The weather forecast says (that) S´V´. 天気予報によると～だ。
- □ according to ～ ～によると
  - 例 According to the weather forecast, ～. 天気予報によると，～。
- □ *be* supposed to 原形 ～しそうだ（直訳は「～すると予想される」）
  - 例 It's supposed to rain this evening. 夕方は雨になるそうだ。
- □ chance of rain 降水確率
  - 例 There's a 30 percent chance of rain today. 本日の降水確率は30％です。

□ **〜, followed by ...** 〜のち…

例 We'll see rain, followed by clouds tomorrow. 明日は雨のち曇りでしょう。

□ **cloudy with occasional rain** 曇り時々雨

□ **toward{s}** 〜に向けて

例 It'll be warmer towards the end of the week.
今週末に向けて暖かくなるでしょう。

□ **partly cloudy** ところにより曇り

□ **partly sunny** ところにより晴れ

□ **widespread** 広い範囲で

□ **scattered** ところにより

□ **flood warning** 洪水警報

□ **storm warning** 暴風警報

□ **advance warning** 事前の警告

今回の長文に出てきましたが，特に難しいためリストには入れていない単語もあります。以下のものは無理に覚える必要はありません。

□funnel-shaped 漏斗(ろうと)状の

□whirling wind 旋風(せんぷう)

□waterspout 水上に起こる竜巻

□storm cellar ストームセラー（暴風雨を避けるための地下室）

文構造の分析

1 [1]Tornadoes are nature's most violent storms. [2](Spawned from powerful thunderstorms), tornadoes can cause fatalities and devastate a neighborhood (in seconds). [3]A tornado appears (as a rotating, funnel-shaped cloud [that extends from a thunderstorm to the ground with whirling winds [that can reach 300 miles per hour (MPH)]]). [4]Damage paths can be in excess of one mile wide and 50 miles long. [5]Every state is at some risk [from this hazard].

訳 [1]竜巻は自然界の最も激しい嵐だ。[2]竜巻は強い雷雨から発生し，数秒のうちに死者を出し，辺りを壊滅させることがある。[3]竜巻は回転する漏斗(ろうと)形の雲のような見た目をしており，時速300マイルにも達することがある旋風を伴って雷雨から地面に伸びる。[4]被害を受ける経路は幅1マイル，長さ50マイルを超えることもある。[5]すべての州がこの災害を被る危険性を一定程度，抱えている。

語句 [1]tornado 名 竜巻／[2]spawn 動 生み出す／fatality 名 死者，災害／devastate 動 破壊する／neighborhood 名 地域，土地／in seconds 数秒で／[3]rotate 動 回転する／funnel 名 漏斗／whirl 動 ぐるぐる回る／[4]in excess of 〜 〜を超えて／[5]hazard 名 災害

文法・構文 [2]Spawned 〜 は過去分詞から始まる分詞構文です（「竜巻が生み出される」という受動関係なので過去分詞形になっています）。[3]rotating／funnel-shapedはどちらも名詞cloudを修飾しています。

2 [1]Some tornadoes are (clearly) visible, (while rain or nearby low-hanging clouds obscure others). [2](Occasionally), tornadoes develop so (rapidly) that little, (if any), advance warning is possible. [3](Before a tornado hits), the wind may die down and the air may become very still. [4]A cloud of debris can mark the location of a tornado (even if a funnel is invisible). [5]Tornadoes (generally) occur (near the trailing edge of a thunderstorm). [6]It is not uncommon to see clear, sunlit skies (behind a tornado).

so 〜 that S'V' 構文

訳 [1]はっきりと目に見える竜巻もあれば，雨や近くに低く垂れ込める雲のせいでよく見えない竜巻もある。[2]ときには，竜巻があまりに急激に発達し，事前の警告がほとんど不可能に等しいこともある。[3]竜巻が襲来する前に，風がやみ，空気が静まり返ることもある。[4]漏斗雲が見えない場合でも，ごみを巻き上げた雲が竜巻の位置を示していることもある。[5]竜巻は通常，雷雨の後端付近で発生する。[6]竜巻の奥によく晴れた，太陽の光が降り注ぐ空が見えることも珍しくない。

語句 [1]visible 形 目に見える／low-hanging 形 低い位置にぶら下がっている／obscure 動 曖昧にする，見えなくする／[2]develop 動 発達する（「ブワ〜ッと広がる」イメージで

したね⇒p.55）／if any たとえあるにしても（few/littleなどを強調する）／advance 形 事前の／[3] die down やむ／still 形 静かな／[4] debris 名 がれき，破片，ごみ／mark 動 印をつける，表す／[5] occur 動 発生する／trailing 形 後端の／[6] sunlit 形 日に照らされた

文法・構文 [1] obscureは「曖昧」なという形容詞が有名ですが，今回のように「曖昧にする，見えなくする」という動詞で使われることもあります（文の構造を考えるとobscureは動詞としか考えられないので，形容詞「曖昧な」→動詞「曖昧にする」という意味を推測することができます）。

3 [1] The following are facts [about tornadoes]:

[2]・They may strike (quickly), (with little or no warning).

[3]・They may appear (nearly) transparent (until dust and debris are picked up or a cloud forms in the funnel).

[4]・The average tornado moves (Southwest to Northeast), but tornadoes have been known to move (in any direction).

[5]・The average forward speed of a tornado is 30 MPH, but may vary (from stationary to 70 MPH).

[6]・Tornadoes can accompany tropical storms and hurricanes (as they move (onto land)).

[7]・Waterspouts are tornadoes [that form over water].

[8]・Tornadoes are (most frequently) reported (east of the Rocky Mountains) (during spring and summer months).

[9]・Peak tornado season [in the southern states] is March through May; (in the northern states), it is late spring through early summer.

[10]・Tornadoes are most likely to occur (between 3 p.m. and 9 p.m.), but can occur (at any time).

訳 [1] 以下は竜巻に関する事実である。

[2]・ほとんど，あるいは一切の予兆なく，すぐに襲来することがある。

[3]・塵（ちり）やごみが巻き上げられたり，雲が漏斗形になったりするまでは，ほとんど透明に見えることがある。

[4]・平均的な竜巻は南西から北東に向かって移動するが，竜巻はあらゆる方角に進むことが知られている。

[5]・竜巻の平均移動速度は時速30マイルだが，動かないものから時速70マイルで動くものまで，さまざまだ。

[6]・竜巻は上陸の際，熱帯低気圧およびハリケーンに伴って生じることがある。

[7]・水上竜巻とは，水上で発生する竜巻のことである。

[8]・竜巻は，春夏のロッキー山脈東側において最も多く報告されている。

[9]・南部の州で竜巻が最も多く発生する時期は，3月～5月の間である。北部の州では，晩春から初夏にかけて最も多く発生する。

[10]・竜巻が最も発生しやすいのは午後3時～午後9時の間だが，どの時間帯でも起こり得る。

語句 [1] following 名 次に述べるもの（単数・複数扱い）／[3] transparent 形 透明の／dust 名 塵／[4] *be* known to 原形 ～することで知られている／[5] vary 動 異なる，さまざまである／stationary 名 止まっているもの／[6] accompany 動 伴う／tropical storm 熱帯（性）低気圧／hurricane 名 ハリケーン／[7] waterspout 名 水上竜巻／[9] peak season 最も盛んな時期

文法・構文 [1] コロン（:）以下で具体的に「竜巻に関する事実」を羅列しています。[3] or は2つの文（dust and debris are ～／a cloud forms ～）を結んでいます。[10] but は動詞2つ（are most likely to occur ～／can occur ～）を結んでいます。

4 （If you are under a tornado WARNING）, seek shelter （immediately）!

訳 竜巻の警報が出ていたら，すぐに避難場所を見つけなさい！

語句 shelter 名 避難場所

5 1段目 **If you are:**

[1] In a structure（e.g. residence, small building, school, nursing home, hospital, factory, shopping center, high-rise building）

Then:

[2] Go （to a pre-designated shelter area such as a safe room, basement, storm cellar, or the lowest building level）. [3]（If there is no basement）, go （to the center of an interior room [on the lowest level （e.g. closet, interior hallway）] [away from corners, windows, doors, and outside walls]）. [4] Get （under a sturdy table） and use your arms （to protect your head and neck）. [5] Do not open windows.

2段目 **If you are:**

[6] Outside with no shelter

Then:

[7] Lie flat （in a nearby ditch or depression） and cover your head （with your hands）. [8] Be aware of the potential [for flooding]. [9] Do not get （under an overpass or bridge）. [10] You are safer （in a low, flat location）. [11] Never try to outrun a tornado （in urban or congested areas）（in a car or truck）. [12]（Instead）, leave the vehicle （immediately）（for safe place）. [13] Watch out （for flying debris）. [14] Flying debris [from tornadoes] causes most fatalities and injuries.

訳 （1段目）**もしあなたが：**[1] 建造物（例：住宅，小さな建物，学校，介護施設，病院，工場，ショッピングセンター，高層ビル）の中にいる場合

そのときは：[2] 安全な部屋，地下室，ストームセラー，あるいは建物の最下階など，指定避

難所に行きなさい。[3] 地下室がない場合は，最下階の屋内スペース（例：クローゼット，屋内廊下）で，角，窓，ドア，外壁から離れた中央部分に行きなさい。[4] 丈夫な机の下にもぐり，腕で頭と首を守りなさい。[5] 窓は開けてはいけない。
(2段目) **もしあなたが**：[6] 屋外にいて避難所がない場合
そのときは：[7] 近くの溝やくぼみに寝そべり，手で頭を覆いなさい。[8] 洪水の危険性に注意しなさい。[9] 陸橋や橋の下に入ってはいけない。[10] 低く平らな場所のほうが安全である。[11] 都心部や混雑した場所で，車やトラックで竜巻から逃げようとしては絶対にいけない。[12] むしろ直ちに車を降りて安全な場所に向かいなさい。[13] 飛来物に注意しましょう。[14] 竜巻から飛んでくるがれきは，人々の死亡や負傷の原因の大半を占める。

語句 [1] e.g. 例えば／nursing home 介護施設／high-rise building 高層ビル／[2] pre-～(動詞・形容詞などについて）前の～，事前に～／designated 形 指定された／basement 名 地下室／storm cellar ストームセラー（暴風雨を避けるための地下室）／[3] interior 形 屋内の／hallway 名 廊下／[4] sturdy 形 丈夫な／[7] lie flat 寝そべる／ditch 名 溝／depression 名 くぼみ／[8] flooding 名 洪水／[9] overpass 名 陸橋／[11] outrun 動 ～から逃げ切る，より速く走る／congested 形 混雑した

音読をしよう！

🔈 07

Tornadoes are nature's most violent storms. // Spawned from powerful thunderstorms, // tornadoes can cause fatalities / and devastate a neighborhood in seconds. // A tornado appears / as a rotating, // funnel-shaped cloud // that extends from a thunderstorm / to the ground / with whirling winds / that can reach 300 miles per hour (MPH). // Damage paths can be in excess of one mile wide / and 50 miles long. // Every state is at some risk from this hazard. //

Some tornadoes are clearly visible, // while rain or nearby low-hanging clouds obscure others. // Occasionally, // tornadoes develop so rapidly / that little, // if any, // advance warning is possible. // Before a tornado hits, // the wind may die down / and the air may become very still. // A cloud of debris can mark the location of a tornado / even if a funnel is invisible. // Tornadoes generally occur near the trailing edge of a thunderstorm. // It is not uncommon to see clear, // sunlit skies / behind a tornado. //

The following are facts about tornadoes: //

・They may strike quickly, // with little or no warning. //

・They may appear nearly transparent / until dust and debris are picked up // or a cloud forms in the funnel. //

・The average tornado moves Southwest to Northeast, // but tornadoes have been known to move in any direction. //

・The average forward speed of a tornado is 30 MPH, // but may vary from stationary to 70 MPH. //

・Tornadoes can accompany tropical storms and hurricanes / as they move onto land. //

・Waterspouts are tornadoes that form over water. //

・Tornadoes are most frequently reported east of the Rocky Mountains / during spring and summer months. //

・Peak tornado season in the southern states / is March through May; // in the northern states, / it is late spring through early summer. //

・Tornadoes are most likely to occur between 3 p.m. and 9 p.m., // but can occur at any time. //

If you are under a tornado WARNING, // seek shelter immediately! //

If you are:	Then:
In a structure // (e.g. // residence, // small building, // school, // nursing home, // hospital, // factory, // shopping center, // high-rise building) //	Go to a pre-designated shelter area / such as a safe room, // basement, // storm cellar, // or the lowest building level. // If there is no basement, // go to the center of an interior room on the lowest level // (e.g. // closet, // interior hallway) // away from corners, // windows, // doors, // and outside walls. // Get under a sturdy table // and use your arms to protect your head and neck. // Do not open windows. //

Outside with no shelter //	Lie flat in a nearby ditch or depression // and cover your head with your hands. // Be aware of the potential for flooding. // Do not get under an overpass or bridge. // You are safer in a low, flat location. // Never try to outrun a tornado in urban or congested areas / in a car or truck. // Instead, leave the vehicle immediately for safe place. // Watch out for flying debris. // Flying debris from tornadoes / causes most fatalities and injuries. //

Lesson 8 解答・解説

▶問題 別冊 p.35

このLessonで出てくるルール

Rule 62 解法 説明問題の解法 ⇒Q1
Rule 70 構文 〈SV that ～〉は「Sは～と思う・言う」の意味！ ⇒Q1
Rule 32 読解 無生物主語・第3文型は「受動態」で訳す！ ⇒Q1

解答

Q1 科学技術のせいで，子どもにとって上手で明瞭な手書き文字が失われた技術になりつつあると，親たちが嘆いていること［～になりつつあるという親たちの不満］。

Q2「文字と文字をつなぐときの，適切な書き方」で筆記体を書く方法を教えることから始めるという指導。

Q3 例1 古代ギリシャのソクラテスは，文字で書き留めないほうがより正確に記憶できると考えていたので，当時新しいと認識されていた，書いてコミュニケーションをとる方法に強く反対し，ギリシャ人による口頭伝承を好んだ。

例2 中世の宗教学者たちは，美しい手書きの写本が時代遅れになってしまう［失われてしまう］恐れがあったので印刷機の発明に反対した。

Q4「学生が筆記体の書き方を学ばなければ，独立宣言を読めなくなるだろう」という，愛国主義に関連した（議員による）主張と，それに対する「大学教授である自分自身も筆記体で書かれた独立宣言の原本は読むことができず，現代人にとって読みやすい書体を使った印刷物で学生が読むことに問題はない」という（トゥルーベックによる）反論。

Q5 ③

Q1 難易度 ★★☆

設問の訳

下線部（1）の「おなじみの不満」とは何のことか，日本語で説明しなさい。

設問のrefer toは「イコール」を表し（***Rule 15*** ⇒p.57），familiar complaint

の内容が問われています。このように，refer toは英文の本文だけでなく，設問でも使われます（大阪府の高校入試でも使われているくらいです）。

>>> Rule 62 解法 説明問題の解法

（1）「説明問題」とは？

「和訳する」問題ではないので，ただ日本語に置き換えただけでは合格点はもらえません。文字どおりの意味（単なる和訳）を踏まえたうえで，**「それが本文でどういう意味を持つのか？」**を具体的に説明する必要があります。

（2）答案作成の手順

1. まずは「型」をつくる

下線部分の「定義」を考え，答案の「型」をつくります。下線部分を一度日本語で説明してみると，そのまま型になることが多いです。例えば，paradoxに下線が引かれていれば，「矛盾・逆説」→「相反していそうで，実は両立すること」のように説明してみて，これをそのまま答案の土台にすればいいのです。

2. 定義を念頭に該当箇所を探す

paradoxの場合なら，心の中で「逆説，逆説…」と思いながら探すと，該当箇所に反応しやすくなる（探しやすくなる）のでオススメです。

3. 該当箇所を型に代入する

該当箇所を見つけたら，その内容をそのまま訳すのではなく，「型に当てはめる」イメージで答案をつくります。

4. 見直し

できあがった解答を下線部に代入し自然に意味が通るかを確認します。

ここではcomplaintを説明する問題なので，「不満」を念頭に読み進めると，直後にParents lament that ～「親たちは～と嘆いている」が見つかり，ここで親の「不満」が書かれていると判断します（ちなみに，It's a familiar complaint. のItは後方のthat ～の内容を指しています）。lament「嘆く」はぜひ押さえてほしい単語ですが，知らなくても**SV that ～**の形に注目して意味を推測できます。

>>> Rule 70 構文 〈SV that ～〉は「Sは～と思う・言う」の意味！

S V that ～という形（直後にthat節）をとる動詞は「思う，言う」の意味になります。直後にthat節をとる動詞は**「認識・伝達」の意味をもつ動詞**に限られるのです。例えば，I think[say] that he is rich. とは言いますが，eat / run / haveなどはNGですよね。

Lesson 8

このルールを逆手に取れば，「**S V that ～.は『思う・言う』って意味**」という必殺技ができあがるわけです。知らない動詞が出てきても**SV that ～**の形に注目するだけで，大体の意味がわかります。

Parents lament that ～ は**SV that ～**の形なので，lamentは「思う，言う」系の意味だと推測できますね。よって，that以下で「思っている，言っている内容」，つまりcomplaint「不満」の内容が書かれていると推測してください。該当箇所はこの文なので，ここをしっかり理解すればOKです。

Parents(S) lament(V) 〈that(O) technology(S′) is turning(V′) good, clear handwriting(O′) (into a lost art form) (for their kids)〉.

turn *A* into *B*「AをBに変える」

that節中はturn *A* into *B*「AをBに変える」の形で，Aはgood, clear handwriting「上手で明瞭な手書き文字」，Bはa lost art form「失われた技術・表現方法」です（artは「技術」，art formは「表現方法」）。that節中の直訳は「科学技術は，子どもにとって上手で明瞭な手書き文字を，失われた技術に変えつつある」です。

このままでもOKですが，さらに「科学技術によって～」と因果関係を意識して訳すと，より自然な和訳になります。technology is turning *A* into *B*は無生物主語の第3文型なので，「技術によって［技術のせいで］AがBに変化しつつある」と考えます。文末は「～と親たちが嘆いていること」や，familiar complaintを意識して「～という親の不満」と締めくくれば完璧です。

>>> Rule 32 読解 無生物主語・第3文型は「受動態」で訳す！

無生物主語の第3文型の文は受動態で訳す，つまり無生物Sを**「Sによって～」という原因**と考えると，自然な和訳になります。例えばTravel broadens the mind.は，直訳の「旅は心を広げる」よりも，「旅によって心が広がる」とするイメージです。

	Travel	broadens	the mind.	
	無生物S	**V**	**O**	
△	旅は	広げる	心を	SがOをVする
◎	旅によって	広げられる	心が	**Sによって Oが Vされる**
	by S		**Oは受動態にするとSになる**	

※「広げられる」は「広がる」と意訳可。

この訳し方を知っておくと,「日本語訳がキレイになる」,「筆者の意図がリアルにわかる」というメリットがあります。

注意 1.「受動態」という用語はわかりやすさ優先で使っているだけなので，決して「『される』と訳さなきゃダメ」ということではありません。

2. 無生物Sの第3文型であっても，状態動詞（特にhaveやmean）は直訳でOKです。ただし小難しいことは気にせず, 和訳がかえって不自然になった場合は直訳すれば問題ありません。

Q2 難易度 ★★☆

設問の訳

下線部（2）に関して, テキサス州の２年生用の筆記体の教育課程［カリキュラム］を日本語で要約しなさい。

下線部（2）の後ろに「イコール」を表すincludeがあります（***Rule 15*** ⇒p.57）。よって，includeの後ろのrequirements for instruction to begin with teaching second-graders how to form cursive letters with the "appropriate strokes when connecting letters." をまとめれば解答となります。特にbegin with ～「～で［から］始まる」，stroke「筆の運び」，letter「文字」に注意してください。

strokeは本来「打つ，なでる」などの動作を表し（strike「打つ」と語源が同じ),「ペンで紙の上を（なでるように）動かす」→「筆の運び，書き方」となります。水泳の「ストローク」=「ひとかき」からも動き自体を連想できそうです（実際，美術用語で「筆の動き」を「ストローク」と言います)。難しい意味ですが，ニュースで使われたこともありますし，日本の紹介で書道について説明するときにも便利です。ちなみに，strokeは他に「打つ」→**「一撃」**,「病気が体を打つ」→**「発作，脳卒中」**の意味も大事です。

以上の点を踏まえて，解答の最後を「～という教育課程·カリキュラム」，または「指導」（解答例）や「指針」のようにします。本来はrequirementsを訳すわけですが，訳が難しいので，主語のguideline，もしくはその前の内容からcurriculumの説明だと判断して，それらを利用すればOKです。

Q3 難易度 ★★☆

設問の訳

下線部（3）の「歴史的伝統主義者」の例を２人挙げ, そのそれぞれが新しいコミュニケーション形式を受け入れたがらなかった理由を説明しなさい。これらの問いには日本語で解答すること。

19行目disagreements between (3) **historical** traditionalist and those who favored **new** writing and communication technologiesでは，disagreement between *A* and *B*「AとBとの意見の相違・論争」の形で，A（古い考えの人）とB（新しい考えの人）が対比されています。**historicalとnewも対比の目印**ですね（***Rule 24*** ⇒p.111）。今回はAの部分に下線が引かれているので，「古いコミュニケーション方法を好む人」の具体例とその理由をまとめます。

■ **1つ目の具体例**

直後の文に「固有名詞（In ancient Greece, Socrates ～）」があるので，**具体例**だとわかります(***Rule 12*** ⇒p.54)。strongly opposed writing, a form of communication perceived new at that timeやpreferred the Greeks' oral traditionなど，「古いコミュニケーション方法を好む」考えにも合致します。

■ **2つ目の具体例**

Later, religious scholars in the Middle Ages ～ で「中世」に時代が移っており，ここから「2つ目の具体例」だと考えます。protested against the invention of the printing pressで，新しい方法（印刷機）に反対しており，これも「古いミュニケーション方法を好む」人の具体例として適切です。

In ancient Greece, Socrates had strongly opposed writing, a form of communication perceived new at that time, Trubek noted.

具体例①　「古代ギリシャ時代のソクラテスは，当時新しいと認識されていた，書いてコミュニケーションをとる方法に強く反対した」

理由

The philosopher preferred the Greeks' oral tradition and felt those who didn't write things down would preserve a "better memory," she said.

具体例①　「ソクラテスは，ギリシャ人による口頭伝承を好んだ」

理由　「文字で書き留めない人のほうがより正確に記憶できると考えていたから」

2つ目の具体例

Later, religious scholars in the Middle Ages protested against the invention of the printing press, which threatened to make their beautiful, hand-copied texts out of date.

理由（make OCの形）

具体例②　「中世の宗教学者たちは，印刷機の発明に反対した」

理由　「印刷機の発明は，美しい手書きの写本を時代遅れにする恐れがあったから」

以上の内容をまとめればOKですが,「歴史的伝統主義者＝古いコミュニケーション方法を好む人」が「新しいコミュニケーション形式を受け入れたがらなかった理由」を述べる点に注意しましょう。答案では「○○は～なので，…だ」という形でまとめます。

Q4 難易度 ★★★ 思考力

設問の訳

下線部（4）に関して，愛国主義に関連した具体的な議論を特定し，それを日本語で説明しなさい。

設問の**identifyは「特定する, つきとめる」**, describeは「説明する」です（「描写する」と覚えている受験生が多いですが，普通に「説明する」で十分なケースがほとんどです）。

下線部はin favor ofで，筆記体を支持する側だけに触れていますが，設問では“debate”を説明するように求められていて，specific「具体的な」とあることからも,「議論」は主張と反論の両方を説明に含む必要があると判断します（***Rule 35*** ⇒p.187）。直後にsome lawmakers complained that ～「～と不満を言う議員もいる」があり，その次の文にthere was nothing wrong with ～「～に何の問題もない」と反論があるので，この2つの意見をまとめればOKです。

■「型」を意識する

設問にthe specific debate related to patriotismとあるので,「～という愛国主義に関連した主張と，…という反論」という型でまとめましょう。皆さんの解答では，**（1）主張があるか，（2）反論があるか，（3）debateを説明する形になっているか**を確認してください。

ここが 思考力 あらかじめ「答案の型」を作る

この問題は，何となく「直後の文を訳せばOK」と考えた人も多いでしょう。訳すのに気をとられて，設問の指示にきちんと従わない解答は上級者でもよくあります。このミスを防ぐために,「まずは解答の型をつくる」ことが大事です。

今回はdebate「議論，論争」の説明なので，**1つの意見では不十分**で，それに対する「反論」が必要だと考えます。英文を読み進めて該当箇所を探す前に，きちんと「主張とそれに対する反論」という型を意識しておくことで,

1つの意見の説明だけで終えてしまうミスを防げるわけです。

また，debateなどの「**反論**」の意味を含む単語は（***Rule 35***⇒p.187）でまとめます。

Q5 難易度 ★☆☆

設問の訳

トゥルーベックの意見を最もうまくまとめた文章を1つ選びなさい。選んだ選択肢の番号（①，②，③または④）を書きなさい。

トゥルーベックの主張は，第3段落後半「学生が筆記体で書かれた独立宣言の原本を読めなくても問題ない」，そして42行目でもI don't think children should be required to learn cursive if they don't want toとあります。一方で，44行目ではBut, still, Trubek said ～. "It's a fine motor skill," and taking time to skillfully perfect the art has positive effects on students' cognitive development.と言っています。

まとめると，「全員が筆記体を学ぶ必要はないが，利点もある」ということなので，③It is not necessary to require all the students to learn cursive writing, while acquiring it can have some positive impacts.が正解です。また，今回は選択肢に「全部」を表すallが含まれていますが，It is not necessary to require all the students to ～「すべての学生に～するよう義務づける必要はない」という部分否定になっており，本文の内容と合致します。

本文のhas positive effects on ～「～によい効果がある」が，選択肢ではcan have some positive impacts「よい影響を与える可能性がある」に言い換えられています。こういった「影響」に関する箇所はかなりの確率で設問に関係してくるので，必ずチェックしておきましょう。〈have a 形容詞 influence[impact/effect] on ～〉「～に形容詞な影響を与える，～に形容詞の効果がある」の形が重要です。onは本来「接触」ですが，*A* on *B*で，Aが単にBに接触するだけでなく，グイグイと力を加えて「影響を与える」イメージです。

「影響・効果」を表す重要表現

- □ have a positive[negative] influence on ～ ～によい[悪い] 影響を与える
- □ have a big[great / significant / profoundなど] influence on ～ ～に大きな影響を与える
- □ have a long-term influence on ～ ～に長期的な影響を与える

□ have little influence on ～ ～にほとんど影響を与えない
※influenceの代わりにimpactやeffectも使うことができる。

今回は細かい該当箇所を照合しなくても，第2～5段落での「英文の方向性」を把握していれば簡単に答えを判別できます。

選択肢の訳

① アメリカの生徒は少なくともアメリカ建国の文書の読み方を習う必要があるので，筆記体を書く技術を欠いているのは，非常に深刻である。

→ 36行目にthere was nothing wrong with students reading the nation's founding documents in typed versions with fonts readable to modern eyesとあるので，選択肢とは真逆です。

② 歴史的議論は，新たな手書き技術を発明して幼い子どもにそれを教えることの重要性を強調してきた。

→ 第2段落で「歴史的に新しいコミュニケーション方法に反対する人も，好む人もいた」と，賛成と反対両方が書かれていますし，そもそも「新たな手書き技術」は出てきません。

③ 筆記体のスキルを身につけるといくつかのよい影響がある一方で，すべての生徒に筆記体を学ぶことを強制する必要はない。

④ 筆記体のサインは，クレジットカードのICチップのような先進技術よりも，法令書類に信憑性をもたらし得る。

→ 40行目にShe said technologies like the chips in credit cards were more effective in preventing crimes than pen-and-paper signatures that can be faked.とあります。「**本文と比較関係が逆**」というひっかけですね（***Rule 47*** ⇒p.110）。ちなみに，本文のlikeが選択肢ではsuch as ～ に言い換えられており，どちらも「**具体例**」を表す重要表現でしたね（***Rule 14*** ⇒p.13）。

文構造の分析

（設問指示文）

Read the following passage [and] answer the questions below.

訳 次の文章を読み，下の問いに答えなさい。

文法・構文 今回のthe questions belowのように，場所を表す副詞が形容詞として名詞を修飾する場合，1語でも名詞の後ろから修飾することがあります。

1 [1] It 's a familiar complaint. [2] Parents lament 〈[that] technology is turning good, clear handwriting (into a lost art form) (for their kids)〉. [3] (In response), lawmakers [in state after state] — particularly in the South — are making time (in classrooms) [to keep the graceful loops of cursive writing alive (for the next generation)]. [4] Alabama passed a law [requiring it] (in 2016). [5] (That same year), Louisiana passed its own cursive law. [6] Others [like Arkansas, Virginia, California, Florida [and] North Carolina], have similar laws. [7] Texas is the latest state [in which educators are pushing to bring back cursive writing in elementary schools]. [8] Each state's curriculum differs (in subtle ways). [9] The guideline [described in the Texas Education Code], (for instance), includes requirements for instruction [to begin with teaching second-graders how to form cursive letters with the "appropriate strokes ([when] connecting letters)]."

SV that ～ →「思う，言う」

keep OCの形

反復表現

不定詞の意味上のS

イコール表現

〈S´＋be動詞〉の省略

[10] Third-graders would focus on writing complete words, thoughts, [and] answers to questions, [and] fourth-graders would need to be able to complete their assignments outright (in cursive).

訳 [1]それはおなじみの不満だ。[2]親は，科学技術のせいで，上手で明瞭な手書きの文字を書く技術が子どもから忘れ去られつつあると嘆いている。[3]それに応えて，多くの州，特に南部の州の議員が，筆記体の優美な弧を次世代に存続させるための授業の時間をつくっている。[4]アラバマ州は，それを義務付ける法律を2016年に可決した。[5]同年，ルイジアナ州は独自の筆記体教育法を成立させた。[6]アーカンソー州，ヴァージニア州，カリフォルニア州，フロリダ州，ノースカロライナ州など他の州にも，同じような法律がある。[7]テキサス州も最近，教育者たちが小学校における筆記体教育を復活させようとしている。[8]各州の教育課程は微妙に異なる。[9]例えばテキサス州の教育規約に記載されている指針には，教育は2年生に「文字と文字をつなぐ際の適切な筆づかい」で筆記体の文字を形作る方法を教えるところから始めるように義務づける内容が記載されている。[10]3年生は単語をフルで書いたり自分の考えや問題の解答を書いたりすることに注力し，4年生は宿題をまるごと筆記体で完成できる必要がある。

語句 [1]familiar 形 よく知られている，なじみの／complaint 名 不満，愚痴／[2]lament 動 残念がる，嘆き悲しむ／turn *A* into *B*　AをBに変える／handwriting 名 手書き／art 名 技術，芸／[3]lawmaker 名 (法律の制定に携わる) 議員，立法者／particularly 副 特に／graceful 形 (物の形などが) 優美な／loop 名 輪形部 (gの下の部分などの，丸い形をした部分)／cursive 形 筆記体の，続け字の／generation 名 世代／[4]pass 動 可決する／law 名 法律／require 動 要求する／[7]latest 形 一番遅い，最新の／educator 名 教師，教育者／push to 原形 ～しようと推し進める／bring back 回復させる，生き返らせる／[8]curriculum 名 教育課程，カリキュラム／differ 動 異なる／subtle 形 微妙な／[9]describe 動 記述する／requirement 名 要求されること，必要条件／instruction 名 指導／letter 名 文字 (ここで使われているletterは「文字」の意味で，「手紙」ではないので注意しましょう)／appropriate 形 適切な／stroke 名 一筆，筆づかい／connect 動 つなぐ／[10]focus on ～ ～に集中する／complete 形 完全な 動 完成させる／assignment 名 課題／outright 副 完全に

文法・構文 [1]文頭Itは次の文のthat technology ～ kidsを指します。このようにitは前の内容だけでなく後ろの内容を指すこともあります。[3]time to 原形「～する時間」の形で，間にin classroomsが入り込んでいます。to不定詞以下はkeep OCの形で，the graceful ～ writingがO，aliveがCです。Oが長いためにつながりが見えにくくなっています。[6]similarは「反復表現」です。similar lawsは前文の「筆記体教育を義務づける法律と似たような法律」だと判断できます。[7]latestは「最新の」という意味で使われることも多いのでチェックしておきましょう。「(これまでに発売された中で) 一番最後の」→「最新の」となります。[9]includeはオーバーに言えば「イコール」と言える動詞でした。またbegin with以降は動名詞のカタマリが続いており，〈teach 人 物〉の形になっています (second-gradersが 人，how to ～ が 物)。[10]wouldは「現在の弱い推量 (～だろう)」を表しています (仮定法ではないので注意しましょう)。

2 [1]Anne Trubek, the author of “The History and Uncertain Future of Handwriting,” told CNN 〈that efforts [to emphasize cursive] have been ongoing “(for years)〉.” [2]And debates [about 〈whether we should preserve handwriting (in general)〉] are not strictly modern phenomena, (as various periods [in history] featured disagreements [between historical traditionalists and those [who favored new writing and communication technologies]]).
[3](In ancient Greece), Socrates had strongly opposed writing, a form of

Sの同格
過去と現在の対比
固有名詞 → 具体例
writingの同格

Lesson 8

communication [perceived new at that time], Trubek noted. [4]The philosopher preferred the Greeks' oral tradition and felt 〈 those [who didn't write things down] would preserve a "better memory〉," she said. [5]Later, religious scholars [in the Middle Ages] protested (against the invention of the printing press, [which threatened to make their beautiful, hand-copied texts out of date]). [6](As inventions like the printing press and the Internet throw humanity forward), "there will be a loss," Trubek said.

make OCの形

訳 [1]『手書き文字の歴史と不確かな未来』の著者であるアン・トゥルーベックはCNNに，筆記体を重要視する努力は「長年にわたって」行われ続けているのだと語った。[2]そして，手書き文字全般を保護すべきかどうかについての議論は，厳密には現代に限った現象ではない。なぜなら，歴史的伝統主義者と新しい字体やコミュニケーション技術を好む人々との意見の相違は，歴史上のさまざまな時代において起こってきたからである。[3]古代ギリシャでは，ソクラテスは筆記という，当時は新しいものだと認識されていたコミュニケーション形式に強く反対していたのだとトゥルーベックは述べた。[4]彼女は，その哲学者はギリシャ人による口頭伝承のほうを好み，物事を書き留めない人のほうがより正確に記憶できるだろうと考えていたのだと述べた。[5]後に中世の宗教学者たちは，彼らの美しい，手書きの写本を時代遅れなものにしてしまう恐れのあった，印刷機の発明に反対した。[6]印刷機やインターネットのような発明により人類が前に突き動かされるのに伴い，「失われるものがある」とトゥルーベックは述べた。

語句 [1]uncertain 形 はっきりとしない／tell 人 that S´V´ 人にS´V´と話す／CNN 名 米国のニュース専門テレビ局（Cable News Networkの略）／effort 名 努力／emphasize 動 重要視する，強調する／ongoing 形 継続中の／[2]debate 名 議論／preserve 動 保存する，保護する／in general ～全体／strictly 副 厳密に（言えば）／phenomena 名 phenomenon「現象」の複数形／feature 動 特徴づける，特色となる／traditionalist 名 伝統主義者／favor 動 ～に好意を示す，～を支持する／[3]ancient 形 大昔の，古代の（発音は［éɪnʃənt］）／Greece 名 ギリシャ／Socrates 名 ソクラテス（発音は［sá(:)krətì:z］）／oppose 動 反対する／perceive OC OをCと認識する／note 動 発言する／[4]philosopher 名 哲学者／prefer 動 ～のほうを好む／Greek 名（the Greeksで）ギリシャ人／oral 形 口頭での／tradition 名 伝承，言い伝え／[5]religious 形 宗教の／scholar 名 学者／Middle Ages 中世（5世紀末から15世紀半ばごろまでのこと）／protest 動 反対する，抗議する／invention 名 発明／printing press 印刷機／threaten to 原形 ～すると脅す／copy 動（文字などを）書き写す／out of date 時代遅れの／[6]throw ～ forward（乱暴に）前に動かす

文法・構文 [2]debate aboutのOに，名詞のカタマリwhether ～が続いています。また，asは「理由」（～なので）を表しています。as ～ 以下は直訳「～の対立は，歴史上のさまざまな時代の特徴になった」→「～の意見の相違は，歴史上のさまざまな時代において起こってきた」と訳してあります。[3]Greece／Socratesという固有名詞から，「具体例」が述べられると判断できます。前文の「歴史的伝統主義者と新しい字体やコミュニケーション技術を好む人々との対立」を具体的に説明しています。またperceived new at that timeは本来

perceive OC「OをCと認識する」の形で，O（a form of communication）が前に出て分詞のカタマリになっています。[4]The philosopherとは，前文のSocratesのことです。[5], which ～ はthe invention of the printing pressを先行詞とする関係代名詞（非制限用法）です。その後ろはmake OCの形が使われています（their beautiful, hand-copied textsがO，out of dateがC）。[6]文頭Asは，forwardという「変化を表す表現」があることから，「比例（～するにつれて）」の意味だと判断できます。throw ～ forwardは「（乱暴に）前に動かす」という意味から，今回は「人類が（否応なく）進歩させられる」というイメージです。

3 [1](In the history of handwriting), we 're in a unique place [in which most Americans alive learned cursive writing], and efforts [to spread cursive again among a new generation of youth] represent a new "reaction" [to ongoing change], she said. [2](Today), debates [in favor of cursive] take the form of "tradition [strangely joined with patriotism]," she said, (noting 〈that some lawmakers complained 〈that (if students didn't learn how to write in cursive), then they wouldn't be able to read the Declaration of Independence〉〉). [3]Trubek, [who is also a professor at Oberlin College], said 〈 she herself can't read the original flowing script of the Declaration of Independence, and there was nothing wrong (with students reading the nation's founding documents (in typed versions with fonts [readable to modern eyes]))〉.

イコール表現
sheの強調
動名詞の意味上のS

訳 [1]手書き文字の歴史において，私たちは，現在生きているアメリカ人の大半が筆記体を学んでいるという珍しい状態にあり，新しい世代の若者たちにおける筆記体を再び普及させようという試みが今起こっている変化への新しい「反応」を表しているのだと彼女は述べた。[2]今日，筆記体を支持する主張は「愛国主義と伝統の奇妙な関連」という形をとっているのだと彼女は述べ，中には，生徒たちが筆記体の書き方を習わなかったらアメリカ独立宣言を読めないだろうと不満を述べる議員がいることに言及した。[3]トゥルーベックは，オーバリン大学の教授でもあるのだが，彼女自身はアメリカ独立宣言の流れるような（筆記体で書かれた）原本の手書き文字を読むことはできず，学生たちが自国の建国文書を現代人の目に読みやすい書体でタイプされた形式で読むことに何の問題もないと言った。

語句 [1]unique 形 無比の，独特の／[2]in favor of ～ ～に賛成の，～を支持する／take the form of ～ ～の形をとる／patriotism 名 愛国主義／the Declaration of Independence アメリカ独立宣言／[3]flowing 形 流れるような／script 名 手書き[筆記体]の文字／there is nothing wrong with ～ ～には何の問題もない／founding 名 創立／type 動 タイプする，打ち込む／readable 形 読みやすい

文法・構文 [1]most Americans aliveのaliveは，most Americansを後ろから修飾しています。most Americans {who are} aliveから〈関係代名詞+be動詞〉が省略されたイメージ

です。[2]ここでのdebatesはarguments「主張」に近い意味で使われていると考えられます。, noting ～ はsheを意味上のSとする分詞構文です。またcomplained that以下は仮定法過去の形〈If S′ 過去形, S would 原形.〉が使われています。

4 [1]Trubek also said 〈students didn't necessarily need cursive (to come up with their own signature [that gives them their "individuality" and "uniqueness" (in signing legal forms)]) either〉. [2]She said 〈technologies [like the chips in credit cards] were more effective (in preventing crimes than pen-and-paper signatures [that can be faked])〉. [3]"I don't think 〈children should be required to learn cursive (if they don't want to)〉," Trubek said.

訳 [1]トゥルーベックはまた，法令書式への署名の際に「個性」や「独自性」を自らにもたらすような独自のサインを考え出すのに使う筆記体も，学生たちにとって必ずしも必要ではないと述べた。[2]彼女は，クレジットカードのICチップのような科学技術は，偽造が可能なペンと紙でのサインよりも防犯において効果的だと言った。[3]「私は，本人が望まないのなら，子どもは筆記体を学ぶことを義務づけられるべきではないと思います」とトゥルーベックは述べた。

語句 [1]come up with ～ ～を考え出す，生み出す／signature 名 署名，サイン／individuality 名 個性／uniqueness 名 独自性／[2]fake 動 偽造する／[3]*be* required to 原形 ～するよう義務づけられている

文法・構文 [1]not necessarily ～ は「必ずしも～ない」という「部分否定」です（all／every／always／altogether など「全部」を表す語が否定語の後ろにくると「すべてが～というわけではない」という「部分否定」の意味になります）。[3]日本語では普通「～ではないと思う」と言いますが，英語の場合，今回の英文のようにI think children should not ～ と言うよりも，I don't think children should ～ と言うのが普通です（「思う」と似た意味を表すsuppose／believe／expect／imagineなどの場合も同様です）。また，後半のif they don't want toはtoの後ろに{learn cursive}が省略されています。

5 [1]But, still, Trubek said 〈being careful and thoughtful has its virtues〉. [2]"It's a fine motor skill," and taking time [to skillfully perfect the art] has positive effects on students' cognitive development. [3]"Handwriting is slower," she said, "And sometimes you just want to slow down."

＊1 cursive writing：a style of handwriting where the characters written in sequence are joined. An example is given below.

＊2 CNN（Cable News Network）：a broadcasting company in the United States which specializes in news delivery

訳 [1]しかしそれでも，トゥルーベックは，慎重かつ思慮深くいることには利点があると言った。[2]「それは微細運動技能であり」，時間をかけてその技術をうまくマスターするこ

とは，生徒の認知発達によい影響をおよぼす。[3]「手書きのほうが，時間がかかります。そして，ただペースを落としたくなることもあるのです」と彼女は言った。
(以下は文章末の注の訳である：
＊1 筆記体：順番に書かれた字をつないだ文字の書き方。以下がその例である。
＊2 CNN（Cable News Network）：ニュース配信を専門とするアメリカの放送会社)

語句 [1]thoughtful 形 思慮深い／virtue 名 長所／[2]fine motor skill 微細運動能力（「微細運動」とは「手や指を使った細かく精密な動作を必要とするもの」のこと）／take time to 原形 時間をかけて～する／skillfully 副 うまく／perfect 動 マスターする／cognitive development 認知発達／[3]slow down ペースを落とす

音読をしよう！

🔊 08

It's a familiar complaint. // Parents lament that technology is turning good, // clear handwriting / into a lost art form for their kids. // In response, // lawmakers in state after state // — particularly in the South — // are making time in classrooms / to keep the graceful loops of cursive writing alive for the next generation. // Alabama passed a law / requiring it in 2016. // That same year, // Louisiana passed its own cursive law. // Others like Arkansas, // Virginia, // California, // Florida // and North Carolina, // have similar laws. // Texas is the latest state / in which educators are pushing / to bring back cursive writing / in elementary schools. // Each state's curriculum / differs in subtle ways. // The guideline described in the Texas Education Code, // for instance, // includes requirements for instruction to begin / with teaching second-graders / how to form cursive letters / with the "appropriate strokes when connecting letters." // Third-graders would focus on writing complete words, // thoughts, // and answers to questions, // and fourth-graders would need to be able to complete their assignments / outright in cursive. //

Anne Trubek, // the author of / "The History and Uncertain Future of Handwriting," // told CNN / that efforts to emphasize cursive / have been ongoing "for years." // And debates about whether we should preserve handwriting in general / are not strictly modern phenomena, // as various periods in history / featured disagreements / between historical traditionalists // and those who favored new writing and communication technologies. // In ancient Greece, // Socrates had strongly opposed writing, // a form of communication perceived new at that time, // Trubek noted. // The philosopher preferred the Greeks' oral tradition // and felt those who didn't write things down / would preserve a "better memory," // she said. // Later, religious scholars in the Middle Ages / protested against the invention of the printing press, // which threatened to make their beautiful, // hand-copied texts out of date. // As inventions like the printing press and the Internet / throw humanity forward, // "there will be a loss," // Trubek said. //

In the history of handwriting, // we're in a unique place // in which most Americans alive learned cursive writing, // and efforts to spread cursive again / among a new generation of youth / represent a new "reaction" to ongoing change, // she said. // Today, // debates in favor of cursive take the form / of "tradition strangely joined with patriotism," // she said, // noting that some lawmakers complained // that if students didn't learn how to write in cursive, // then they wouldn't be able to read the Declaration of Independence. // Trubek, who is also a professor at Oberlin College, // said she herself can't read the original flowing script / of the Declaration of Independence, // and there was nothing wrong with students reading the nation's founding documents / in typed versions / with fonts readable to modern eyes. //

Trubek also said students didn't necessarily need cursive / to come up with their own signature / that gives them their "individuality" and "uniqueness" / in signing legal forms either. // She said technologies like the chips in credit cards / were more effective in preventing crimes / than pen-and-paper signatures that can be faked. // "I don't think children should be required to learn cursive / if they don't want to," // Trubek said. //

But, still, // Trubek said being careful and thoughtful has its virtues. // "It's a fine motor skill," // and taking time to skillfully perfect the art / has positive effects on students' cognitive development. // "Handwriting is slower," // she said, // "And sometimes you just want to slow down." //

Lesson 8

Lesson 9 解答・解説

▶問題 別冊 p.39

このLessonで出てくるルール

Rule 31 読解 more than ～ は3つの意味を考える！ ⇒問1

Rule 35 読解 長文単語・語句をマスターする！（ladder）⇒問2

Rule 74 構文 「強制倒置」のパターン ⇒問4

解答

問1〔A〕① 〔B〕④ 〔C〕③ 〔D〕② 〔E〕④ 問2 ②

問3〔 3 〕① 〔 5 〕② 問4〔 3 〕② 〔 5 〕⑤ 問5 ②

問1

〔 A 〕難易度 ★★★

空所の前にある"American dream"は，空所直後のIt is not a dream of motor car and high wages merely, but a dream of social order in which ～で説明されます（not ～ merely, but ...「単に～ではなく，…」)。これに合致する①amounted to more than the materialismが正解です（amount to ～「～を意味する，～に等しい」という意味)。このmore than ～ は「～だけでない」という意味で考えると，後ろのnot ～ merelyとうまくつながるのがわかります。

>>> ***Rule 31*** 読解 more than ～ は3つの意味を考える！

more than ～は「～より多い」だけでは上級レベルには足りないので，以下のように整理しておきましょう。

more than ～ の3つの意味

(1) **～より多い** (2) not **～でない** (3) not only **～だけでない**

※（2）と（3）の区別は文脈判断となります。

「～より多い」とは，「その範囲を超えて，もはや～でない」と，否定的に解釈できます。そして**「否定の後ろに主張がくる」**（***Rule 1*** ⇒p.107）ことがよくあります。

選択肢の訳

① **単なる物質主義を超えた**
② 一切の物質的な成功を否定した
→ ②は「言いすぎ」選択肢です。本文では「物質的な成功だけでなく，社会秩序も」で，物質的な成功をすべて否定しているわけではありません。
③ 物質主義のよい例となった
④ 物質主義的な文化を促進した

〔 B 〕 **難易度** ★★★

〔 B 〕の前にある they are innately capable「生まれながらにできる」や what they are「現在の自分，ありのままの自分」という内容とつながるのは，④ regardless of the circumstances of their birth or positionです。また，このあとのFor people to realize the potential they were born withで示される「持って生まれた自らの可能性を発揮する」もヒントになります。

選択肢の訳

① 生まれながらの特権的な地位によって［誕生によって特権を与えられた立場に応じて］
② 生まれと，受け継がれた社会的地位に基づいて
③ 生まれと地位の産物である夢が理由で
→ ①～③はすべて逆方向の内容です。
④ **生まれや地位などの環境にかかわらず**

Lesson 9

〔 C 〕 **難易度** ★★★

「消えたbutに気づけるか」がポイントです（***Rule 1*** ⇒p.107）。9行目のIt was **not** about becoming rich or famous; {**but**} it was about having the opportunity 〔 C 〕, and being appreciated for who you are as an individual.は，**"not *A*. {~~But~~} *B*."**の形です。空所部分が「主張（本来のアメリカンドリーム）」の説明になるので，8行目のFor people to realize the potential they were born withなどと似た内容になると考えて，選択肢を見ます。

③を選んでthe opportunity to develop all your possibilitiesとすれば，「アメリカンドリームとは，裕福・有名になることではなく，生まれ持ったあらゆる可能性を高める機会を持つこと」となり，空所直後のand以降「1人の個人としてありのままの自分を認めてもらうこと」ともつながります。

ここまでの主張の確認と〔C〕のポイント整理も兼ねて本文を見ると，次ページのようになります。それぞれ同じ形で下線部が対応しているので，**「同じ形」**→**「同じ意味」**という原則（***Rule 25*** ⇒p.103）を活用することもできます。

"It is not a dream of motor car and high wages merely, but a dream of social order in which each man and each woman shall be able to attain to the fullest stature of which they are innately capable, and be recognized by others for what they are, regardless of the circumstances of their birth or position."

「それは単なる自動車や高賃金という夢ではなく，生まれや地位などの環境にかかわらず，一人一人の男女が生まれもった能力における最高水準を達成することができ，また，他の人々にありのままの自分を認めてもらえるという，社会秩序の夢である」

It was not about becoming rich or famous; {but} it was about having the opportunity to develop all your possibilities, and being appreciated for who you are as an individual, not because of your type or rank.

「それは裕福になったり，有名になったりすることが目的なのではなかった。それは自らのあらゆる可能性を高める機会を持つこと，そして，自分のタイプや階級によってではなく，1人の個人としてありのままの自分を認めてもらうことだった」

選択肢の訳

① 習得した技能を示す

② 習得した能力についてよく考える

→ acquiredとlearnedは両方「(後天的に) 習得した」なので，本文の「持って生まれた(先天的)」と合いません。

③ 自らのあらゆる可能性を高める

④ 潜在能力をまるまる押さえ込む

〔 D 〕**難易度**★★★

空所前のaveragarianismについて，14行目にthe idea that individuals can be evaluated, sorted, and managed by comparing them to the average，19行目にgave "no regard for the individuals to whom alone any system could mean anything."とあります。

元々のアメリカンドリームは「生まれ持った可能性を高める，その人らしさを重視するもの」でしたが，averagarianismによって（平均と比べることで），「自分自身の可能性，その人らしさに目を向けなくなった」と考えられます。

この流れに合うのは② less personal fulfillmentです（実際にはこれをズバリ選ぶのは難しいでしょうから，消去法を利用してもOK)。ちなみに，空所直前**signify「示す，意味する」**は**「イコール」を示す**表現です（***Rule 15*** ⇒p.57)。

選択肢の訳

① (signify less individual attachmentで) 個人の愛情を意味するものではなくなっていく
→ less individualはOKですが，attachment「愛着，愛情」は関係ありません。
② (signify less personal fulfillmentで) 自己実現を意味するものではなくなっていく
③ (signify more distinct individualityで) ますます，他とは異なる個性を意味するようになっていく
④ (signify more unique subjectivityで) ますます独自の主観性を意味するようになっていく
→ ③・④共に，本文「平均主義により個性が重視されなくなる」と真逆です。

〔 E 〕 難易度 ★★☆

ダッシュ（—）以下は〈not *A*, but *B*〉の形で対比されていて，but以下はof howとの間に{in terms}が省略されています。この英文は「平均（他者との比較）」⇔「それぞれ個人（自分の可能性を発揮）」という対比なので，**個人を軸にした内容**を選択肢から探せば，④to the standard we set for ourselvesが正解になります。「平均との差」⇔「自分の基準との距離」という対比関係です。他の選択肢はすべて空所に入るべき「個人を重視」と真逆です。英文そのものは難しいのですが，対比関係をつかめばその方向の選択肢を探すことで解ける問題です。

選択肢の訳

① 私たちの文化に広く普及した模範に
② 社会で認められている個性の原則に
③ 私たちが自ら作り出した一次元的な考え方に
④ 自分が設定した基準に

問2 難易度 ★★★ 思考力

英文の構造はwe worry that ～ and that ... の形で「**2つのthat節は似た内容になる**，（worryの目的語なので）心配する内容になる」と推測できます。

～, we(S) worry(V) {
〈that(O) we(S') might not (fully) ascend(V') them(O')〉
and
人 is denied 物「人は物を与えられない」
〈that(O) we(S') will be denied(V') those opportunities(O') [that are
物 is afforded to 人「物は人に与えられる」
(only) afforded to those [who muscle their way up the one-dimensional ladder]]〉.

最後にあるladderは**比喩的に「成功への道」**を表しています（実際に「はしごを登る」話ではありません）。

>>> Rule 35 読解 長文単語・語句をマスターする！（ladder）

ladderは本来「はしご」ですが，長文では「成り上がるためのはしご」→**「出世の手段，道」**という比喩的な意味でよく使われます。例えばclimb the ladder of successは，直訳「成功のはしごを上る」→「出世する」を表すわけです。このように，**長文でよく使われる比喩**を知っておくことが重要です（ほぼ間違いなく設問に絡みます）。

下線部のare only afforded to ～は，〈afford 物 to 人〉「人に物を与える」の物が主語になった受動態で，those who muscle their way up the one-dimensional ladderは「一次元的なはしご（成功への道）を力ずくで進む人々」です（muscle *one's* way「強引に押しのける，押しのけて進む」は，受験生は知らなくて当然ですが，muscleが動詞なので「（筋肉を使って）力ずくで進む，押しのけて進む」くらいに推測したいところです）。

この内容に近いのは，②are only given to the people who push other people out of their way in moving up the one-dimensional ladderです。以下のように，本文と選択肢で4種の下線部がきれいに対応しています。

本文	are only afforded to those who muscle their way up the one-dimensional ladder
選択肢	are only given to the people who push other people out of their way in moving up the one-dimensional ladder

選択肢の訳

① 一次元的なはしごを登れるだけの体力が十分ある人々だけに与えられる
→ physical strength「体力」がアウトです。
② 一次元的なはしごを登るときに他の人々を押しのける人々だけに与えられる
③ 自分が登りたい一次元的なはしごを作れる人だけに与えられる
→ buildがアウトです。
④ 一次元的なはしごを登ることによってもっと筋肉を鍛えたい人々だけに与えられる
→ become more muscular「もっと筋肉を鍛えたい」がアウトです。

ここが 思考力 「比喩」を見抜く

今回の問題では難しい表現が含まれていて，苦労した人も多いと思います。しかし実際には「ladderが比喩的に使われている／muscleが動詞」さえ意識すれば，消去法で解けてしまいます。誤りの選択肢ではladderを「実際のはしご」，muscleを「肉体的なもの」と捉えているので，本文の比喩とズレるわけです。

今回のような「英文での常識（ladderは比喩で使われること）」は「長文単語のルール」で解説していくので，本書のルールをしっかり押さえていけば，この手の思考力問題も難なく解けますよ。

問3 難易度 ★★☆

語群のbeとdemandsに注目して，〈demand that S´ 原形〉の形を考えます（詳しくは下記参照）。選択肢にthatはないので省略して主語をweにし，その後はthe same as ～「～と同じ」の形を利用して，a world that demands we be the same as ～とします。最後はeveryone elseとつなげればOKです（実際には，everyone elseをつなげてから主語はweと判断してもOK）。

ちなみに，〈demand that S´ 原形〉の形は下線部（3）の直前にもあります。

suggest型の動詞　基本形：S suggest that S´ should 原形 ／ 原形

提案	□ suggest / propose 提案する　□ recommend 勧める
	□ advise 忠告する
主張	□ urge / advocate 主張する
要求	□ insist / request / require / demand 要求する
命令	□ order / command 命じる
決定	□ decide / determined 決定する　□ arrange 取り決める

これらの動詞はすべて**「命令」**がベースになっています。例えば「提案（suggest）」＝「優しい命令」,「決定（decide）」＝「度がすぎた命令」ですね。「命令」という意味を意識すれば，「提案・主張・要求…」なんて暗記する必要はありません。

Lesson 9

問4 難易度 ★★☆

下線部直後に**but also**があるので，語群でnot onlyをまとめます。すでに主語weの位置が指定されていて，not onlyを文頭に置きます。文頭にnot onlyを置くと**「倒置」が起きる**ので，will we haveの語順になるのがポイントです。その後はhaveの目的語にmore individual opportunityをつなげば完成です。

>>> *Rule 74* 構文 「強制倒置」のパターン

文法・読解を問わず「倒置」という用語が頻繁に使われますが，「倒置」には2種類があり，「強制倒置（文頭に否定語）」と「任意倒置（文型ごとに形が決まっている）」で考え方は異なるので，別々にきちんと考えないといけません。ここでは「強制倒置」を確認します。

強制倒置の形
文頭の否定語＋**倒置**
　→疑問文と同じ語順（do / does / didを使うこともある）

強制倒置は「文頭に否定語がきたら倒置が起きる（疑問文の語順になる）」というものです。否定語は以下をチェックしておきましょう。

（1）完全否定　**Not / Never / Little**（倒置で使うLittleは「完全否定」の意味）
（2）準否定語　**Hardly / Scarcely** ほとんど～ない
　　　　　　　Rarely / Seldom めったに～ない　※「頻度」を表す。
（3）要注意の否定語　**Only**　※「～しかない」という否定語。

※「任意倒置」は***Rule 73*** ⇒p.192にて。

問5 難易度 ★★☆

全体を通じて「本来のアメリカンドリーム」⇔「平均主義」という対比になっており，14行目にAnd this dream has been corrupted by what I call "averagarianism," the idea that individuals can be evaluated, sorted, and managed by comparing them to the average.とあります。

このthis dreamは「本来のアメリカンドリーム」を指し，「平均主義かつ一次元的な考え方によって，自分の能力を最大限に発揮できていない」とわかるので，これに合致する② The one-dimensional thinking widespread in our culture of averagarianism has kept us from becoming the best we could possibly be.が正解です。ちなみにこのwidespreadは過去分詞でThe one-dimensional thinkingを修飾しています。has keptが動詞で，〈**keep** 人 **from –ing**〉「人が～するのを妨げる」の形です（prevent型は⇒p.101）。

他に，44行目の ～ reduces the American dream to a narrow ambition to be *relatively* better than the people around us, rather than the best version of ourselves.や，49行目のIf we overcome the barriers of one-dimensional thinking, ～ we will change the way we think about success — not ～, but of how close we are to the standard we set for ourselves.などもヒントになります。

選択肢の訳

① アダムズは，個人が効率的な制度の中で働くことの重要性を主張したテイラーの説を支持するために「アメリカンドリーム」という言葉を作り出した。

→ 17行目にAdams originally coined his term in direct response to the growing influence of Frederick Winslow Taylor's theory of scientific management, which valued efficient systems but gave "no regard for the individuals to whom alone any system could mean anything."とあります。本文は「Adams：個人を重視」⇔「Taylor：平均主義」という対比関係なので，選択肢のin order to support Taylor's theoryはアウトです。

② 私たちの平均主義の文化に普及している一次元的な考え方によって，私たちは，なり得る最高の自分になれずにいる。

③ コンピテンシーに基づいた評価は，授業への出席や宿題が，よい成績を得るために最も重要な要因であることを示唆している。

→ competency-based evaluationについて，57行目にIn the evaluation, instead of awarding grades for never being absent in a course, completing all your homework on time, and getting an A on your midterm exam, credits would be given if, and only if, you demonstrate competency in the relevant skills, abilities, and knowledge needed for the fulfillment of that particular course.とあります。instead of ～「～ではなく」を使って，「講座に欠席しない・宿題を期限内に終わらせる・試験でAを取る」ではなく，「必要なスキル・能力・知識」で評価されると言っているので，選択肢とは真逆です。**instead of ～ が対比表現**だと気づくのがポイントです（***Rule 22*** ⇒p.188）。

④「平均の時代」の終焉は，私たちが，いくつかの分野で試されている，新しいタイプの平均主義を築けるかどうかだ。

→ 73行目のWe can break free of the rule of averagarianism by choosing to value individuality over conformity to the rigid system.で平均主義の支配から抜け出す可能性は述べられていますが，選択肢のset up a new style of averagarianism「新しいタイプの平均主義を築く」がアウトです。本文でそもそも言及されていませんし，平均主義ではなく「個人を重視する・自分の能力を最大限に発揮する」という主旨ですね。ちなみに，depend on ～は「～に頼る」だけでなく「～次第だ」という意味で使われることがよくあります。

文構造の分析

1 [1] James Truslow Adams coined the phrase "American dream" (in his 1931 book *The Epic of America*), [which he published φ (in the depths of the Great Depression)]. [2] Adams argued for a view of the American dream [that amounted to more than the materialism of his time]: "It is not a dream of motor car and high wages (merely), but a dream of social order [in which each man and each woman shall be able to attain to the fullest stature [of which they are (innately) capable], and be recognized (by others) (for 〈what they are〉), (regardless of the circumstances of their birth or position)]."

具体化

訳 [1]ジェームズ・トラスロー・アダムズは，世界大恐慌のさなかに出版した1931年の著書『アメリカの叙事詩』の中で「アメリカンドリーム」という言葉を生み出した。[2]アダムズは，彼の時代の単なる物質主義を超えるアメリカンドリームという考え方を主張した。「それは単なる自動車や高賃金という夢ではなく，生まれや地位などの環境にかかわらず，一人一人の男女が生まれもった能力における最高水準を達成することができ，また，他の人々にありのままの自分を認めてもらえるという，社会秩序の夢である」

語句 [1]coin 動（言葉を）作る（「硬貨を作る」→「新しい言葉を作る」となりました）／publish 動 出版する／[2]argue for ～ ～に賛成の主張をする／amount to ～ ～に相当する／materialism 名 物質主義（精神よりも物質的なものを第一とする考え方）／time 名 時代／wage 名 賃金／merely 副 単に／order 名 秩序／attain to ～ ～を達成する／stature 名 水準，達成度／innately 副 生まれながらにして／regardless of ～ ～のいかんにかかわらず

文法・構文 [1], which ～ は関係代名詞（非制限用法）で，先行詞は*The Epic of America*です（先行詞が固有名詞の場合，それ以上制限（限定）しようがないので，非制限用法を用いることが多いです）。[2]the fullest stature of which they are innately capable は，they are innately capable of the fullest statureを元の文として，the fullest statureがwhichに変わり，of whichが丸ごと前に出た形です。また最後のandは，be able to attain ～ とbe recognized by ～ を結んでいます。

2 [1] For people to realize the potential [they were born with φ]: this was the original concept [of the American dream]. [2] It was not about becoming rich or famous; it was about having the opportunity [to develop all your possibilities], and being appreciated (for 〈who you are (as an individual)〉), (not because of your type or rank). [3] (Though America was one of the first places [where

意味上のS

this was a possibility] (for many of its citizens)), the dream is not limited (to any one country or people); it is a universal dream [that we all share φ]. [4] And this dream has been corrupted (by ⟨what I call φ "averagarianism⟩)," "averagarianism"の同格 the idea ⟨that individuals can be evaluated, sorted, and managed (by comparing them to the average)⟩.

同格のthat

訳 [1]人々が持って生まれた自らの可能性を発揮すること。これがアメリカンドリームのもともとの概念であった。[2]それは裕福になったり，有名になったりすることが目的なのではなかった。それは自らのあらゆる可能性を高める機会を持つこと，そして，自分のタイプや階級によってではなく，1人の個人としてありのままの自分を認めてもらうことだった。[3]アメリカはその多くの国民にとって，これが実現できる可能性の高い最初の場所の1つだったのだが，この夢は一国や一国の国民に限定されているものではない。私たち誰もが持っている世界共通の夢なのだ。[4]そしてこの夢は，私が「平均主義」と呼ぶものによって損なわれている。それは，個人を平均と比較することによって評価し，分類し，管理できるという考えである。

語句 [1]realize 動 実現する／potential 名 潜在能力／original 形 本来の／concept 名 概念，考え／[2]opportunity 名 機会／develop 動 発達させる／possibility 名 可能性／appreciate 動 正当に評価する／individual 名 個人／[3]citizen 名 国民，市民／universal 形 世界中の，普遍的な（すべてのものにあてはまること）／share 動 共有する／[4]corrupt 動 腐敗させる，汚す／evaluate 動 評価する／sort 動 分類する／manage 動 管理する／compare *A* to [with] *B*　AをBと比較する／average 名 平均

文法・構文 [1]thisは直前のto不定詞句の内容，つまり「人々が持って生まれた自らの可能性を発揮すること」を受けています。[2]not *A*, but *B*「AではなくB」から「butが消える」パターンですね（詳細は ***Rule 1*** ⇒p.107／butがセミコロンで代用されているとも考えられます）。またS is about *A*「Sの本質はAだ」は重要表現です。直訳「SはAの周りにある」→「（SはいつもAから離れないので）Sの重要な点（本質）はAだ」となります。またandは，having the opportunity ～ とbeing appreciated ～を結んでいます。[3]thisは前文のbeing appreciated ～ as an individual「一個人としてありのままの自分を認めてもらうこと」を指しています。また，ここでもnot *A*; *B*というbutが消えるパターンが使われていますね。[4]what I call "averagarianism"は，⟨I call 名詞 "averagarianism"⟩の名詞がwhatに変わり，先頭に出た形です。また"-ism"とは「○○主義」という意味です（この他にも，第1段落第2文のmaterialism「物質主義」も参照）。

3 [1]Adams (originally) coined his term (in direct response to the growing influence [of Frederick Winslow Taylor's theory of scientific management], [which valued efficient systems but gave "no regard (for the individuals [to

過去を表す語句（現在と対比）

Lesson 9

whom alone any system could mean anything]))." [2] (For Adams), Taylor's view of the world was not only altering the fabric of society, but it was altering the way [people viewed themselves and one another], the way [they determined their priorities], and the way [they defined the meaning of success]. [3] (As averagarianism reshaped the educational system and workplace), the American dream came to signify less personal fulfillment and changed (into a belief) 〈that even the lowliest of citizens could climb (to the top of the economic ladder)〉.

訳 [1]アダムズはもともと，フレデリック・ウィンスロー・テイラーの科学的管理法の理論の影響力の高まりに直接反応してその言葉を作りだした。彼（テイラー）の理論は，効率的な制度は高く評価する一方で，「どんな制度でも個人に対してのみ何かしらの意味を持ち得るのに，その個人を無視」したものだった。[2]アダムズにとって，テイラーの世界観は，社会の構造を変えるだけでなく，人々の自分自身やお互いに対する見方，優先順位の決め方，そして成功の意味を定義する方法も変えてしまうものだった。[3]平均主義が教育制度や職場を再建するにつれ，アメリカンドリームは，自己実現を意味するものではなくなっていき，最下層の国民でさえも経済のはしごの頂上に登ることができるのだという考え方に変わっていった。

語句 [1]term 名 用語／in response to ～ ～に応じて／influence 名 影響（力）／theory 名 理論／value 動 重んじる／efficient 形 効率的な／regard 名 配慮，関心，敬意／mean 物 to 人 人にとって 物の重要性を持つ（物にはeverything / anything / nothingなどがきます）／[2]alter 動 変える／fabric 名 構造／the way S´V´ S´V´する方法／determine 動 決定づける／priority 名 優先順位／define 動 定義する／[3]reshape 動 作り変える，再形成する／educational 形 教育の／signify 動 表す，意味する（≒ mean）／personal 形 個人の／fulfillment 名 実現，達成／belief 名 信念／lowly 形 身分の低い／economic 形 経済の／ladder 名 はしご（「成り上がるためのはしご」→「出世の道・手段」という意味でよく使われます）

文法・構文 [1]his termはAmerican dreamを指しています。また，... , which ～ は関係代名詞（非制限用法）で，先行詞は直前のFrederick Winslow Taylor's theory of scientific managementです。to whom以下は本来any system could mean anything to the individuals aloneという形でした（aloneは強調する言葉の後ろに置いて「～だけ」の意味）。the individualsがwhomに変わり，to whom aloneが丸ごと前に出た形です。[2]not only *A* but {also} *B*からalsoが省略されています。またbut以下は*A*, *B*, and *C*の形で，the way ～ のカタマリ3つが結ばれています。[3]文頭のAsは，reshapedやcame toやchanged intoなど「変化を表す動詞」があることから**「比例のas（～につれて）」**だと判断できます（***Rule 81*** ⇒p.209）。

4 [1] It is easy to see 〈why this shift [in values] occurred〉, and it is not (nearly) as straightforward as simple materialism. [2] We all feel the weight of the one-dimensional thinking [that has spread so widely (in our averagarian culture)]: a standardized educational system [that always sorts and ranks us]; a workplace [that hires us (based on these educational rankings), then (frequently) imposes new rankings (at every annual economic performance)]; a society [that gives out rewards, esteem, and praise (according to our professional ranking)]. [3] (When we look up at these artificial and meaningless steps [that we are expected to climb ϕ]), we worry 〈that we might not (fully) ascend them〉 and 〈that we will be denied those opportunities [that are (only) afforded to those [who muscle their way up the one-dimensional ladder]]〉.

〈this＋名詞〉→まとめ表現

コロン (:) →具体化

〈these＋名詞〉→まとめ表現

訳 [1] このような価値観の変化が起こった理由は容易に理解できるが，単純な物質主義のようなわかりやすさからは程遠いものだ。[2] 私たちは皆，私たちの平均主義文化の中にとても広く普及してきた，一次元的な思考の重みを感じている。それは常に私たちを分類しランク付けする標準化された教育制度や，そういった教育制度上の順位付けに基づいて人を雇用し，毎年の経済的成果に応じて頻繁に新たな順位付けを行う職場，そして職業の序列に応じて報酬，評価，称賛を与える社会のことである。[3] 私たちが進むことが期待されている，こういった人為的で無意味な道のりを見上げると，最後まで進めないのではないか，一次元的なはしごを強引に押し進む人々だけに与えられる機会を自分には与えられないのではないかと心配になる。

語句 [1] value 名（通例valuesで）価値観／not nearly まったく～でない／straightforward 形 わかりやすい／[2] one-dimensional 形 一次元的な／standardize 動 標準化する／based on ～ ～に基づいて／impose 動 課す／annual 形 毎年の／reward 名 報酬／esteem 名 高い評価／praise 名 称賛／according to ～ ～に応じて／[3] ascend 動 登る／deny *A B* AにBを与えない／afford *A* to *B*　BにAを与える（afford *B A*「BにAを与える」の第3文型への書き換え表現）／muscle 動 強引に押し進む

文法・構文 [1] 〈this＋名詞〉は「まとめ表現」で，第3段落をshift in values「価値観の変化」とまとめています。またnearlyはnot nearlyの形では「ほとんど」ではなく「まったく～ない」という意味になることにも注意しましょう。[2] コロン（:）以下で，「一次元的な思考が普及してきた場所」の具体例が羅列されています。[3] 〈these＋名詞〉は「まとめ表現」の目印です。ここまでの内容をartificial and meaningless steps「人為的で無意味な階段」とまとめていると同時に，ここまでで具体例が終わったと判断できます。ちなみにwe will be denied ～はdeny us those opportunitiesのusがSになり受動態になった形です。

5 [1] We worry 〈that (if we, or our children, are labeled "different")," we will have no chance of succeeding (in school) and will be destined (to a life [on the lower position])〉. [2] We worry 〈that (if we do not attend a leading school and earn high grades), the employers [we want to work for φ] may not (even) look at us〉. [3] We worry 〈that (if we answer a personality

even → 反復表現　構文反復

test (in the wrong way)), we may not get the job [we want φ]〉. [4] We live in a world [that demands 〈we be the same (as everyone else), only better,〉 and reduces the American dream (to a narrow ambition [to be *relatively* better than the people around us]), (rather than the best version of ourselves)].

訳 [1] 自分たちが，あるいは自分の子どもたちが「普通ではない」というレッテルを貼られたら，学校で成功する可能性はなくなり，低い地位の人生を送ることになるのだろうと心配になる。[2] 一流の学校に通い，好成績を収めなければ，自分が働きたい職場の雇用主には見向きもされないのではないかと心配になる。[3] 性格検査で間違った回答をしたら，希望する職に就けないのではないかと心配になる。[4] 私たちは，他人と同じでありながら，他人より優れていることを私たちに求め，アメリカンドリームを，自分自身の最高の状態になることではなく，周りの人々よりも「相対的に」優れた人間になるという狭い願望にまで引き下げてしまう世界に住んでいる。

語句 [1] label OC OにCというラベル［レッテル］を貼る／have a chance of -ing ～の可能性がある／*be* destined to[for]～ ～に運命づけられる／[2] leading 形 一流の／earn 動 稼ぐ，得る／[3] personality 名 性格／[4] demand 動 要求する／narrow 形 狭い，偏狭な／ambition 名 大望／relatively 副 比較的に，相対的に

文法・構文 [1] *be* destined to a life ～ は直訳「低い地位の人生へと運命づけられる」→「低い地位の人生を送ることになる」となります。[3] ここまで，We worry that if ～ という同じ形が3回使われていて，どれも「普通でないことを恐れる」という内容です（構文反復）。また，2文目のevenも反復表現の目印です。[4] demand「要求する」が導くthat節中の動詞は，原形もしくは〈should + 原形〉です。今回はwe be the same ～と原形になっていますね（まさにこの部分が整序問題で問われています）。

6 [1] The principles of individuality present a way [to restore the original meaning of the American dream] — and, (even better), the chance for everyone [to attain it]. [2] (If we overcome the barriers [of one-dimensional thinking]),

不定詞の意味上のS　If節の同格

(if we demand 〈that social institutions value individuality (over the average)〉), (then) not only will we have more individual opportunity, but also we will change the way [we think about success] — not (in terms of 〈how different we are (from the average)〉, but of 〈how close we are (to the standard [we set φ for ourselves]〉〉).

訳 [1]個人主義は，アメリカンドリームの本来の意味を取り戻す道筋を示し，さらによいことに，皆がそれを成就するチャンスを与えてくれる。[2]私たちが一次元的な考え方という壁を乗り越えたら，つまり社会的機関が平均よりも個性を重視することを求めたら，個人のチャンスが広がるだけではなく，成功についての考え方も変わるだろう。平均とどれくらい異なるのかではなく，自分が設定した基準にどれだけ近づいているかという観点で考えるようになるはずだ。

語句 [1]present 動 提示する／restore 動 取り戻す／attain 動 成し遂げる／[2]overcome 動 乗り越える／institution 名 組織，機構／individuality 名 個性／in terms of ～ ～の観点から／standard 名 基準

文法・構文 [1]evenは「～さえ」ではなく「なおいっそう～」という比較級強調表現です。[2]2つ目のif節は1つ目のif節と同格で，If we overcome ～ thinkingの内容をより具体的に説明しています。また，主節はnot only（否定の副詞）が文頭に置かれているため，will we have ～という「疑問文の語順」になっています。

7 [1]We are not talking about a future utopia; we are talking about a practical reality [that is already happening all around us today]. [2]Our healthcare system is moving (toward personalized medicine). [3]Competency-based evaluation is being tried out — (successfully) — (at leading universities). [4](In the evaluation), (instead of awarding grades (for never being absent in a course, completing all your homework on time, and getting an A on your midterm exam)), credits would be given (if, and only if, you demonstrate competency (in the relevant skills, abilities, and knowledge [needed for the fulfillment of that particular course])). [5]Enterprises [that have committed themselves to valuing the individual] are achieving global success, (like Costco, Zoho, and Morning Star). [6]These are the places [that provide us with a glimpse of 〈what designing a flexible system [fit for all] will (actually) look like〉]. [7]It 's time for *all* institutions [to embrace individuality and adopt this relationship [between people and the system] (as the necessary principle [to restore the dream])].

対比表現

不定詞の意味上のS

〈this + 名詞〉→ まとめ表現

訳 [1]将来のユートピアについて話しているのではない。すでに今日そこらじゅうで起こっている実際の現実について話しているのだ。[2]医療制度は，個々の患者に合わせた医療に移行しつつある。[3]一流大学では，コンピテンシーに基づいた評価の試験的運用が行われ，うまくいっている。[4]その評価では，講座を一度も欠席せず，すべての宿題を期限内に終わらせ，中間試験でAを取ればよい評価が与えられるのではなく，その特定の講座を修了するために必要な，関連するスキルや能力，知識におけるコンピテンシーを示した場合

にのみ単位が与えられる。[5]個人の尊重に本気で取り組む企業は，コストコ，ゾーホー，モーニングスターのように，世界的な成功を収めている。[6]こういった企業は，全員に合った柔軟なシステムの設計とは実際どのようなものになるのかを垣間見ることができる場所である。[7]「すべての」機関が個性を受け入れ，人とシステムのこういった関係を，夢を取り戻すために必要な原則として採用するときが来ているのだ。

語句 [1]utopia 名 ユートピア，理想郷／practical 形 実際の／[2]toward{s} 前 ～の方向に／personalize 動 個々に合ったものにする／[3]competency 名 コンピテンシー（能力，適格性のこと）／-based ～に基づいた／try out 試験的に使ってみる／[4]instead of ～ ～ではなく／award 動 授与する／on time 時間どおりに／credit 名 単位／demonstrate 動 示す／relevant 形 関係のある／particular 形 特定の／[5]enterprise 名 企業／commit *oneself* to -ing ～に本気で取り組む／achieve 動 達成する／[6]provide *A* with *B* AにBを与える／glimpse 名 垣間見ること／flexible 形 柔軟な／fit 形 ぴったりの／actually 副 実際に／[7]it's time (for 人) to 原形 人が～するときがきた（今回は人ではありませんが便宜上人としています）／embrace 動 受け入れる／principle 名 原則／restore 動 復活させる

文法・構文 [1]not *A*, but *B*「AではなくB」から「butが消える」パターンです（***Rule 1*** ⇒p.107／butがセミコロンで代用されているとも考えられます）。[4]1つ目のandは，*A*, *B*, and *C*の形で，never being ～／completing ～／getting ～という動名詞句のカタマリ3つを結んでいます。3つ目のandも*A*, *B*, and *C*の形でrelevant skills／abilities／knowledgeの3つを結んでおり，分詞句のカタマリ（needed for ～）は3つそれぞれにかかっています。[6]provide *A* with *B*「AにBを与える」が使われており，直訳「私たちに～を垣間見ることを与える」→「（私たちは）～を垣間見ることができる」となります。what以下はWhat will S look like?「Sはどのようなものになるだろう？」が間接疑問になった形で，Sには動名詞のカタマリ（designing ～ all）がきています。[7]the systemとは，前文で述べられたa flexible system（fit for all）のことです。

8 [1]The ideal [that we call φ the American dream] is one [that we all (once) shared φ] — the dream [of becoming the best [we can be], (on our own terms)], and [of living a life of excellence [as we define it]]. [2]It 's a dream [worth striving for] and (while it will be difficult to achieve), it has never been closer (to becoming a reality) than it is (right now). [3]We no longer need to be limited (by the constraints [imposed on us (by the Age of Average)]). [4]We can break free of the rule of averagarianism (by choosing to value individuality over conformity to the rigid system). [5]We have a bright future (before us), and it begins (where the average ends).

強調のright

訳 [1]私たちがアメリカンドリームと呼ぶ理想は，自分の思うがまま，なり得る最高の自分になるという夢，また自分の定義する素晴らしい人生を送るという夢として，私たちみんながかつて共有していたものである。[2]それは，それを目指して努力する価値のある夢

であり，達成するのは困難だが，今ほど現実に近づいたことはない。[3]私たちはもう，「平均の時代」によって課される制約に縛られる必要はない。[4]私たちは，厳格な制度に合わせることよりも個性を重視するほうを選ぶことによって，平均主義の支配から抜け出すことができる。[5]私たちの前には明るい未来が広がっており，それは平均が終わるところから始まるのだ。

語句 [1]ideal 名 理想／on *one's* own terms 自分のやり方で／of excellence（＝excellent）素晴らしい，優秀な（〈of＋抽象名詞〉＝形容詞）／[2]worth –ing ～する価値のある／strive for ～ ～を目指して努力する／[3]no longer もはや～ない／constraint 名 制約／impose *A* on *B* AをBに課す／[4]break free of ～ ～から自由になる／rule 名 支配／choose *A* over *B* Bよりも優先してAを選ぶ／conformity 名 服従，一致／rigid 形 厳格な

文法・構文 [1]代名詞oneはan idealの代わりになる代名詞です。andは，ofのカタマリ2つ（of becoming ～ とof living ～）を結んでいます。またas we define itのasは「名詞限定のas」と呼ばれるもので，名詞a life of excellenceを修飾しています（このasは接続詞ですが，本書では意味を優先して形容詞節と考えます）。[2]a dream worth ～ はa dream that is worth striving forのthat isが省略された形です。S is worth -ing以下には，Sと同じOが欠けた不完全な形がきます（今回もforのOであるa dreamが欠けていますね）。またit has never been closer to becoming a reality than it is right nowは，直訳「今よりも現実に近づいたことはない」→「今が最も現実に近づいている」ということで，最上級に近い意味です。〈否定表現＋比較級〉を見たら，「最上級相当表現」ではないかと意識できるようにしておきましょう。[4]choose *A* over *B*の形で，Aにはto value ～ という不定詞の名詞的用法，Bにはconformity to ～ という名詞句がきています。[5]ここでのwhereは「接続詞」で，「～するところで［から］」という意味です。

音読をしよう！

◀))) 09

James Truslow Adams coined the phrase "American dream" / in his 1931 book // *The Epic of America*, // which he published in the depths of the Great Depression. // Adams argued for a view of the American dream / that amounted to more than the materialism of his time: // "It is not a dream of motor car / and high wages merely, // but a dream of social order / in which each man and each woman / shall be able to attain to the fullest stature / of which they are innately capable, // and be recognized by others for what they are, // regardless of the circumstances of their birth / or position." //

For people to realize / the potential they were born with: // this was the original concept of the American dream. // It was not about becoming rich or famous; // it was about having the opportunity to develop all your possibilities, // and being appreciated for who you are as an individual, // not because of your type or rank. // Though America was one of the first places / where this was a possibility for many of its citizens, // the dream is not limited to any one country or people; // it is a universal dream that we all share. // And this dream has been corrupted / by what I call "averagarianism," // the idea that individuals can be evaluated, // sorted, // and managed / by comparing them to the average. //

Adams originally coined his term / in direct response to the growing influence / of Frederick Winslow Taylor's theory / of scientific management, // which valued efficient systems / but gave "no regard for the individuals / to whom alone any system could mean anything." // For Adams, // Taylor's view of the world / was not only altering the fabric of society, // but it was altering the way people viewed themselves and one another, // the way they determined their priorities, // and the way they defined the meaning of success. // As averagarianism reshaped the educational system and workplace, // the American dream came to signify less personal fulfillment // and changed into a belief / that even the lowliest of citizens / could climb to the top of the economic ladder. //

It is easy to see why this shift in values occurred, // and it is not nearly as straightforward as simple materialism. // We all feel the weight of the one-dimensional thinking / that has spread so widely in our averagarian culture: // a standardized educational system / that always sorts and ranks us; // a workplace that hires us based on these educational rankings, // then frequently imposes new rankings / at every annual economic performance; // a society that gives out rewards, // esteem, // and praise / according to our professional ranking. // When we look up at these artificial and meaningless steps / that we are expected to climb, // we worry that we might not fully ascend them / and that we will be denied those opportunities / that are only afforded / to those who muscle their way up the one-dimensional ladder. //

We worry that if we, // or our children, // are labeled "different," // we will have no chance of succeeding in school / and will be destined to a life on the lower position. // We worry that if we do not attend a leading school / and earn high grades, // the employers we want to work for may not even look at us. // We worry that if we answer a personality test in the wrong way, // we may not get the job we want. // We live in a world that demands we be the same as everyone else, // only better, // and reduces the American dream to a narrow ambition / to be *relatively* better than the people around us, // rather than the best version of ourselves. //

The principles of individuality / present a way to restore the original meaning of the American dream // — and, // even better, // the chance for everyone to attain it. // If we overcome the barriers of one-dimensional thinking, // if we demand that social institutions value individuality over the average, // then not only will we have more individual opportunity, // but also we will change the way we think about success // — not in terms of how different we are from the average, // but of how close we are to the standard we set for ourselves. //

We are not talking about a future utopia; // we are talking about a practical reality / that is already happening all around us today. // Our healthcare system is moving toward personalized medicine. // Competency-based evaluation is being tried out // — successfully — // at leading universities. // In the evaluation, // instead of awarding grades for never being absent in a course, // completing all your homework on time, // and getting an A on your midterm exam, // credits would be given if, // and only if, // you demonstrate competency in the relevant skills, // abilities, // and knowledge / needed for the fulfillment / of that particular course. // Enterprises that have committed themselves to valuing the individual / are achieving global success, // like Costco, // Zoho, // and Morning Star. // These are the places that provide us with a glimpse / of what designing a flexible system fit for all / will actually look like. // It's time for *all* institutions to embrace individuality / and adopt this relationship between people and the system / as the necessary principle to restore the dream. //

The ideal that we call the American dream / is one that we all once shared // — the dream of becoming the best we can be, // on our own terms, // and of living a life of excellence as we define it. // It's a dream worth striving for / and while it will be difficult to achieve, // it has never been closer to becoming a reality / than it is right now. // We no longer need to be limited by the constraints / imposed on us by the Age of Average. // We can break free of the rule of averagarianism / by choosing to value individuality / over conformity to the rigid system. // We have a bright future before us, // and it begins where the average ends. //

Lesson 10 解答・解説

▶問題 別冊 p.45

このLessonで出てくるルール

Rule 23 読解 「対比」は繰り返される！ ⇒ 問1〔B〕
Rule 35 読解 長文単語・語句をマスターする！（question）⇒ 問1〔F〕
Rule 35 読解 長文単語・語句をマスターする！（on the contrary）⇒ 問1〔F〕
Rule 17 読解 「前後関係」の表現に注目！（accompany）⇒ 問2（イ）

解答

問1〔A〕① 〔B〕① 〔C〕④ 〔D〕② 〔E〕③ 〔F〕③
問2（ア）② （イ）① （ウ）② （エ）②

問1

〔 A 〕 **難易度** ★★☆

空所〔A〕を含む文にはandが3つあるので，接続関係をしっかり把握しましょう。

> folk wisdom that ～「～という民衆の知恵」（thatは同格）
>
> ～, but they reflect the folk wisdom that
> *ums* and *uhs* { are the mark of a nervous, ignorant, and careless speaker,
> and このandは，areとshould beを結んでいる
> should be〔 A 〕at all costs.
>
> 「しかしこれは「うーん」や「えーっと」が，緊張していて，無知で，不注意な話し手の印［特徴］であり，何としてでも避けるべきだという民衆の知恵を反映している」

1つ目のandは*ums*と*uhs*を結び，2つ目のandはnervous, ignorant, carelessを結び，3つ目のandはare ～とshould be ～を結びます。are以降の「緊張，無知，不注意な話し手の印［特徴］」から，①avoidedを入れて「言いよどみを避けるべき」という流れにすると自然になります。

選択肢の訳

① **避けられる**　② 無視される　③ 練習[実践]される　④ 保存される
→ ③は訳語だけで考えるとOKに思えるかもしれませんが，そもそも主語は*ums* and *uhs*なので，「言いよどみが練習[実践]される」は不自然ですね。

〔 B 〕 **難易度** ★★☆

空所〔B〕の前にあるthough「けれども」から，**対比関係**を考えます（***Rule 22*** ⇒p.52）。この前では「言いよどみは好ましくない，避けるべき」とあるので，空所の文は反対になるはずなので，正解は①deeply mistakenです。

>>> *Rule 23* 読解 「対比」は繰り返される！

例えば「*A* vs. *B*」とAとBの対比について述べたあとで，「*A′* vs. *B′*」と**少し見た目を変えて繰り返す**ことがよくあります。皆さんはこれを逆手にとって，対比を見つけたら「このあとも対比関係が繰り返されるのでは」と考えてみてください。これによって，知らない単語や表現があっても，大まかな意味がとれてしまうことはよくあります。

今回は，「言いよどみはよくない」⇔「言いよどみはOK」という対比が3回繰り返されています。それぞれ**though「けれども」**，**no *A*, but *B*「AではなくB」**，**far from 〜「決して〜ではない」**が対比の目印です。この書かれ方を「（広い意味での）**構文反復**」と捉えることもできます（***Rule 25*** ⇒p.103）。

〜, but they reflect the folk wisdom that *ums* and *uhs* are the mark of a nervous, ignorant, and careless speaker, and should be avoided at all costs. Many scientists, **though**, think our cultural obsession with eliminating what they call "disfluencies" is deeply mistaken.

「しかしこれは「うーん」や「えーっと」が，緊張していて，無知で，不注意な話し手の印[特徴]であり，何としてでも避けるべきだという民衆の知恵を反映している。しかし多くの科学者は，いわゆる「言いよどみ」を撲滅しなくてはいけないという私たちの文化的強迫観念はまったくの誤りだと考えている」

二重下線部＝言いよどみはよくない　　波型下線部＝言いよどみはOK

Saying *um* is **no** weakness of character, **but** a natural feature of speech;

「「うーん」と言うことは性格の弱点ではなく，スピーチの自然な特徴である」

far from distracting listeners, there's evidence that it focuses their attention

Lesson 10

in ways that improve comprehension.

「聞き手の気を散らすどころか，理解度が高まるように聞き手の注意を集中させることが証明されている」

選択肢の訳

① **大いに間違っている**　② 根本的に重要である
③ きわめて当然のことである　④ ときに忘れられる

〔 C 〕**難易度** ★★☆

「言いよどみが発生する原因」が問われています。直後の文(13行目)にSpeakers have to talk and think at the same time, launching into speech with only a vague sense of how a sentence will unfold, confident that by the time they've finished the earlier parts of the sentence, they'll have worked out exactly what to say in the later parts.とあります。この「話しながら同時に考えること」を時間的制約と考え，④time pressuresを選べばOKです（そのあとのMostly the timing works out, but occasionally it takes longer ～もヒントになります)。the time pressures {which} speakers face「話者が直面する時間的制約」となります（faceは動詞)。

今回は本文でmainly because ～「主に～の理由で」の形が使われましたが，becauseの前に副詞がつくことがよくあります。因果関係の表現は英文理解において大事なので，以下のまとめで細かいニュアンスをきちんと理解しておきましょう。英作文でも役立ちますよ。

副詞 because ～

- □ **mainly** because ～ 主に～の理由で
- □ **partly** because ～ 1つには～の理由で
- □ **precisely** because ～ まさに～の理由で　※60行目に出てきます。
- □ **probably** because ～ おそらく～という理由で
- □ **possibly** because ～ もしかしたら～という理由で　※53行目に出てきます。
- □ **just** because ～ 単に～という理由で

「単に～だからと言って，…というわけではない」

- □ **Just** because ～, it does not mean[follow] that ...

※Just because ～ が名詞節として使われ，Just because ～ doesn't mean ... となる場合もあります。

選択肢の訳

① 理解の難しさ　② 一般的な批判　③ 長期にわたる訓練　④ **時間的制約**

〔 D 〕 **難易度** ★★☆

空所を含むbut occasionally it takes longer (than expected) to〔 D 〕.は**〈It takes 時間 to 原形〉「〜するのに 時間 がかかる」**の形で，間に**than expected「思ったより」**が割り込んでいます（このthan 〜 の割り込みはよく使われます）。空所は「思ったより時間がかかること」が入ると考えて，②find the right phraseを選べばOKです。

選択肢の訳

① 言いよどみをチェックする　**② 正しいフレーズを見つける**
③ 最後まで読む　④ 時間を覚えている

〔 E 〕 **難易度** ★★☆

主張と具体例の発見がポイントです。第5段落の冒頭（33行目）で「言いよどみによって聞き手は理解しやすくなる」と主張し，その後は**「固有名詞」**を使って具体例を挙げていきます（***Rule 12*** ⇒p.54）。

主張：「言いよどみによって聞き手は理解しやすくなる」

Disfluencies can also improve our comprehension of longer pieces of content.

固有名詞 →「具体例」！

Psychologists Scott Fraundorf and Duane Watson experimented with recordings of a speaker retelling passages from *Alice's Adventures in Wonderland* and compared how well listeners remembered versions from which all disfluencies had been removed as opposed to ones that contained an average number of *ums* and *uhs*.

「言いよどみなし」vs.「言いよどみあり」の対比

They found that hearers remembered details better after listening to〔 E 〕. Stripping a speech of *ums* and *uhs*, as Toastmasters aim to do, appears to be doing listeners no favors.

実験結果は「主張」と同じ内容になるはず

主張→具体例の流れから，空所〔E〕を含む文は「言いよどみありのほうが覚えている」という内容だと考えて，③the disfluent versionsを選べばOKです。

選択肢の訳

① より上手な録音　② 『不思議の国のアリス』
③ 言いよどみが含まれるもの　④ 「うーん」や「えーっと」のない話

〔 F 〕**難易度** ★★★

空所〔F〕の直前（45行目）They also produced more complex sentences, and a greater number of disfluencies, calling into question the idea that disfluencies reflect a lack of control over one's material. とあります（calling into question ～は分詞構文で，call ～ in question「～を疑問視する」の「～」が後ろに配置されています）。

>>> Rule 35 読解 長文単語・語句をマスターする！（question）

> **question「質問／質問する，疑問／疑問に思う・疑う」**
> 長文ではquestionに反応するようにしてください。**「疑問（に思う）」**という意味で使われることがよくあり，**「一般論や従来の考えを疑う」→「新しい内容（主張）」**という流れになることが多いです。

ちなみに41行目でthere's reason to question the assumption that ～「～という前提を疑うべき根拠がある」と，動詞questionが使われています。

空所には③On the contraryを入れて，「知識不足が原因で言いよどみが起こるのは疑わしい」→「いやむしろ，知識が豊富だから言いよどみが増える」という流れが自然です。空所直前のcalling into question ～「～に疑問を投げかける」という否定的な内容を，On the contrary「それどころか～」で補強するイメージです。

>>> Rule 35 読解 長文単語・語句をマスターする！（on the contrary）

on the contraryは「反対に」と訳されるだけのことが多いのですが，実際には直前の**否定的内容**に対して「**（とんでもない）それどころか**」という意味でよく使われます。「～じゃないよ。それどころかむしろ…だ」という流れです。

> **on the contraryの使い方**
> **否定的な内容**. On the contrary ～「（とんでもない）それどころか～」

ちなみに，on the other hand「他方で」は，前後の内容を「対比」させるときに使います（この「on the contraryとon the other handの区別」は，早稲田，慶應などでも問われたことがあります)。

選択肢の訳

① 例えば　② それにもかかわらず　**③ それどころか**　④ 他方で

問2

(ア) 難易度 ★★☆

指示語が問われているので,**「答えは前, ヒントは後ろ」**という発想で考えます(***Rule 50*** ⇒p.69)。(ア)This is the method used by the Toastmasters public-speaking club. とあり, This = the method「(話し方を上達させる)方法」だとわかります。そのあと(5行目)はAs part of the training, one person has the job of counting the speaker's *uhs*. と続くので, Thisは「話者の言いよどみを数えること」と考え, ②Strictly monitoring *ums* and *uhs*を選びます。本文のcount「数える」が, 選択肢でmonitor「チェックする, 監視する」に言い換えられています(monitorは「モニターを見ながら監視する」と覚えるといいでしょう)。

選択肢の訳

① プレゼンテーションを大声で発表すること

→ 3行目にthis person loudly announces how many of these have spoiled your presentationとあり, 大声で発表するのは「プレゼンを台無しにした言いよどみの数」です。

②「うーん」や「えーっと」を厳密にチェックすること

③ 聴衆の前で話すこと

→ 1行目にImagine standing up to give a speech in front of an audience.とありますが,「人前で話すこと」自体が話し方を上達させる方法ではなく, 話しているときに「言いよどみを数えること」です。

④ スピーチの時間を計る手助けとなるクリッカーカウンタを使うこと

→ 1行目にWhile you are speaking, someone in the room uses a clicker to count your every stumble and hesitation — every one of your *ums* and *uhs*.とあります。clickerを使うのは「言いよどみを数えるため」で,「スピーチの時間を計る(time a speech)」ためではありません(ここではtimeは動詞で「計る」の意味)。

(イ) 難易度 ★★★

文の構造は, Experiments (...) show that ～「(…) 実験は～を示している, 実験によって～がわかっている」のthat節中にwhen (S)(V), S′V′.「(S)(V)するときS′V′だ」がきています。

(when (s) words (v) are accompanied (by disfluencies)),
listeners s´ recognize v´ and remember v´ (イ) them o´ faster them o´ more accurately.

「言葉がいいよどみを伴ったときのほうが，聞き手が言葉をより速く理解し，より正確に覚えている（ことが証明されている）」

代名詞は「同じ格」を第一候補にするのでしたね。ただし受動態の場合は「**受動態の主語」＝「能動態（元の文）の目的語**」で，注意が必要でした（***Rule 50*** ⇒p.69）。つまり，今回は（when節の中で）are accompanied byの目的語（動作主）"disfluencies"と主語"words"を同じ重要度で検討する必要があります。主語のwordsをthemに当てはめてみると，listeners recognize them［= words］faster「聞き手は言葉をより速く理解する」となり文意がとおります。そのあともremember them［= words］more accurately「言葉をより正確に覚えている」となるので，これがベストと判断するわけです。2つの候補を比較→文脈で考える→決め手はandをしっかり意識する，という問題でした。

>>> *Rule 17* 読解 「前後関係」の表現に注目！（accompany）

accompany「伴う」は，よく受動態で使われますが，「～によって伴われる」などと訳すと混乱してしまいます。〈サブ **accompany** メイン〉のように考えるのが現実的です。

accompanyの使い方

〈サブ accompany メイン〉	サブはメインに伴う
〈メイン is accompanied by サブ〉	メインにはサブが伴う

例 Children under twelve years of age must be accompanied by an adult.
「12歳に満たない子どもには，大人が同伴しなくてはならない（12歳未満の子どもは大人の同伴が必要です）」
※「子ども（メイン）には大人（サブ）がついてくる」という関係。

今回のwords are accompanied by disfluenciesも，「言葉（メイン）に言いよどみ（サブ）がついてくる」と考えればOKです。「言葉は言いよどみによって伴われる」では意味不明ですよね。

選択肢の訳

① 言葉　② 「うーん」や「えーっと」　③ 言いよどみ　④ 実験

(ウ) 難易度 ★★☆

It's (ウ) a performanceは**It = a performance**で，Itは「主格」なので，前の文にて**最も近い「主語」**public speakingを第一候補にします（主節の主語an argumentよりもthat節中の主語public speakingのほうが近くにある）。当てはめてみると，It［=Public speaking］is a performance in which the speaker is meant to demonstrate mastery over language and make speaking look easy「演説は，話し手が言語を使いこなせることを示し，話すことを簡単に見せようとするパフォーマンスである」となり，意味がとおるので，正解は②です。

選択肢の訳

① 主張　**② 人前で話すこと**　③ 言語の熟達度　④ 日々の会話

(エ) 難易度 ★★☆

66行目の**just as ～「～とまったく同じように」**をヒントに，前半と後半の関係を対応させて考えます。asについては***Rule 81***（⇒p.209）でまとめます。

It's an irony of our age that robots, unconcerned with ego, may be busy putting disfluencies into their speech

「自我を気にしないロボットがせっせと話に言いよどみを差し込んでいるのかもしれないと思うと，それはこの時代の皮肉である」

just as humans, occupied with their self-images, are undergoing tough training to (エ) take them out.

「自分がどう見られるかで頭がいっぱいの人間がきつい訓練を受けて言いよどみを排除しようとしているのとまったく同じように」

この対応を見ると，下線部 (エ) take them outの，themはdisfluenciesを受けていると考えられます（themは「代名詞の目的格」，disfluenciesはputの目的語）。つまり，take them［= disfluencies］out「言いよどみを取り除く」なので，②speak without disfluenciesを選べばOKです。

選択肢の訳

① 自己像をよりよくする
② 言いよどみなく話す
③ より優れたタイプの人工音声を作る
④ 人間のように自らを表現するロボットを開発する

文構造の分析

1 [1]Imagine standing up (to give a speech (in front of an audience)). [2](While you are speaking), someone [in the room] uses a clicker (to count your every stumble and hesitation) — every one of your *ums* and *uhs*. [3](Once you 've finished), this person (loudly) announces 〈how many of these have spoiled your presentation〉. [4]This is the method [used by the Toastmasters public-speaking club]. [5](As part of the training), one person has the job of counting the speaker's *uhs*. [6]The club's measures may be extreme, but they reflect the folk wisdom 〈that *ums* and *uhs* are the mark of a nervous, ignorant, and careless speaker, and should be avoided (at all costs)〉. [7]Many scientists, (though), think 〈our cultural obsession [with eliminating 〈what they call φ "disfluencies"〉] is (deeply) mistaken〉. [8]Saying *um* is no weakness of character, but a natural feature of speech; (far from distracting listeners), there 's evidence 〈that it focuses their attention (in ways [that improve comprehension])〉.

命令文 → 具体例

your every stumble and hesitation の同格

同格の that

同格の that

訳 [1]立って聴衆の前で話をしているところを想像してほしい。[2]あなたが話している間，その部屋にいる誰かがクリッカーカウンタを使って，あなたの口ごもりや言いよどみをすべて,「うーん」や「えーっと」を1つ残さず数えている。[3]あなたが話し終えると，この人は声高に，そのうちいくつの言いよどみがあなたのプレゼンテーションを損なったかを発表する。[4]これは，トーストマスターズ・パブリックスピーキングクラブで使われている手法である。[5]訓練の一環として，1人の人が話し手の「えーっと」を数える係を務める。[6]このクラブのやり方は極端かもしれないが,「うーん」や「えーっと」が，緊張していて，無知で，不注意な話し手の印［特徴］であり，何としてでも避けるべきだという民衆の知恵を反映している。[7]しかし多くの科学者は，いわゆる「言いよどみ」を撲滅しなくてはいけないという私たちの文化的強迫観念はまったくの誤りだと考えている。[8]「うーん」と言うことは性格の弱点ではなく，スピーチの自然な特徴である。それは聞き手の気を散らすどころか，理解度が高まるように聞き手の注意を集中させることが証明されている。

語句 [2]clicker 名 カウンター，カチッと音のするもの（ここではカウント用）／stumble 名 口ごもり／hesitation 名 言いよどみ，口ごもり／[3]once S´V´, SV. いったんS´V´すると，SVする／loudly 副 大声で，声高に／spoil 動 損なう，台無しにする／[4]method 名 手法／public speaking 演説，弁論／[5]have the job of ～ ～という仕事がある，～しなくてはいけない／[6] measure 名（通例measuresで）手段／extreme 形 極端な／reflect 動 反映する／folk wisdom 民衆の知恵／mark 名 印，特徴，現れ／ignorant 形 無知な／at all costs[at any cost] 何としてでも／[7] obsession 名 執着／eliminate 動 撲滅する，取り除く／[8] character 名 性格，性質／far from ～ ～どころか，決して～ではない／comprehension 名 理解

文法・構文 [1] Imagine／Think／Suppose などで始まる命令文は「具体例」の目印になります（***Rule 10*** ⇒p.207）。今回は導入的に具体的状況が設定されているイメージです。[2] everyは「単数扱いする形容詞」なので，後ろの名詞はevery stumble and hesitationと「単数形」になっています。[3] 文頭のonceは「接続詞」で，once S′V′, SV.「いったんS′V′すると，SVだ」の形で使われます（「副詞」のonce「一度，かつて」と区別してください）。[6] 3つ目のandは，are the mark of ～ と should be avoided ～ を結んでいます。the folk wisdom that ～ は「同格のthat」で，「民衆の知恵」の内容を具体的に説明しています。[7] what they call "disfluencies" は，本来call O "disfluencies"「Oを『言いよどみ』と呼ぶ」で，Oが関係代名詞whatに変わって文頭に出た形です。直訳「彼らが『言いよどみ』と呼ぶもの」→「いわゆる『言いよどみ』」となります。[8] no weakness of character, but ～ は，not *A* but *B*「AではなくB」のバリエーションだと考えてOKです（noは「決して～ではない」という，not「～ではない」よりも強い否定を表します）。

2 [1] Disfluencies arise (mainly) (because of the time pressures [speakers face φ]). [2] Speakers have to talk and think (at the same time), (launching into speech (with only a vague sense of 〈how a sentence will unfold〉)), (confident 〈that (by the time they 've finished the earlier parts of the sentence), they 'll have worked out (exactly) what to say (in the later parts)〉). [3] (Mostly) the timing works out, but (occasionally) it takes longer than expected to find the right phrase. [4] Saying *um* is the speaker's way [of signaling 〈that processing is still going on〉]. [5] People (sometimes) have more disfluencies (while speaking in public), (ironically), (because they are trying (hard) not to make mistakes).

因果表現

〈S′＋be動詞〉の省略

訳 [1] 言いよどみは主に，話し手がさらされる時間的制約が原因で生じる。[2] 話し手は話しながら同時に考える必要がある。文章の前半を話し終える頃には後半で何を話すかを正確に練り上げているだろうという自信をもって，文章がどのように展開するのかを漠然としか把握していない状態で話し始めるのだ。[3] たいてい時間の調整はうまくいくが，ときには正しいフレーズを見つけるまでに予定より時間がかかることもある。[4]「うーん」と言うのはその処理がまだ進行中であることを話し手が示す方法なのだ。[5] 人々は，人前で話すときのほうが言いよどみが多くなることがあるが，皮肉なことにそれは，間違いをおかさないように必死だからである。

語句 [1]face 動 直面する，身に迫る／[2]launch into ～ ～を始める／vague 形 漠然とした／sense 名 意識／unfold 動 展開する／confident 形 確信している／by the time S´V´ S´V´するまでには／work out ひねり出す，練り上げる／[3]timing 名 タイミング，時間調整／work out うまくいく／occasionally 副 ときどき（=sometimes）／[4]signal 動 示す，明らかにする／processing 名 処理／*be* going on 進行中である／[5]in public 公然と／make mistakes 間違いをおかす

文法・構文 [2]launching into ～ と confident that ～ はどちらも分詞構文で，confidentの直前にはbeingが省略されています。またthat以下はby the time S´V´, SV「S´V´するまでにはSVする」の形が使われています。 [3]〈It takes 時間 to 原形〉「～するのに 時間 がかかる」の形で，間にthan expected「思ったより」が割り込んでいます。直訳「～するのは予想したよりも長くかかる」→「～までに予定より時間がかかる」となります。

3 [1]（Since disfluencies show 《that a speaker is thinking carefully about 〈what she is about to say φ〉》）, they provide useful information（to listeners）,（helping them to focus attention on 〈what's being said〉）. [2]One famous example comes（from the movie *Jurassic Park*）. [3]（When Jeff Goldblum's character is asked 〈whether a group of only female animals can breed〉）, he replies, "No, I'm ..., I 'm（simply）saying 〈that life, uh ... finds a way〉." [4]The disfluencies emphasize 〈that he 's coming to grips with something [not easy to explain]〉 — an idea [that turns out to be a key part of the movie].

旧情報 → 後ろに主張を予想

somethingの同格

「重要な表現」を表す形容詞

訳 [1]言いよどみは，話し手が言おうとしていることについて慎重に考えていることを示しているので，それらは聞き手に有益な情報を与え，聞き手が話されている内容に意識を集中させるのに役立っている。[2]ある有名な例が映画『ジュラシック・パーク』にある。[3]ジェフ・ゴールドブラムの演じる登場人物が，雌の動物だけで構成された集団が繁殖できるかどうかを尋ねられたときに，彼は「いや，私は……，私は単に，生命は，その……道を見つけるのだと言っているのです」と答える。[4]この言いよどみは，彼が何か説明しにくいことに直面していることを強調している。そしてそれは，映画の鍵を握ることになることである。

語句 [1]*be* about to 原形 ～しようとしている／help 人 {to} 原形 人 が～するのに役立つ／[3]breed 動 繁殖する／[4]come [get] to grips with ～ ～に真剣に取り組む，直面する／turn out to 原形 結局～であることが判明する，～することになる

文法・構文 [1]「理由（～だから）」の意味で使われているsinceは「旧情報」を表し，後ろには「主張」がくることが多いです。今回も主節に「言いよどみが役立つ」という主張がきています。ちなみにhelping ～ はthey（= disfluencies）を意味上のSとする分詞構文です。[3]life finds a wayは直訳「生命は道を見つける」→「生命に不可能はない，生命は勝手に進化する」という意味です。映画『ジュラシック・パーク』で，恐竜たちは雌しかいない

ように操作しているから繁殖する可能性はないはずなのに，一部の雌が雄化して繁殖していたことがわかったときの（焦った）博士のセリフです。

4 [1] Experiments [with *ums* or *uhs* either added to or taken out of speech] show 〈that (when words are accompanied (by disfluencies)), listeners recognize them faster and remember them more accurately〉. [2] (In some cases), disfluencies allow listeners to make useful predictions [about 〈what they're about to hear φ〉].

データ表現

訳 [1]実験で，「うーん」や「えーっと」が話に含まれたときと含まれなかったときを比べたところ，言葉が言いよどみを伴ったときのほうが，聞き手が言葉をより速く理解し，より正確に覚えていることが証明されている。[2]中には，言いよどみがあることで聞き手が，次に耳にすることに関する有用な予測を行うことができる場合もある。

語句 [1] (*be*) taken out of ～ ～から外される／*be* accompanied by ～ ～を伴う／accurately 副 正確に／[2] make a prediction 予測する／*be* about to 原形 ～するところである

文法・構文 [1] with *ums* or *uhs* either added to or taken out of speechはwith OCのカタマリで，名詞Experimentsを修飾しています（*ums* or *uhs*がO，either added ～ speechがC）。Cであるeither added to or taken out of speechはeither *A* or *B*の構造になっており，Aに当たるのがadded to，Bに当たるのがtaken out ofで，speechはその両方につながります（added to speech, taken out of speechということ）。直訳「『うーん』や『えーっと』を足されるか，もしくは外されたスピーチの実験が～を示した」→「『うーん』や『えーっと』を話に含んだ場合と含まなかった場合の実験で，～が証明されている」という意味です。

5 [1] Disfluencies can (also) improve our comprehension of longer pieces of content. [2] Psychologists Scott Fraundorf and Duane Watson experimented (with recordings [of a speaker retelling passages from *Alice's Adventures in Wonderland*]) and compared 〈how well listeners remembered versions [from which all disfluencies had been removed] (as opposed to ones [that contained an average number of *ums* and *uhs*])〉. [3] They found 〈that hearers remembered details better (after listening to the disfluent versions)〉. [4] Stripping a speech of *ums* and *uhs*, (as Toastmasters aim to do), appears to be doing listeners no favors.

動名詞の意味上のS

固有名詞 → 具体例

訳 [1]言いよどみはまた，長い話の内容についての理解も高めてくれる。[2]心理学者のスコット・フラウンドーフとドウェイン・ワトソンは，話し手が『不思議の国のアリス』から引用した数節を読み上げた録音を用いて実験を行い，平均的な回数の「うーん」や「え

Lesson 10

ーっと」が含まれるものに対して，言いよどみが一切含まれないものを聞き手がどれほどよく覚えているかを比較した。[3]彼らは，聞き手は言いよどみが含まれるものを聞いた後のほうが細かい内容をよく覚えていることがわかった。[4]トーストマスターズクラブがやろうとしているように，話から「うーん」や「えーっと」を排除することはどうやら，一切聞き手のためにならないようである。

語句 [1]content 名 内容，コンテンツ／[2]retell 動 再び語る／*Alice's Adventures in Wonderland*『不思議の国のアリス』（ルイス・キャロルの児童向けの小説）／as opposed to ～ ～に対立するものとして／contain 動 含む／[3]detail 名 細部／[4]strip *A* of *B*　AからBを取り去る／appear to 原形 ～するようである／do 人 a favor 人のために役立つ

文法・構文 [1]our comprehension of longer pieces of contentは，ourがS，comprehensionがV，longer pieces ～ がOというイメージで読むと「私たちが長いコンテンツを理解する」となり，理解しやすくなります。[2]Scott Fraundorf／Duane Watson／*Alice's Adventures in Wonderland*などの固有名詞に注目して「具体例」だと判断できます。「言いよどみが，長いコンテンツの理解を高める」ということを具体的に説明しています。またones that contained ～ のonesは代名詞で，直前の複数形の名詞versionsを受けていることもチェックしておきましょう。[4]Stripping ～ のカタマリを分詞構文と誤読してしまっても，appears to be ～ というVが現れていることから，Sになる動名詞のカタマリだったと予想を修正できることが大切です（as S′V′は「様態（～するように）」）。

6 [1](Moreover), there 's reason [to question the assumption] 〈that disfluencies reveal a speaker's lack of knowledge〉. [2](In a study [led by Kathryn Womack]), experienced physicians and newly qualified doctors looked at images of various skin conditions (while talking their way to a diagnosis). [3](Not surprisingly), the expert doctors were more accurate (in their diagnoses) (than the new doctors). [4]They (also) produced more complex sentences, and a greater number of disfluencies, (calling into question the idea 〈that disfluencies reflect a lack of control [over one's material]〉). [5](On the contrary), the authors of the study suggest 〈that the experienced doctors had more disfluent speech (because they had a larger body of knowledge [to work with] and were constructing more detailed explanations (while planning their speech))〉.

同格のthat／固有名詞 → 具体例／〈S′＋be動詞〉の省略／同格のthat／〈(S)＋be動詞〉の省略

訳 [1]さらに，言いよどみによって話し手の知識不足がばれるという前提を疑うべき根拠がある。[2]キャサリン・ウーマックが中心となった研究で，ベテラン医師たちと医師免許

を取ったばかりの医師たちが，さまざまな皮膚病の画像を見て，自分の考えを口に出しながら診断をしていった。[3]当然ながら，診断は新人医師たちよりもベテラン医師たちのほうが正確だった。[4]彼らはまた，より複雑な文章で話し，そしてより何度も言いよどんだ。このことは，言いよどみはその話に関して知識が不足していることの表れなのだという考えに疑問を投げかけるものであった。[5]それどころか，この研究を行った人たちは，ベテラン医師たちのほうが使える知識体系が膨大で，話す内容を考えながら詳細な説明を組み立てていたので，話に言いよどみが多かったのだと示唆する。

語句 [1]question 動 疑う，疑問を投げかける／assumption 名 思い込み，想定／reveal 動 明らかにする，暴露する／[2]experienced 形 ベテランの，経験豊富な／newly qualified 免許[資格]を取ったばかりの／condition 名 病気，疾患／diagnosis 名 診断／[3]accurate 形 正確な／diagnoses 名 diagnosis「診断」の複数形（発音は［daɪəgnóusìːz］）／[4]call ～ into question ～に疑問を投げかける／[5]author 名（計画などの）立案者，張本人／disfluent 形 流暢(ちょう)でない，言いよどみの多い／a body of ～ 大量の～／work with ～ ～を操る／construct 動 組み立てる

文法・構文 [1]～ disfluencies reveal a speaker's lack of knowledgeは，直訳「言いよどみが～を明らかにする」→「言いよどみによって～がばれる」と訳してあります。[2]固有名詞Kathryn Womackに注目して，「具体例」だと判断できます。「言いよどみによって知識不足がばれるという前提が間違っている」ということを具体的な研究をもとに説明しています。[4]calling ～ は分詞構文ですが，意味上のSは前の節の内容（ベテランの医師たちがより複雑な文章で話し，何度も言いよどんだこと）です。またcalling into question the idea ～ は，〈call 名詞 into question〉「～に疑問を投げかける」の名詞のカタマリが長いため後ろに配置された形です。[5]andは，because節中のhad ～ とwere constructing ～ を結んでいます。

7 [1](If disfluencies appear to help communication), why are they so stigmatized? [2]Language expert Michael Erard argues (in his book *Um ...*) 〈that (historically), public speakers were unconcerned with disfluencies (until the 20th century) — possibly (because neither hearers nor speakers consciously noticed them (until it became possible to record and replay spoken language))〉. [3]The aversion to disfluencies may well have arisen (from speakers' horror [at hearing their own recorded voices]).

段落冒頭の疑問文 → テーマの提示

因果表現

訳 [1]言いよどみが会話に役立つようであるなら，どうしてこれほど悪者扱いされているのだろうか。[2]語学専門家のマイケル・エラルドは自著『うーん…』で，歴史的に見て，20世紀になるまでは，人前でスピーチを行う人は言いよどみを気にしていなかったと主張している──それはもしかしたら，話された言葉を録音して再生することができるようになるまでは，聞き手も話し手も言いよどみにはっきり気づいていなかったからかもしれない。[3]言いよどみへの嫌悪感は，話し手が録音された自分の声を聞いてゾッとしたところから生じたのだろう。

語句 [1] stigmatize 動 汚名を着せる／[2] be unconcerned with ～ ～を気にしていない／consciously 副 意識的に，はっきりと／replay 動 再生する／[3] aversion 名 嫌悪，反感／may well 原形 きっと～だろう（may「～かもしれない」を強めた表現）／arise from ～ ～から生じる

文法・構文 [1] 段落冒頭の疑問文は，「テーマ」を表します。第7段落は「言いよどみが悪者扱いされている理由について」がテーマだと判断できます。 [2] noticed them until ～ の them は disfluencies を指しています。

8 [1] (Perhaps) there 's an argument [to be made] 〈that public speaking is different (from day-to-day communication)〉. [2] It 's a performance [in which the speaker is meant to demonstrate mastery over language and make speaking look easy (precisely because of the absence of signals like disfluencies [that reveal its complexity])]. [3] (Maybe) so. [4] But the removal of *ums* should be recognized (for 〈what it is〉) — a display [focused on presenting the speaker (in a favorable light)] — and not a kindness [directed at the listener]. [5] (In fact), designers of synthesized voice systems have begun adding naturalistic disfluencies (into artificial speech). [6] It 's an irony of our age 〈that robots, (unconcerned with ego), may be busy (putting disfluencies into their speech) (just as humans, (occupied with their self-images), are undergoing tough training (to take them out))〉.

同格の that

訳 [1] ひょっとしたら，人前で話すのは日々の会話とは違うという主張が出るかもしれない。[2] それは，話し手が言語を使いこなせることを示し，まさに話すことの複雑さを明らかにする言いよどみのようなサインを一切出さないことで話すことを簡単に見せるのが目的のパフォーマンスなのだと。[3] それはそのとおりかもしれない。[4] しかし，「うーん」を排除することは，あるがままに―話し手をよく見せることに重点を置いた見せ方として―受け入れられるべきであり，聞き手に向けられた優しさとして評価されるべきではない。[5] 実際に，合成音声システムの設計者たちは人工音声に自然な言いよどみを付け加え始めている。[6] 自分がどう見られるかで頭がいっぱいの人間がきつい訓練を受けて言いよどみを排除しようとしているのとまったく同じように，自我を気にしないロボットがせっせと話に言いよどみを差し込んでいるのかもしれないと思うと，それはこの時代の皮肉である。

語句 [1] make an argument 主張をする，議論をする／day-to-day 形 日々の／[2] be meant to 原形 ～することを目的［意図］としている／demonstrate 動 示す／precisely because まさに～の理由で／complexity 名 複雑さ／[4] for what it is あるがままに／present ～ in a favorable light よく見せる，好意的に見せる／direct *A* at *B* AをBに向ける／[5] synthesized voice 合成音声／naturalistic 形 自然な／artificial speech 人工音声／[6] irony 名 皮肉／age 名 時代／ego 名 自我，エゴ／*be* busy -ing せっせと～している，～するのに忙しい／(*be*) occupied with ～ ～で忙しい，～で頭がいっぱいの／undergo 動

受ける，経験する／take ～ out ～を排除する

文法・構文 [1]同格のthatは，argumentの内容を具体的に説明しています。[2]andは，demonstrate ～ とmake ～ を結んでいます。mastery over languageはmaster language「言語を習得する，操る」を名詞化した表現です。またprecisely以下は，because signals like disfluencies ～ are absentを名詞化した形で，直訳「言いよどみのようなサインがないために」→「言いよどみのようなサインを一切出さないために」となります。[6]just as ～ は，asにjustがついているので「様態（まったく～と同じ）」の意味だと判断できます。また，occupied with their self-imagesはhumansを意味上のSとする分詞構文です。文の意味としては，「本来言いよどみがあることが自然な人間が，言いよどみを無くそうとする一方で，本来言いよどみなどないロボットがあえて言いよどみを作ろうとする」という様子を悲観的に述べています。

音読をしよう！ 🔊 10

Imagine standing up to give a speech in front of an audience. // While you are speaking, // someone in the room uses a clicker / to count your every stumble and hesitation // — every one of your *ums* / and *uhs*. // Once you've finished, // this person loudly announces / how many of these have spoiled your presentation. // This is the method used by the Toastmasters public-speaking club. // As part of the training, // one person has the job of counting the speaker's *uhs*. // The club's measures may be extreme, // but they reflect the folk wisdom / that *ums* and *uhs* are the mark of a nervous, // ignorant, // and careless speaker, // and should be avoided at all costs. // Many scientists, // though, // think our cultural obsession with eliminating / what they call "disfluencies" // is deeply mistaken. // Saying *um* is no weakness of character, // but a natural feature of speech; // far from distracting listeners, / there's evidence that it focuses their attention / in ways that improve comprehension. //

Disfluencies arise / mainly because of the time pressures speakers face. // Speakers have to talk and think at the same time, // launching into speech with only a vague sense / of how a sentence will unfold, // confident that by the time they've finished the earlier parts of the sentence, // they'll have worked out exactly what to say / in the later parts. // Mostly the timing works out, // but occasionally it takes longer than expected / to find the right phrase. // Saying *um* is the speaker's way of signaling / that processing is still going on. // People sometimes have more disfluencies while speaking in public, // ironically, // because they are trying hard not to make mistakes. //

Since disfluencies show that a speaker is thinking carefully / about what she is about to say, // they provide useful information to listeners, // helping them to focus attention on what's being said. // One famous example comes from the movie / *Jurassic Park*. // When Jeff Goldblum's character is asked / whether a group of only female animals can breed, // he replies, / "No, // I'm ..., // I'm simply saying that life, / uh ... // finds a way." // The disfluencies emphasize / that he's coming to grips with something not easy to explain // — an idea that turns out to be a key part of the movie. //

Experiments with *ums* or *uhs* / either added to or taken out of speech / show that when words are accompanied by disfluencies, // listeners recognize them faster / and remember them more accurately. // In some cases, // disfluencies allow listeners to make useful predictions / about what they're about to hear. //

Disfluencies can also improve our comprehension / of longer pieces of content. // Psychologists Scott Fraundorf and Duane Watson / experimented with recordings / of a speaker retelling passages / from *Alice's Adventures in Wonderland* // and compared how well listeners remembered versions / from which all disfluencies had been removed / as opposed to ones that contained / an average number of *ums* and *uhs*. // They found that hearers remembered details better / after listening to the disfluent versions. // Stripping a speech of *ums* and *uhs*, // as Toastmasters aim to do, // appears to be doing listeners no favors. //

Moreover, // there's reason to question the assumption / that disfluencies reveal a speaker's lack of knowledge. // In a study led by Kathryn Womack, // experienced physicians and newly qualified doctors / looked at images of various skin conditions while talking their way to a diagnosis. // Not surprisingly, // the expert doctors were more accurate in their diagnoses than the new doctors. // They also produced more complex sentences, // and a greater number of disfluencies, // calling into question the idea that disfluencies / reflect a lack of control over one's material. // On the contrary, // the authors of the study suggest that the experienced doctors / had more disfluent speech / because they had a larger body of knowledge to work with // and were constructing more detailed explanations / while planning their speech. //

If disfluencies appear to help communication, // why are they so stigmatized? // Language expert Michael Erard argues in his book / *Um* ... // that historically, // public speakers were unconcerned with disfluencies / until the 20th century // — possibly because neither hearers / nor speakers / consciously noticed them / until it became possible to record and replay spoken language. // The aversion to disfluencies / may well have arisen from speakers' horror / at hearing their own recorded voices. //

Perhaps there's an argument to be made / that public speaking is different from day-to-day communication. // It's a performance / in which the speaker is meant to demonstrate / mastery over language / and make speaking look easy // precisely because of the absence of signals like disfluencies / that reveal its complexity. Maybe so. But the removal of *ums* should be recognized for what it is // — a display focused on presenting the speaker in a favorable light — // and not a kindness directed at the listener. // In fact, // designers of synthesized voice systems / have begun adding naturalistic disfluencies into artificial speech. // It's an irony of our age that robots, // unconcerned with ego, // may be busy putting disfluencies into their speech / just as humans, // occupied with their self-images, // are undergoing tough training to take them out. //

Lesson 11 解答・解説

▶問題 別冊 p.51

このLessonで出てくるルール

Rule 35 読解 長文単語・語句をマスターする！（assumption）⇒ 問1〔A〕
Rule 35 読解 長文単語・語句をマスターする！（反論・異論表現）⇒ 問1〔B〕
Rule 22 読解 「対比」を表す表現に反応する！ ⇒ 問1〔C〕
Rule 73 構文 「任意倒置」のパターン ⇒ 問2（エ）

解答

問1〔A〕③ 〔B〕③ 〔C〕④ 〔D〕④ 〔E〕④ 〔F〕① 〔G〕②
問2（ア）① （イ）④ （ウ）④ （エ）③

問1 思考力

〔 A 〕 難易度 ★★☆

9行目に **For a long time**, the theory behind childhood amnesia rested on **the assumption** that the memory-making parts of babies' brains were undeveloped, and that around age 3, children's memory capabilities rapidly developed to adult levels. とあります。For a long time, ～「長い間～だった」から，**この内容はあとでくつがえる**と予想できます（***Rule 24*** ⇒p.59）。さらにここではassumption「考え，思い込み」もそう予想する1つの要因になります。

>>> *Rule 35* 読解 長文単語・語句をマスターする！（assumption）

assumption「思い込み」
assumptionは「推定，仮定」という意味ですが，**「思い込み」**のイメージを持ってください。長文では「最初は～という思い込み（assumption）があった」→**「でも実際は違う」**という展開がよくあるからです。

assume「取り入れる」
動詞assumeも長文で見つけた場合は，assumptionと同様の展開を予想してください。また，assumeは大事な多義語で，核心**「取り入れる」**からいろいろな意味に派生します。

「考えを取り入れる」→**「思う，思い込む」**，「責任を取り入れる」→**「引き受ける」**，「態度を取り入れる」→「**(態度・性質を) とる，ふりをする**」となります。

※assumptionはLesson 10の41行目でも出ています。

〔A〕のあとにpsychologists have **recently** discovered that ～という「最近の発見」が出てきます。「**長い間**：3歳ごろに記憶機能が発達するという思い込み」⇔「**最近**：生後3～6か月で長期記憶を形成できる」という対比関係なので，③ Howeverが正解です。さらに直後（13行目）のThe difference「その違い」からも「対比」だと確認できます。

選択肢の訳

① その結果として　② 明らかに　**③ しかし**　④ さらに

〔 B 〕 **難易度** ★★☆

空所の前後で**Recent** studies「最近の研究」とthe **long-held** thinking「昔からの考え方」があるので，ここでも**「過去と現在の対比」**がポイントで，それに合うのは③rejectedです。rejectのように反論・異論を表す表現は対比の合図になり，解答のキーになることも多いので，以下でチェックしておきましょう。

>>> Rule 35 読解 長文単語・語句をマスターする！（反論・異論表現）

反論・異論表現

- ☐ oppose 反対する　☐ counter 反論する　☐ reject 拒絶する
- ☐ challenge 異論を唱える　☐ dispute 動 議論する 名 議論，討論
- ☐ debate 動 議論する 名 議論，討論，論争
- ☐ conflict 動 対立する，矛盾する 名 対立，矛盾
- ☐ contradict 否定する，矛盾する
- ☐ controversial 賛否両論ある，物議を醸す　※名詞はcontroversy「論争」。

選択肢の訳

① 無視した　② 認めた　**③ 否定した**　④ 裏づけた

→①は紛らわしい選択肢ですが，あくまで「最近の研究」⇔「昔からの考え」という対比関係であり，「昔の考えを無視した」わけではありません。

〔　C　〕難易度 ★★☆

空所直後の **instead of 〜「〜ではなくて」** により，空所部分と in one significant burst「突然の大幅な発達」が対比されていると考えます。この「突然」のニュアンスと逆になるのは，④gradually with time です。

>>> Rule 22 読解「対比」を表す表現に反応する！

対比表現は必ず注目できるようにしておきましょう。以下が必須表現です。

□ SV while [whereas] S´V´. SVだ。その一方でS´V´だ
□ despite 〜 / in spite of 〜 〜にもかかわらず
□ in contrast to 〜 〜とは対照的に
□ compared to 〜 〜と比べると
□ instead of 〜 〜の代わりに，〜ではなく
□ unlike 〜 〜とは違って
□ rather than 〜 〜よりむしろ，〜ではなく
□ aside from 〜 〜は別として
□ far from 〜 〜ではない

選択肢の訳

① できる限り速く　② 生まれるやいなや
③ 生後3か月になる前に　**④ 時間をかけて徐々に**

〔　D　〕難易度 ★★★

直前（44行目）に〜, which indicates that childhood amnesia may stem from faulty explicit memory retrieval. とあり，そのあと（45行目）に However, 〜, it takes something to〔　D　〕an explicit memory in all age groups. と続いています。「幼児期は顕在記憶を取り戻す機能が不完全だけれど，（幼児期に限らず）どの年齢層でも顕在記憶を取り戻すのは難しい」という流れを考え，④trigger を選びます。

trigger はもともと「（拳銃の）引き金」の意味で，「引き金を引く」→「引き起こす，きっかけになる」となりました（〈**原因** **trigger** **結果**〉の関係）。本文の **retrieval「取り戻すこと，回復」** を，選択肢では trigger「引き起こす，呼び起こす」で表しているわけです（trigger a memory「記憶を呼び起こす」はよく使われる表現です。6行目に trigger more とあり，これは「より多くの記憶を呼び起こす」ことを表しています）。

ちなみに，動詞 retrieve「回収する，回復する，検索する」の名詞形が retrieval です。「ゴールデンレトリバー（golden retriever)」という犬は，「ハンターが撃ち落とした獲物を持って返ってくる犬」という意味なんです。

ここが 思考力 **対比の「軸」が問われている**

この問いを含む部分はHoweverによって前後が「反対」の関係になっているわけですが，今回は，対比されている部分というよりは**対比の前提（条件）**が問われています。つまり「子どもの頃，顕在記憶を取り戻すのが難しい」⇔「どの年齢層でも，顕在記憶を取り戻すのは難しい」という対比において，「子どもの頃」と「どの年齢層でも」の箇所（対比されている箇所）ではなく，「顕在記憶を検索する」という対比の「軸」が問われているわけです。

～, which indicates that childhood amnesia may stem from faulty explicit memory retrieval.

「このことは，幼児性健忘は顕在記憶を引き出す機能が不完全なことが原因かもしれないということを示している」

幼児期 vs. すべての年齢層

However, unless we're thinking specifically about a past event, it takes something to trigger an explicit memory in all age groups.

「しかし，過去の出来事について具体的に考えている場合を除いて，どの年齢層でも顕在記憶を呼び起こすためには，何かが必要だ」

Howeverから「対比だ！」と反応するのはよいのですが，安易に「異なるもの，反対のもの」を選ぶのではなく，きちんと**「何と何を比べているか？」**を考えることが大切です。難関大になればなるほど，この意識がポイントになります。

Lesson 11

選択肢の訳

① 妨げる　② 取り除く　③ 形成する　**④ 引き起こす**

→ ①・②は「顕在記憶を阻害する，なくす」というマイナスなので，流れに合いません。Howeverを見て，安易に「explicit memory retrievalの逆」と考えるとひっかかってしまいます。③は少し紛らわしいですが，空所にはあくまでretrieval「取り戻すこと，回復」に近い内容がくるはずです。formだと「（ゼロから）形成する」という意味になり，本文の「すでに存在するexplicit memoryを取り戻す，回復する」とは合いません。

〔 E 〕 **難易度** ★☆☆

空所直後（49行目）に〈**A＋名詞**〉や「数字」があるので，ここが空所内容の**具体例**だと予想します（***Rule 8*** ⇒p.89）。A 2004 study traced the verbal developmentとあり，その後（51行目）もThe researchers found that if the children didn't know the words to describe the event when it happenedと続いているので，ここから④language skillsを選びます。

選択肢の訳

① 幼少期の経験　② 考え　③ 興味　**④ 言語能力**

〔 F 〕 **難易度** ★★☆

空所直後のit（目的格）はthe event（目的語）を指します（***Rule 50*** ⇒p.69）。「出来事を説明する言葉を知らなければ，それ（出来事）を〔F〕できない」となることから，①explainが自然です。空所の前にあるthe words to describe the eventも大きなヒントになります（describeは「説明する」という意味）。

「イベント」と聞くと楽しい感じですが，英語eventは「場合，出来事」で，「よいこと」にも「悪いこと」にも使われます。今回も別に「（楽しい）イベント」ではありませんね。

選択肢の訳

① 説明する　② 発明する　③ 計画する　④ 拒む

〔 G 〕 **難易度** ★★☆

空所直前はResearch has shown that the way parents verbally recall memories with their small children influences their style for retelling memories later in life.とあり，空所直後は「どんな影響を与えるか」を詳しく説明しています。「影響を与える」→「（その影響とは）親が子どもに出来事について詳しく語ると，子どもは大きくなった時にその記憶を鮮明に表現する」という流れで，前後が「同じ内容」と考えて，②In other wordsを選びます。

選択肢の訳

① さらに　**② つまり**　③ それにもかかわらず　④ 一方で

問2

（ア） 難易度 ★★☆

(ア)this inability of most adults to remember events from early life「ほとんどの大人がこのように幼少期の出来事を思い出せないこと」に最も近い選択肢は，①

the inability to recall our first experiencesです。本文のrememberが選択肢でrecall「思い出す」に，events from early life「幼少期の出来事」がour first experiences「最初の経験」に言い換えられています。ちなみに今回の〈**this＋名詞**〉は，この前にある「幼い頃の出来事を思い出せない」という内容をまとめているわけです（***Rule 4*** ⇒p.71）。

なお，this inability of most adults to 原形は，〈the ability of 人 to 原形〉のabilityが，否定inabilityになっているだけです。ofは「主格（～が）」を表し，inabilityを動詞っぽく「**人が～できないこと**」と訳すと自然になります。ここでは「ほとんどの大人が，～を思い出せないこと」となります。

選択肢の訳

① 最初の経験を思い出せないこと
② 記憶を言葉で表現できないこと
③ 記憶の手助けをする写真アルバムを利用できないこと
④ 生涯を通じて特別な出来事が思い出せないこと

（イ） 難易度 ★★☆

25行目にBy kicking their legs, the babies learned that the motion caused the mobile to move. Later, placed under the same mobile without the ribbon, the infants remembered to kick their legs.とあります。実験内容は「足をバタバタさせるとモビールが動くという関連性を赤ちゃんが記憶するか？」なので，これに合致する④testing whether babies can relate kicking with moving a mobileが正解です。下線の後ろにあるthey picked up the kicking relationship much more quicklyもヒントになります。

選択肢の訳

① 赤ちゃんがベッドにいるときに足をバタバタさせられるかどうかを検証すること
② 赤ちゃんがモビールを動かすのにリボンを必要としたかどうかを検証すること
③ 赤ちゃんが，おもちゃに繋がっているリボンを引っ張れるかどうかを検証すること
④ 赤ちゃんが，足をバタバタさせることとモビールを動かすことを関連づけられるかどうかを検証すること

（ウ） 難易度 ★★☆

(ウ)This is important because the hippocampus determines what sensory information to transfer into long-term storage.の，Thisが指すものは，直後の内容から「重要（important）である理由（because以下）は，海馬がどの知覚情報

を長期記憶に移行するかを決めるから」ということを念頭に探します。

すると，直前の文（35行目）にAlso, the size of the hippocampus at the base of the brain steadily grows until your second or third year.とあります。「海馬の成長」に合致する，④The growth of a key part of the brainが正解です。本文のimportantが，選択肢のkeyに対応しています。

選択肢の訳

① 特定の記憶の機能　② 潜在記憶の発達
③ 脳内のシナプスの数　**④ 脳の重要な部分の成長**

（エ） **難易度** ★★☆

thisの直前（55行目）にMemories of these types help to define our sense of self and our relationship to people around us.とあり，これを言い換えた③identifying who we are in connection to othersが正解です。本文のdefine「明確にする，区別する」が，選択肢ではidentify「特定する，誰であるかわかる」に言い換えられています。さらに，本文のour sense of selfがwho we areに，our relationship to people around us「私たちの周りの人々との関係」がin connection to others「他者との関係」にそれぞれ対応しています。

identify「特定する」の名詞形がidentity「自分らしさ，正体」（58行目で使われています）です。きちんと意味を理解している受験生が少ないので，ここで確認しておきましょう。

選択肢の訳

① 身の周りの人々と関係を築くこと
② 子どもに正しい語彙を教えること
③ 他者との関係の中で自分が何者なのかを認識すること
④ 過去の出来事を説明するために自分の個人的な記憶を明確にすること

ここでもルール

Rule 73 構文「任意倒置」のパターン

設問とは関係ありませんが，56行目に**Closely linked to this is the ability to recognize yourself.**という，倒置が起きた文があるので，ここできっちり理解しておきましょう。倒置については，既に**強制倒置**のルールは解説しました（***Rule 74*** ⇒p.156）。今回は「任意倒置」で，こちらは「カードをシャッフルするイメージ（英単語の順番が入れ替わるだけ）」で，文型ごとにパターンが決まっています。

任意倒置：文型ごとのパターン

第1文型　SVM　→ **MVS**（Mは場所・方向を示す副詞）
※Mが前に出て，SVが入れ替わる。
※Sが代名詞の場合には倒置しないことが多い。

第2文型　SVC　→ **CVS**　※S＝Cの左右が入れ替わるだけ。

第3文型　SVO　→ **OSV**　※Oが文頭に出るだけ。

第4文型　SVO_1O_2 → **O_2SVO_1**　※O_2が文頭に出るだけ。

第5文型　SVOC　→ **OSVC**　※Oが文頭に出るだけ。
→ **SVCO**　※O＝Cの左右が入れ替わるだけ。

ちなみに訳すときは「元の形に戻して訳す」でも「英文と同じ語順で訳す」でも，どちらでもOKです（きちんと構文を理解できていることをアピールできそうなほうを優先してください）。

今回の英文は，元々はThe ability to recognize yourself is closely linked to this. で，これはisを使ったSVCの文ですが，このSとCを入れ替えているわけです。倒置することによって「**旧情報**（既に出た内容・常識的なこと）」→「**新情報**（新しく伝えること）」という流れになり，前の文とのつながりもよくなります。最初に前の内容をthisで受け，後半で「新たな情報を付け加える」わけです。このように，文のつながりをよくするために「**thisなど前の内容を受ける表現**」が前に出ることがよくあります。

※ちなみに本書の「文構造の分析」では，S is p.p.は原則的にSVと判断していますが，本来の細かな分析ではSVCとみなすことも可能です。

文構造の分析

1 [1] Think back (to your earliest memory). [2] (Perhaps) images of a birthday party or scenes [from a family vacation] come (to mind). [3] (Now) think about your age [when that event occurred]. [4] Chances are 〈that your earliest recollection extends (no further back than your third birthday)〉. [5] (In fact), most adults can (probably) come up with no more than a handful of memories [from between the ages of 3 and 7] — (although family photo albums or other things may trigger more) — and most likely none [before that]. [6] Psychologists refer to this inability of most adults to remember events [from early life], [including their birth], (as childhood amnesia).

因果表現

〈this＋名詞〉→ まとめ表現

訳 [1] 自分の一番古い記憶を思い出してほしい。[2] おそらく，誕生日パーティーの様子や家族との休暇の光景が頭に浮かぶだろう。[3] 次に，その出来事が行われたときの自分の年齢について考えてほしい。[4] ひょっとしたら一番古い思い出でも，3歳の誕生日より前にはさかのぼれないかもしれない。[5] 実際のところ，ほとんどの大人はおそらく，せいぜい3歳から7歳の間のことについてはほんのわずかの記憶しか頭に浮かばないだろう──家族写真のアルバムなどをきっかけにもっと色々思い出すかもしれないが──そして，それより前については十中八九，何も記憶にないだろう。[6] 心理学者は，このようにほとんどの大人が，自分が生まれたときを含めて幼少期の出来事を思い出せないことを，幼児期健忘と呼ぶ。

語句 [1] think back to ～ ～を思い出す／[2] scene 名 光景／come to mind 頭に浮かぶ／[3] occur 動 起きる／[4] Chances are that S´V´. ひょっとしたらS´V´かもしれない（直訳「可能性はS´V´である」）／recollection 名 思い出／extend back さかのぼる／[5] come up with ～ ～を頭に浮かべる，～を思いつく／no more than ～ たったの～，せいぜい～／a handful of ～ 一握りの～／trigger 動 引き起こす，引き金を引く／[6] refer to *A* as *B* AをBと呼ぶ／inability to 原形 ～ができないこと

文法・構文 [1] Think／Imagine／Considerなどで始まる命令文は「具体例」の目印になります。今回は導入的に具体的状況を設定しているイメージです。[5] triggerは因果関係を表す表現です。また，trigger moreの後ろにはtrigger more {memories} が省略されています。[6]〈this＋名詞〉は「まとめ表現」です。直前の内容がわからなくてもinability of most adults to remember ～「ほとんどの大人は幼少期の出来事を思い出せない」という内容だと判断できます。さらにこの部分はmost adults are not able to remember ～ を名詞化した表現だと気づけると，より理解しやすくなります（not able → inabilityになるイメージ）。

2 [1] (For a long time), the theory [behind childhood amnesia] rested on the

対比を予想

assumption 〈that the memory-making parts of babies' brains were undeveloped〉, and 〈that (around age 3), children's memory capabilities (rapidly) developed (to adult levels)〉. [2] (However), psychologists have recently discovered 〈that children [as young as 3 months old and 6 months old] can form long-term memories〉. [3] The difference lies (in 〈which memories stay with us〉). [4] (For instance), it appears that babies are born (with more implicit, or unconscious, memories). [5] (At the same time), the explicit memory [that records specific events] does not carry information (over that three-year gap), (explaining 〈why people do not remember their births〉). [6] But why does this happen and what changes take place (in those first years)? [7] And ((if we can form memories (as babies)), why don't we retain them (into adulthood)? [8] Let's look at some of the research.

対比を予想　同格のthat　過去との対比（今は違う）　同格のor

訳 [1] 長い間，幼児期健忘の背後にある理論は，幼児の脳では記憶を形成する部位が十分に発達しておらず，3歳ごろに子どもの記憶機能が急速に大人レベルまで発達するのだという仮説に基づいていた。[2] しかし，心理学者たちは最近，わずか生後3か月や生後6か月の子どもが長期記憶を形成できることを発見した。[3] 違いが出るのは，どの記憶が私たちのもとに残るのかという点だ。[4] 例えば赤ちゃんは，より潜在的な，つまり無意識の記憶を持った状態で生まれてくるようである。[5] その一方で，特定の出来事を記録する顕在記憶は，その3年間の期間にわたって情報を保持し続けることはない。このことが，人々が自分の生まれたときのことを覚えていない理由である。[6] しかし，なぜこのようなことが起こり，そしてその生後数年の期間でどのような変化が起こるのだろうか。[7] そして，私たちが幼児期に記憶を形成することができるのなら，それをどうして大人になるまで覚えていないのだろうか。[8] いくつかの研究を見ていこう。

語句 [1] rest on ～ ～に基づく／assumption 名 仮説，想定，思い込み／[2] long-term memory 長期記憶（long-term memory / short-term memory「短期記憶」は，最近では注や説明なしで登場することが多いです）／[3] lie in ～ ～にある／[4] it appears that S´V´ S´V´のようである／*be* born with ～ ～を持って生まれてくる／implicit 形 潜在的に含まれた／unconscious 形 無意識の／[5] at the same time 同時に，その一方で／explicit 形 顕在的な／record 動 記録する／[6] take place 起こる／[7] retain 動 持ち続ける

文法・構文 [1] andは，2つのthat節（that the memory-making parts ～／that around age 3 ～）を結んでおり，どちらのthat節もthe assumptionの内容を説明する「同格のthat」です。ちなみにassumptionは「間違った考え，思い込み」というニュアンスで使われることが多く，のちにそれが覆されることが多いです（今回も次の文でHowever, ～ と覆されていますね）。[3] whichは疑問詞で，「どの記憶が私たちのもとに残るのか」という名詞節を作っています。[5] explaining why ～ は分詞構文ですが，意味上のSは前の内容（顕在記憶が情報

Lesson 11

を保持し続けないこと）です。[7] as babiesのasは「時（～のとき）」を表します。

3 [1] Recent studies have (largely) rejected the long-held thinking 〈that babies cannot encode information [that forms the foundation of memories]〉. [2] (For instance), (in one experiment [involving 2- and 3-month-old infants]), the babies' legs were attached (by a ribbon) (to a mobile), a toy [that hung (above the baby's bed)]. [3] (By kicking their legs), the babies learned 〈that the motion caused the mobile to move〉. [4] (Later), (placed (under the same mobile without the ribbon)), the infants remembered to kick their legs. [5] (When the same experiment was performed (with 6-month-olds)), they picked up the kicking relationship (much more quickly), (indicating 〈that their encoding ability must develop (gradually with time) (instead of in one significant burst [around 3 years old])〉).

過去との対比　反論表現　過去を表す語句　同格のthat　a mobileの同格　因果表現　対比表現

訳 [1]最近の研究はそのほとんどが，幼児は記憶の土台となる情報を記号化することができないのだという，古くから信じられてきた考えを否定している。[2]例えば，生後2か月および生後3か月の幼児を対象にしたある実験で，赤ちゃんたちの足には，モビールという，その赤ちゃんのベッドの上につるされたおもちゃに繋がっているリボンが結びつけられた。[3]足をバタバタさせることで，その動きでモビールが動くことを赤ちゃんたちは学んだ。[4]その後，リボンは着けずに同じモビールの下に寝かされると，その乳児たちは足をバタバタさせることを覚えていた。[5]同じ実験を生後6か月の子どもに行ったところ，足をバタバタさせること（とモビールの動き）の関連性に気づくのがはるかに早かった。このことは，記憶を記号化する能力が，3歳前後で突然大幅に発達するのではなく，時間をかけて徐々に発達するに違いないことを示している。

語句 [1] reject 動 否定する／long-held 形 古くから信じられてきた（直訳「長年（long）考えられてきた（held）」→「長年抱いてきた，長年の」です）／encode 動 符号化する（「情報を取り込み，記憶として保持する過程」のこと）／foundation 名 土台，基礎／[2] infant 名 幼児／attach *A* to *B*　AをBに取りつける／mobile 名 モビール（天井や壁につるし，ゆらゆらと揺れ動く飾り，おもちゃ）／hang 動 つるす（hungは過去形，過去分詞）／[3] motion 名 動き／[4] place 動 置く／remember to 原形　忘れずに～する／[5] pick up 気づく／gradually 副 徐々に／burst 名 突発，一気

文法・構文 [1] that babies cannot ～は「同格のthat」で，the long-held thinkingの内容を具体的に説明しています。ちなみにlong-held「古くから信じられてきた」は「過去と現在の対比」を示すために用いられることもポイントです。[2] a toy that ～はa mobileの同格で，a mobileがどんなおもちゃなのかを説明しています。[4] placed under ～はthe infantsを意味上の主語とする分詞構文です（赤ちゃんは「置かれる」という受動関係なので，過去

分詞で始まっています)。 [5]indicating ～ は分詞構文ですが，意味上のSは前の内容（赤ちゃんが～に気づくのが早かったこと）です。また後半は*A* instead of *B*「BではなくA」の形で，Aにはgradually with time，Bにはin one ～ oldが来ています。

4 [1]This memory encoding could relate to a baby's development of the prefrontal cortex [at the forehead]. [2]This area, [which is active (during the encoding and retrieval of explicit memories)], is not (fully) functional (at birth). [3](However), (by 24 months), the number of synapses [in the prefrontal cortex] has reached adult levels. [4](Also), the size of the hippocampus at the base of the brain (steadily) grows (until your second or third year). [5]This is important (because the hippocampus determines what sensory information to transfer into long-term storage).

〈This＋名詞〉→まとめ表現

訳 [1]この記憶の記号化は，幼児の，前頭部にある前頭前野の発達に関係があるかもしれない。[2]この部位は，顕在記憶を記号化したり顕在記憶を引っ張り出したりしているときに活性化されるところで，生まれた時点では十分に機能していない。[3]しかし，生後24か月までには，前頭前野のシナプスの数が成人レベルに達する。[4]また，脳の基底部にある海馬の大きさも，2歳から3歳まで着実に大きくなっていく。[5]この海馬がどの知覚情報を長期記憶に移行するかを決めるので，このことは重要である。

語句 [1]relate to ～ ～に関係がある／forehead 名 前頭部／[2]functional 形（*be* functionalの形で）機能を果たせる／[3]synapse 名 シナプス（神経興奮を伝達するときの2つの神経細胞の連接部）／[4]hippocampus 名 海馬／steadily 副 着実に／[5]determine 動 決める，左右する／transfer 動 移行する

文法・構文 [1]〈This＋名詞〉は「まとめ表現」の目印です。ここまでの内容はmemory encoding「記憶の記号化」についてだと判断できます。また，ここでのcouldは「～できた」という過去の意味ではなく，「(ひょっとしたら) あり得る」という意味です。 [5]what sensory ～ は〈what to 原形〉「何を～するか」のwhatがwhat sensory informationに膨らみ，「どの知覚情報を～するか」となった形です。

5 [1]But what about implicit memory? [2]It is essential (for newborns), (allowing them to associate feelings of warmth and safety (with the sound of their mother's voice), and to instinctively know how to feed). [3](Confirming this early presence), studies have revealed few developmental changes [in unconscious memory] (as we age). [4](Even in many adult amnesia cases), implicit skills [such as riding a bicycle or playing a piano] (often) survive the brain damage.

段落冒頭の疑問文 → テーマの提示

「重要な」を表す単語

データ表現

Even → 反復表現

Lesson 11

5 (Now) we know 〈that babies have a strong implicit memory and can encode explicit ones (as well)〉, [which indicates 〈that childhood amnesia may stem (from faulty explicit memory retrieval)〉]. 6 (However), (unless we're thinking (specifically) about a past event), it takes something to trigger an explicit memory (in all age groups).

因果表現　因果表現

訳 1 しかし，潜在記憶についてはどうなのだろうか。2 それは新生児にとって極めて重要なものであり，それのおかげで，新生児は温かい感情や安心感があると母親の声を思い出したり，食べ物の食べ方を本能的に理解したりすることができるのだ。3 研究によって，この幼児期段階での存在が確認され，私たちが年齢を重ねるにつれて潜在記憶に発達上の変化が起こることはほとんどないことが明らかになっている。4 成人発症の健忘でさえも多くの場合，自転車に乗ったりピアノを弾いたりといったような，潜在的なスキルは脳障害があっても失われないことが多い。5 現在，赤ちゃんには優れた潜在記憶力があること，また顕在記憶も記号化できることがわかっており，このことは，幼児性健忘は顕在記憶を引き出す機能が不完全なことが原因かもしれないということを示している。6 しかし，過去の出来事について具体的に考えている場合を除いて，どの年齢層でも顕在記憶を呼び起こすためには，何かが必要だ。

語句 1 What about ～? ～についてはどうだろうか／2 newborn 名 新生児／allow 人 to 原形 人が～することを可能にする／associate *A* with *B*　AとBを結びつける，AでBを連想する／instinctively 副 本能的に／feed 動 食べ物を食べる／3 confirm 動 確認する／developmental 形 発達上の／age 動 年を取る（日本語でも「アンチエイジング」（老化防止）などと使われています）／4 survive 動 切り抜けて生き残る，乗り切る／5 stem from ～ ～が原因である／faulty 形 不完全な／retrieval 名 回復，復旧，検索／6 trigger 動 引き金になる，引き起こす

文法・構文 1 段落冒頭の疑問文は「テーマ」を表します。第5段落は「潜在記憶について」がテーマだと判断できます。 2 allowing ～ はIt（= implicit memory）をSとする分詞構文です。また2つ目のandは，to associate ～ と to instinctively know ～ を結んでいます。 3 Confirming ～ は分詞構文で，直訳「（研究は）～を確認し」→「研究によって～が確認され」としています。またasは，近くにage「年を取る」という変化を表す動詞があることから「比例（～につれて）」の意味だと判断できます。 4 Evenは反復表現の目印です（⇒p.162（第5段落第2文））。「潜在記憶に変化が起こらない」ということを繰り返し述べています。 5 stem from ～ は因果関係を表す表現です。また，～, which indicates ～ は前のthat節の内容を先行詞とする関係代名詞（非制限用法）です。

6 1 Our earliest memories may remain blocked (from our consciousness) (because we had no language skills (at that time)). 2 A 2004 study traced the verbal development [in 27- and 39-month-old boys and girls] (as a measure

〈A＋名詞／数字〉→ 具体例

of 〈how well they could recall a past event〉). [3] The researchers found 〈that (if the children didn't know the words [to describe the event] (when it happened)), they couldn't explain it (later) (after learning the appropriate words)〉.

訳 [1] 私たちの一番古い記憶は，当時私たちには言語能力が一切なかったために，私たちの意識から遮断されたままかもしれない。[2] ある2004年の研究では，生後27か月および生後39か月の男の子と女の子を対象に，彼らがどれほどしっかりと過去の出来事を思い出せるのかを測る1つの指標として，彼らの言語的発達を追跡調査した。[3] 研究者たちは，出来事が起こったときにそれを言い表す言葉を子どもが知らなかったら，のちに適切な表現を知ったあとでもそれを説明することはできないということを発見した。

語句 [2] trace 動 追跡調査する／verbal 形 言語の／measure 名 指標／recall 動 思い出す

文法・構文 [2] 〈A + 名詞〉や2004という数字から「具体例」だと判断できます。前文の「一番古い記憶は意識から遮断されたままかもしれない」ということを具体的な研究をもとに説明しています。[3] 文の動詞が過去形foundなので，that節中もif the children didn't know ～, they couldn't explain ～と「過去形」になっています（仮定法過去ではありません）。

7 [1] Expressing our personal memories of events (in words) contributes to our autobiographical memories. [2] Memories of these types help to define our sense of self and our relationship [to people around us]. [3] Closely linked to this is the ability [to recognize yourself]. [4] Some researchers have proposed 〈that children do not develop self-recognition skills and a personal identity (until 16 or 24 months)〉. [5] (In addition), we develop knowledge of our personal past (when we begin to organize memories (into a context of time and place)). [6] Many preschool-age children can explain the different parts of an event (in sequence), [such as 〈what happened (when they went to a circus)〉]. [7] But it isn't (until their fifth year) that they can understand the ideas of time and the past, and are able to place that trip [to the circus] (on a mental time line).

因果表現

強調構文

訳 [1] 出来事に関する個人的な記憶を言葉にして表現することによって，自分についての記憶の形成が促進される。[2] こういった種類の記憶は，私たちの自己意識や身の回りの人々との関係性をはっきりさせるのに役立つ。[3] これと密接に関連しているのが自己認識力である。[4] 一部の研究者は，子どもは生後16か月あるいは生後24か月になるまで，自己認識力が身についたり個人のアイデンティティが確立されたりすることはないと提唱している。[5] さらに，記憶を時間と場所の状況の中で整理するようになると，自分の個人的な過去についての知識は深まる。[6] 多くの未就学年齢の子どもは，サーカスに行ったときに起こったことのような，出来事のさまざまな部分について順を追って説明することができる。

[7]しかし，時間や過去の概念が理解できるようになり，そのサーカス旅行を脳内の時間軸上に配置することができるようになるのは，彼らが5歳になってからのことである。

語句 [1]contribute to ～ ～に貢献する，～を引き起こす一因となる／[2]help to 原形 ～するのに役立つ／define 動 はっきりさせる／[4]propose 動 提唱する／[5]organize 動 整理する／context 名（事柄の）状況，関係／[6]preschool-age 形 未就学年齢の／in sequence 順を追って／[7]it is not until ～ that SV ～して初めてSVする／mental 形 脳内の

文法・構文 [1]contribute to ～ は因果関係を表す表現です（「～に貢献する」という訳語がよく知られていますが，よいことにも悪いことにも用いられるので，訳語にこだわりすぎず〈原因 contribute to 結果〉という関係をすぐに把握できるようにしましょう）。[3]Closely linked to ～ という過去分詞のカタマリのあとにisが続いていることから，第2文型SVC→CVSの倒置形だと判断できます。[7]it isn't until ～ that SV は強調構文を使った慣用表現です。直訳「～するまでSVしない」→「～して初めてSVする」となります。また2つ目のandは，that節中の動詞2つ（can understand ～／are able to ～）を結んでいます。

8 [1]Parents play a central role (in developing children's autobiographical memory as well). [2]Research has shown 〈that 〈the way [parents (verbally) recall memories with their small children]〉 influences their style [for retelling memories (later in life)]〉. [3](In other words), children [whose parents tell them (about past events) (in detail)], [such as birthday parties or trips to the zoo], will be more likely to (vividly) describe their own memories (when they grow up).

データ表現

訳 [1]親もまた，子どもの自分についての記憶の発達において中心的役割を果たしている。[2]研究によって，親が言葉に出して幼い子どもとの記憶を呼び起こすやり方が，のちの人生で子どもが記憶を再び語るやり方に影響を与えることが証明されている。[3]つまり，誕生日パーティーや動物園へのお出かけなどの過去の出来事について詳しく子どもに語る親の子どもは，大きくなったときに自分の記憶を鮮明に表現する可能性が高いのである。

語句 [1]play a role in ～ ～において役割を果たす／central 形 中心的な／[2]verbally 副 言葉で／retell 動 再び語る／[3]in detail 詳しく／vividly 副 鮮明に／describe 動 表現する，説明する

文法・構文 [3]such as ～ zoo はpast eventsを修飾しています。

音読をしよう！ 🔈 11

Think back to your earliest memory. // Perhaps images of a birthday party / or scenes from a family vacation come to mind. // Now think about your age when that event occurred. // Chances are / that your earliest recollection / extends no further back than your third birthday. // In fact, // most adults can probably come up / with no more than a handful of memories / from between the ages of 3 and 7 // — although family photo albums / or other things may trigger more — // and most likely none before that. // Psychologists refer to this inability of most adults / to remember events from early life, // including their birth, // as childhood amnesia. //

For a long time, // the theory behind childhood amnesia rested on the assumption / that the memory-making parts of babies' brains / were undeveloped, // and that around age 3, // children's memory capabilities rapidly developed to adult levels. // However, // psychologists have recently discovered / that children as young as 3 months old and 6 months old / can form long-term memories. // The difference lies in which memories stay with us. // For instance, // it appears that babies are born with more implicit, // or unconscious, // memories. // At the same time, // the explicit memory that records specific events / does not carry information over that three-year gap, // explaining why people do not remember their births. // But why does this happen / and what changes take place in those first years? // And if we can form memories as babies, // why don't we retain them into adulthood? // Let's look at some of the research. //

Recent studies have largely rejected the long-held thinking / that babies cannot encode information / that forms the foundation of memories. // For instance, // in one experiment involving 2- and 3-month-old infants, // the babies' legs were attached by a ribbon to a mobile, // a toy that hung above the baby's bed. // By kicking their legs, // the babies learned that the motion caused the mobile to move. // Later, placed under the same mobile without the ribbon, // the infants remembered to kick their legs. // When the same experiment was performed with 6-month-olds, // they picked up the kicking relationship much more quickly, // indicating that their encoding ability must develop gradually with time // instead of in one significant burst around 3 years old. //

This memory encoding could relate to a baby's development / of the prefrontal cortex at the forehead. // This area, // which is active during the encoding and retrieval of explicit memories, // is not fully functional at birth. // However, // by 24 months, // the number of synapses in the prefrontal cortex / has reached adult levels. // Also, // the size of the hippocampus at the base of the brain / steadily grows until your second or third year. // This is important / because the hippocampus determines / what sensory information to transfer into long-term storage. //

But what about implicit memory? // It is essential for newborns, // allowing them to associate feelings of warmth and safety / with the sound of their mother's voice, // and to instinctively know how to feed. // Confirming this early presence, // studies have revealed few developmental changes / in unconscious memory as we age. // Even in many adult amnesia cases, // implicit skills such as riding a bicycle / or playing a piano / often survive the brain damage. // Now we know that babies have a strong implicit memory / and can encode explicit ones as well, // which indicates / that childhood amnesia may stem from faulty explicit memory retrieval. // However, // unless we're thinking specifically about a past event, // it takes something to trigger an explicit memory in all age groups. //

Our earliest memories may remain blocked from our consciousness / because we had no language skills at that time. // A 2004 study traced the verbal development / in 27- and 39-month-old boys and girls / as a measure of how well they could recall a past event. // The researchers found that if the children didn't know the words / to describe the event when it happened, // they couldn't explain it later / after learning the appropriate words. //

Expressing our personal memories of events in words / contributes to our autobiographical memories. // Memories of these types help to define our sense of self / and our relationship to people around us. // Closely linked to this is the ability to recognize yourself. // Some researchers have proposed / that children do not develop self-recognition skills / and a personal identity until 16 or 24 months. // In addition, // we develop knowledge of our personal past / when we begin to organize memories into a context / of time and place. // Many preschool-age children can explain / the different parts of an event in sequence, // such as what happened when they went to a circus. // But it isn't until their fifth year / that they can understand the ideas of time and the past, // and are able to place that trip to the circus / on a mental time line. //

Parents play a central role / in developing children's autobiographical memory as well. // Research has shown / that the way parents verbally recall memories / with their small children / influences their style for retelling memories / later in life. // In other words, // children whose parents tell them about past events in detail, // such as birthday parties or trips to the zoo, // will be more likely to vividly describe their own memories / when they grow up. //

Lesson 12 解答・解説

▶問題 別冊 p.57

このLessonで出てくるルール

Rule 35 読解 長文単語・語句をマスターする！（common）⇒ Q3
Rule 3 読解 In factを意識する！ ⇒ Q4
Rule 10 読解 命令文は「具体例」の合図！ ⇒ Q4
Rule 81 構文 「接続詞as」の識別をマスターする！ ⇒ Q5

解答

Q1 ③　Q2 ③→①→②　Q3 ④　Q4 ②
Q5 ⑤than／⑦way／①is（rather than the way it is）　Q6 ②

Q1 難易度 ★☆☆

3〜7行目に「研究者は1匹のサルには大好きなブドウを，2匹目のサルにはキュウリをあげた」とあり，そのあとでNow, this offer was insulting. Some monkeys would throw the cucumber back at the researcher in anger and disgust. とあります。これに合うのは③felt upset that other monkeys were getting better treatment. です。

upsetは本来「ひっくり返す」で，「冷静な心をひっくり返す」→「うろたえさせる，イライラさせる」となりました（活用はupset-upset-upsetという無変化型）。feel upset（このupsetは過去分詞）で，「イライラさせられたように感じた」→「イライラした，腹を立てた」です（**感情動詞は*Rule 20*** ⇒p.33）。

ちなみに，そのあとにIn other words, the monkeys cared deeply about fairness. や，What mattered to them was not just what they received but also what others got. とあり，「他のサルが何をもらったかも重要だった（他のサルが自分より優遇されているか気になる）」とあるのもヒントになります（**matter**は動詞「重要である」で，***Rule 2*** ⇒p.37で出てきました）。

設問と選択肢の訳

下の選択肢から，次の文を完成させるのに最も適切なものを選びなさい。
研究者にキュウリのスライスを投げ返したサルたちは

①渡されていたキュウリの種類が好みではなかった。
②公平性の重要さが理解できなかった。
③他のサルたちが自分よりもよい待遇を受けていることに腹を立てた。
④研究者に向かって投げることのできる小石をもう1つも持っていなかった。
⑤研究者がそれを欲しがっていると思った。

Q2 難易度 ★★★ 思考力

①は,「しかし（However）真ん中から乗り込む飛行機もある」では前の英文とつながらないので，これが最初にはこないと判断します。②は，these two scenariosを指すものが前の文にないので，これも最初にはきませんね。よって，③が最初にくるとわかります。③はtypically「通常は，典型的に」を使って,「エコノミークラスの乗客はファーストクラスを通って座席に向かう」と一般的な状況を説明しています。

次に①のHoweverで「しかし，真ん中から乗り込む飛行機もある」と続きます。③のeconomy passengersを①のtheyで受けています(theyは「主格」で，economy passengersは「主語」なので***Rule 50*** ⇒p.69のとおりですね)。

最後に②で，この2つの状況をthese two scenarios（**〈these＋名詞〉**の形）でまとめています(***Rule 4*** ⇒p.71)。②の後半にwhen economy passengers had to walk through first class compared with when they bypassed itとあり，①と③の状況を比較しているわけです。

When there is a first-class section, it is at the front of the plane, and economy passengers typically walk through it to reach their seats.

「ファーストクラスがある場合，その区画は機内の前方にあり，エコノミークラスの乗客は通常そこを通って自分の座席に向かう」

However, in some flights, they get on in the middle of the plane.

「しかし，飛行機によっては，真ん中から機内に乗り込む場合もある」

〈these＋名詞〉でまとめている

Looking at these two scenarios, the researchers found that an air-rage incident in economy was three times as likely when economy passengers had to walk through first class compared with when they bypassed it.

「研究者たちはこの2パターンの状況を比べ，エコノミークラスにおける機内逆上事件は，エコノミークラスの乗客がファーストクラスの区画を通り抜けなければいけない場合のほうが，そこを通らない場合に比べて3倍起こりやすいことを突き止めた」

ここが 思考力 **文を適切な順番に並び替える問題**

「文を並び替える問題」は多くの受験生が苦手意識を持っており，思考力を問う問題とも言われますが，今回は**代名詞**や〈**this**[**these**]**+** 名詞〉が大きなヒントになりました。本書で学んだルールは問題形式にかかわらず，様々な場面で役立ちます。何となく訳して考えるのではなく，思考力を要しそうな難しい問題ほど，「形から答えを絞れないか？」「ルールが使えないか？」と意識してみてください。

設問と選択肢の訳

下の選択肢から，空欄（A）を埋めるのに最も適切な文の順番を選びなさい。

① しかし，飛行機によっては，真ん中から機内に乗り込む場合もある。

② 研究者たちはこの2パターンの状況を比べ，エコノミークラスにおける機内逆上事件は，エコノミークラスの乗客がファーストクラスの区画を通り抜けなければいけない場合のほうが，そこを通らない場合に比べて3倍起こりやすいことを突き止めた。

③ ファーストクラスがある場合，その区画は機内の前方にあり，エコノミークラスの乗客は通常そこを通って自分の座席に向かう。

Q3 難易度 ★★☆

設問文はKeith Payne suggests that we are mistaken to think thatに続くものなので，「我々一般人の勘違い，広く知れわたっている一般論」で，かつ「Keith Payneが反論している内容」です（このように設問文にare mistakenなどがある場合は，解答が求めるものを強く意識しないと混乱してしまいます。今回は①にひっかかりやすいのです）。

26行目にAnd what's becoming clearer is the weakening of the ties that hold society together.，28行目にPayne challenges a common perception that the real problem isn't inequality but povertyとあり，Payneは一般論（a common perception that ～）に異議を唱えているので，この一般論の中身がそのまま解答につながるはずです（その中身では「（社会の結びつきの弱体化の要因は）不平等ではなく貧困」とあり，これに合致する④poverty is the reason for the weakening of social ties.が正解です。

ちなみに，今回のポイントとなった動詞**challenge**「**異議を唱える**」は，すでに**反論表現**として紹介してありますが（***Rule 35*** ⇒p.187），名詞「挑戦」の意味しか知らない受験生が多いので，しっかりチェックしておきましょう。

challengeは動詞「従来の考えに異議を唱える」の意味で使われて，**主張の合図**になることがよくあるのです。ちなみに，テニス・バドミントン・バレーボールなどで「審判の判定に異議を唱える」ことを「チャレンジ」と言います。

>>> Rule 35 読解 長文単語・語句をマスターする！（common）

common「共通の，よくある」

「共通の」という訳語が有名ですが，実際には「みんなに共通した」→**「よくある，ありふれた」**という意味でもよく使われます。長文では「ありふれた考え方・一般的な考え方」のように，**「一般論」の目印**になります。

設問と選択肢の訳

下の選択肢から，次の文を完成させるのに最も適切なものを選びなさい。

キース・ペインは，私たちは間違って〜と考えていると言う。

① 不平等の問題に関するデータが実際の状況を正確に反映している
② 最低賃金を稼ぐことで家族の絆が強くなる
③ 人間は社会的な生き物と言い表すのが一番合っている
④ 貧困は社会の結びつきの弱体化の要因である
⑤ 貧困であることのデメリットは，私たちの食べ物の価値に対する感覚を変えてしまう

Q4 難易度★★☆ 思考力

35行目のone might think that pay inequality creates incentives for better performance and more winsで一般論を示したあと（oneは「一般的な人」で，one might think that 〜で「〜だと思う人もいるかもしれない」），37行目でIn fact, economists have analyzed the data and（　B　）.と主張しています。「〜と考えるかもしれないが，実際には…」という流れで，空所には**「その一般論は正しくなかった」**といった内容がくると予想できます。

さらに，空所前後で「賃金格差はよい影響を与える」⇔「平等性が高いチームのほうが，結果がよい」と真逆の内容になっていることも踏まえて，②found that the opposite was trueを選べばOKです。「一般論・譲歩 → 主張」の流れです。

>>> Rule 3 読解 In factを意識する！

in factは「実際に」の訳語が有名ですが，意外な意味や使い方があります。実は**主張を補強する**役割と**前の文と反対の意見を述べる**役割の2つがあるのです。

A. In fact *B*

(1) 「実際に，もっと言えば」

前の文の補強・さらなる具体例を出す　(A ≒ B)

(2) 「しかし実際は，実際はそれどころではなく」　(A ⇔ B)

1. 否定文のあとで，butのバリエーションとして

not *A* but *B*という基本形において，**but→in fact**になるイメージです。イメージとしては，*A*（notの文）. In fact *B*. という形になります。

2. 肯定文のあとで，その内容と相反することを述べる

※in factの前にbutやhoweverが置かれることも多いが，ない場合もある。

今回は上記の **(2)-2.** の用法で，「〜と考えるかもしれない」のあとでIn factが**「しかし実際は」**という意味で使われています。このin factの使い方は受験生にはほとんど知られていませんが，現実にはよく使われます。

51行目In fact, the average president at the largest American public companies earns about 350 times as much as the average worker.でも同じ意味です。他にもこの本の中でin factはたくさん使われているのですが，余裕があれば復習するときにどちらの意味か考えてみてください。

また，設問とは絡みませんが，今回は33行目で主張（The breakdown affects not only those at the bottom, but also the lucky ones at the top.）があり，そのあとに具体例（Consider baseball 〜）が続いています。この具体例のパターンは「命令文」がポイントになるのです。

>>> *Rule 10* 読解　命令文は「具体例」の合図！

文章中で**命令文**を見つけたら，そこから**具体例が始まる**と考えます。

主張. 命令文〜.

→この文から具体例になる！

何かを主張したあとで,「例えばこんな場合を考えてみてください」という感じで，具体的な状況を説明するわけです。特に，以下のような思考系の動詞「考える，想像する」が頻繁に使われます。

☐ Think　☐ Consider　☐ Suppose　☐ Imagine

※命令文は動詞で始まるので大文字で表記しています。

この英文では，あくまで「野球」の話は具体例なので，空所部分も「不平等はよくない」というPayneの主張と同じ内容がくるはずです。さらに，その後のWhat's more ～で「不平等は底辺層だけでなく，上位層にも影響を与える」という主張の裏づけをしています。

ここが 思考力 **一般論と主張の整理+大きな視点が必要な問題**

今回の問題では，「一般論」と「Payneの主張」を把握して，さらに野球の話は「具体例」だと整理する視点が必要な問題です。

皆さんは，なんとなく「これは主張っぽいな」と，場当たり的に読むのではなく，本書で学んだ「in factの使い方」「命令文に注目する」などのルールを活用して，確実な読み方をしてください。

設問と選択肢の訳

下の選択肢から，空欄（B）を埋めるのに最も適切なものを選びなさい。

① そのオーナーたちが正しいことが判明した
② 事実は逆であることが判明した
③ このことが賃上げに役立ったことが判明した
④ 彼らの発見にはほとんど価値が認められなかった
⑤ 関連性を立証することはできなかった

Q5 難易度 ★★☆

設問の訳

次の単語7つのうち6つを使って，最も適切な方法で空欄（C）を埋めなさい。**2番目**，**4番目**，**6番目**にくる選択肢を記すこと。

空所直前のthe world as we want it to be「私たちがそうであってほしいと願うような世界」のasは「名詞限定（～のような）」で，the worldを説明しています。整序問題ではまず動詞に注目するわけですが，今回の問題はisで特に特別な形が浮かぶわけではありませんね。ですから単純に**つなげるものをつなぐ**という発想で，語群からrather than ～「～ではなく」を組み合わせます。

次に語群のtheとwayから，**the way S´V´「S´V´する様子・方法」**を考え，the way it isとすればOKです。itはthe worldを指し，直訳「世界が（実際に）存在する様子」→「現実の世界，ありのままの世界」となります。つなげると，the world as we want it to be rather than the way it is「実際の世界ではなく私たちがそうであってほしいと願うような世界」となり，④soが不要です。

「名詞限定のas」は難関大で問われます。asの基本用法（**比例・様態・譲歩**）も合わせてチェックしておきましょう。

>>> Rule 81 構文「接続詞as」の識別をマスターする！

接続詞asにはたくさんの意味がありますが，入試で狙われるのは以下の4つです（ここに載せていない「理由・時」の意味も，英文の中では出てきますが，設問でポイントになることはありません）。たくさんあるasの意味ですが，核心は**「同時に」**です。どの意味であれ，すべてそれらの根底には「同時に」という意味が潜んでいるのです。

■比例「～するにつれて」

「変化」を表す表現が使われていれば，「比例」を考えてみてください。100%ではありませんが，ほぼすべて**「～するにつれて」**という意味になります。「変化のある単語」は以下のとおりです。

「比例のas」の識別方法

1. 比較級

2. 変化動詞（become / grow / turn / get / change / varyなど）

3. 移動動詞（go / pass / increase / rise / climb / appear / disappearなど）

例 **As** smartphones **become more and more** powerful, we rely on them **more and more**.
スマートフォンがますます高性能になるにつれて，私たちはますますスマートフォンに頼ってしまう。

※変化動詞become，比較級more and more powerful，more and moreがある／「高性能になる」と「頼る」が同時に起きているニュアンス。

■様態「～するのと同じように」

「様態のas」の識別方法　以下のどれかが使われている。

1. 似た表現の繰り返し　**2. 代動詞（do／does／did）**　**3. 省略**

例 When you are in Rome, do **as** the Romans **do**.
郷に入っては郷に従え。

※直訳は「ローマにいるときは，ローマ人のするようにしなさい」。「相手がする方法」と「ローマ人のする方法」が同じということ。

Lesson 12

■ **譲歩「〜だけれども」**

「譲歩のas」の識別方法

特殊な形になる。

X as S´V´, SV. S´V´はXだけれども，SVだ。

※As 形容詞・副詞 as S´V´, SV. の形になることもある。「順接（〜なので）」の意味になることもある（文脈から判断する）。

例 Old **as** it is, the DVD player still works perfectly.
そのDVDプレーヤーは古いが，まだ何の問題もなく動く。

※it（the DVD player）is oldが変形したイメージ／「古い」と「動く」が同時に起きている。

■ **名詞限定「〜のような」**

名詞を修飾する（形容詞的な働きをする）特殊な用法です。

「名詞限定のas」の識別方法

as節中に**代名詞（itなど）**がある（その代名詞は「as直前の名詞」を指す）。

※as節中の〈S´＋be〉は省略されることが多い（その結果，〈as 形容詞〉や〈as p.p.〉の形になる）。

例 Lifetime employment, **as** Japanese workers knew **it** during the bubble economy, is becoming rarer.
日本の労働者がバブル経済のときに知っていたような終身雇用制度は，今はますます減ってきている。

※itはLifetime employmentを指す。「名詞限定のas」は，ある名詞の「一面を切り取って説明する」感覚で，ここでは「あくまで"日本人労働者がバブル経済のときに認識していたような"終身雇用制度」に限定している。

Q6 難易度 ★★★

今回の長文は,「サルの実験」→「不平等の影響」→「アメリカの現状とその考察」という流れになっています。特に最終文はI suspectで筆者が自分の意見を述べています。構造が複雑なので，構文把握の練習も兼ねて確認してみましょう（下線部和訳問題にしたいくらいよい英文です）。

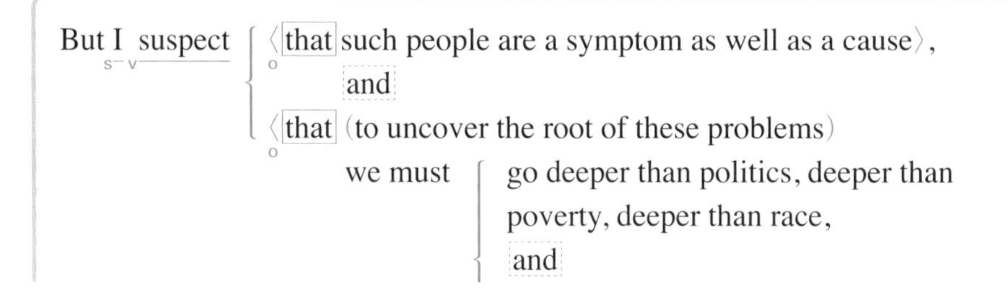
But I suspect
S V
〈that such people are a symptom as well as a cause〉,
O
and
〈that (to uncover the root of these problems)
O
we must
go deeper than politics, deeper than poverty, deeper than race,
and

confront the inequality [that is America today]〉.

「しかし私は，そのような人々は原因であるとともに，兆候でもあるのではないかと思っており，そういった問題の根底を明らかにするためには，政治よりも，貧困よりも，人種よりも深く潜って，この不平等—今日のアメリカは不平等そのものである—に立ち向かわなくてはいけないのではないかと考えている」

この英文の内容（特に2つ目のthatから最後まで）に合致する②focus on how unequal American society has become.が正解です。

本文のto uncover the root of these problemsが設問のdealing with the problems he describesに，we mustがrequires us to ～に，そしてconfront the inequality that is America todayがfocus on how ～に言い換えられています。

ちなみに，これとまったく同じ「サルの実験の話」→「アメリカでの不平等」という，同じ話，同じ展開の報道がCNN（アメリカのニュースチャンネル）でもなされたことがあるので，現代の受験生にはぜひ知っておいてほしい内容でもあります。

設問と選択肢の訳

下の選択肢から，次の文を完成させるのに最も適切なものを選びなさい。

筆者は，彼の述べている問題に対処するために，私たちは～ことが必要であると結論づけている。

① 不幸の要因と兆候[現れ]を区別する

② アメリカ社会がいかに不平等になってしまったかに焦点を当てる

③ 社会の底辺層の人々の収入を増やす

④ 公職から物議を醸している個人を追放する

⑤ 米国における人種間の緊張[敵対意識]の重要性を理解する

文構造の分析

（設問指示文）

Read this article and answer the questions below.

訳 この記事を読み，下の問いに答えなさい。

1 [1] Monkeys were taught (in an experiment) to hand over small stones (in exchange for cucumber slices). [2] They were happy (with this deal).

訳 [1] ある実験で，サルたちは，スライスしたキュウリと引き換えに小石を渡すようにと教え込まれた。[2] サルたちは，この取引に嬉々としていた。

語句 [1] teach 人 to 原形 人に～の仕方を教える／in exchange for ～ ～と引き換えに／cucumber 名 キュウリ／[2] deal 名 取引

文法・構文 [1] taught monkeys to hand over ～「サルたちに～を渡すように教えた」が受動態になった形です（今回は 人 の位置に monkeys がきています）。

2 [1] (Then) the researcher (randomly) offered one monkey — (within sight of a second monkey)— an even better deal: a grape for a stone. [2] Monkeys love grapes, so this fellow was thrilled.

「交換」の for

訳 [1] その後，研究者は無作為に選んだ1匹のサルに，2匹目のサルから見えるところで，さらに好条件の取引を持ちかけた。それは，小石と引き換えにブドウをあげるというものだった。[2] サルはブドウが大好きなので，このサルは大喜びだった。

語句 [1] randomly 副 無作為に／offer 動 提示する／sight 名 視野，見える範囲／[2] fellow 名 片割れ，やつ，仲間，同輩／thrilled 形 興奮した

文法・構文 [1] even は「～さえ」ではなく比較級の強調表現「なおいっそう～」です。

3 [1] The researcher (then) returned (to the second monkey), but presented just some cucumber (for the pebble). [2] (Now), this offer was insulting. [3] Some monkeys would throw the cucumber back (at the researcher) (in anger and disgust).

訳 [1] 研究者はそれから，2匹目のサルのもとに戻ったが，そのサルには小石に対してキュウリを何スライスかあげただけだった。[2] 今や，この申し出は侮辱的なものだった。[3] 中には，怒って不快そうにキュウリを研究者に投げ返すサルもいた。

語句 [1] present 動 あげる／pebble 名 小石／[2] insulting 形 侮辱的な／[3] disgust 名 嫌悪感，むかつき

文法・構文 [1] 第1段落1文目に cucumber slices と出てきましたが，ここでも同様に cucumber

を不可算名詞として使っているので「キュウリを何スライスか」と訳してあります（some cucumbersと可算名詞として使っていれば「何本かのキュウリ」という意味になります）。
3 wouldはSの「過去の強い意志（どうしても～しようとした）」を表しています。

4 1 (In other words), the monkeys cared (deeply) about fairness. 2 What mattered (to them) was not just what they received but also what others got.

「重要」を意味する動詞

訳 1 つまり，そのサルたちは公平性をかなり気にしていたのだ。2 彼らにとっては，自分が何をもらったかだけではなく，他のサルが何をもらったのかも重要だったのである。

語句 1 care 動 気にする／fairness 名 公平性／2 matter 動 重要である／not just *A* but also *B*　AだけでなくBも

文法・構文 2 not just *A* but also *B*は，not only *A* but also *B*のonlyがjustに変わった表現で，意味の違いはほとんどありません。

5 1 It is not only monkeys that are offended (by inequality). 2 (For example), two scholars examined data [from millions of flights] (to identify 〈what factors resulted in "air rage" incidents〉), [in which passengers become angry or (even) violent]. 3 One huge factor: a first-class cabin.

強調構文

因果表現

訳 1 不平等に気分を害するのはサルだけではない。2 例えば，2人の学者が何百万ものフライトデータを調べて，乗客が怒ったり，さらには暴力をふるったりする「機内逆上」事件を引き起こした要因を特定した。3 1つの大きな要因は，ファーストクラスの客室だった。

語句 1 offended 形 気分を害した／2 scholar 名 学者／identify 動 特定する／result in ～ 結果として～になる／rage 名 激怒

文法・構文 1 It is not only ～ thatの時点で強調構文だと予想できます（***Rule 75*** ⇒p.20）。
2 result in ～ は因果関係を表す表現です。また，, in which ～ は"air rage" incidentsを先行詞とする関係代名詞（非制限用法）で，"air rage" incidentsを補足説明しています。

6 1 An incident [in an economy section] was four times as likely (if the plane also had a first-class cabin); a first-class section increased the risk of a disturbance as much (as a nine-hour delay did). 2 (When there is a first-class section), it is at the front of the plane, and economy passengers (typically) walk through it (to reach their seats). 3 (However), (in some flights), they get on (in the middle of the plane). 4 (Looking at these two scenarios), the

〈these＋名詞〉→まとめ表現

Lesson 12

researchers found 〈that an air-rage incident [in economy] was three times as likely (when economy passengers had to walk through first class) (compared with when they bypassed it)〉.

訳 [1]エコノミークラスでの事件は，同じ飛行機にファーストクラスの客室もある場合では4倍起こりやすかった。ファーストクラスがあることによって，9時間の遅延が起こった場合と同じくらい，騒ぎが起きる危険性が高まっていたのだ。[2]ファーストクラスがある場合，その区画は機内の前方にあり，エコノミークラスの乗客は通常そこを通って自分の座席に向かう。[3]しかし，飛行機によっては，真ん中から機内に乗り込む場合もある。[4]研究者たちはこの2パターンの状況を比べ，エコノミークラスにおける機内逆上事件は，エコノミークラスの乗客がファーストクラスの区画を通り抜けなければいけない場合のほうが，そこを通らない場合に比べて3倍起こりやすいことを突き止めた。

語句 [1]disturbance 名 騒ぎ／delay 名 遅延／[4]scenario 名 シナリオ，状況／compared with ～ ～と比較すると／bypass 動 回避する，迂回する

文法・構文 [1]An incident in an economy section was four times as likely if the plane also had a first-class cabin {as it was if the plane did not (have a first-class cabin)}から，比較対象のas以下が省略されています。比較対象が文脈などから明らかな場合，省略される場合があるのでした（⇒p.24（第3段落第5文））。また，文末の～ a nine-hour delay did.は～ a nine-hour delay increased the risk of a disturbance.をまとめて表しています。[4]比較対象がas ～ではなく，compared with ～で示されている特殊なパターンです。

7 [1]Keith Payne, a professor of psychology at the University of North Carolina at Chapel Hill, tells of this research (in a brilliant new book, *The Broken Ladder*, [about 〈how inequality destabilizes societies〉]). [2]It 's an important, fascinating work [arguing 〈that inequality creates a public-health crisis (in America)〉].

Keith Payneの同格

訳 [1]ノースカロライナ大学チャペルヒル校で心理学の教授を務めるキース・ペインは，この研究を，不平等が社会をいかに揺るがすのかについて書かれた彼の見事な新著『The Broken Ladder』の中で取り上げている。[2]これは，不平等がアメリカの公衆衛生上の危機を生むと主張している，重要かつ興味深い本である。

語句 [1]tell of ～ ～について（詳しく）説明する／destabilize 動 揺るがす，不安定にする／[2]public-health 形 公衆衛生の／crisis 名 危機

文法・構文 [2]an important, fascinating workとworkを可算名詞として使っていることから，「作品，著作」の意味だと判断できます。また，arguing ～はworkにかかる分詞のカタマリです。

8 [1]The data [on inequality] reveals the shocking truth. [2]The top 1 percent [in

データ表現　数字 → 具体例

America] owns more than the bottom 90 percent. [3] The annual Wall Street bonus pool alone is more than the annual year-round earnings of all Americans [working full time (at the minimum wage of $7.25 an hour)], (according to the Institute for Policy Studies). [4] And what's becoming clearer is the weakening of the ties [that hold society together].

数字 → 具体例　固有名詞／数字 → 具体例　固有名詞／数字 → 具体例

訳 [1] 不平等に関するデータは，衝撃的な真実を明らかにしている。[2] アメリカの上位1パーセントが，下位90パーセントの合計よりも多く（の資産）を保有しているのだ。[3] 政策研究所によると，年間のウォールストリートのボーナス基金だけでも，全アメリカ人が最低賃金の時給7.25ドルでフルタイム勤務をして得られる年間所得よりも多い。[4] そして，社会を1つにまとめる絆が弱体化していることが明らかになりつつある。

語句 [1] on 前 ～に関する／[3] pool 名 基金，共同出資／year-round 形 一年間の／earning 名 稼ぎ／minimum wage 最低賃金／[4] tie 名 絆，結びつき／hold ～ together ～をまとめる，～を団結させる

9 [1] Payne challenges a common perception 〈that the real problem isn't inequality but poverty〉, and he 's persuasive 〈that societies are shaped not just (by disadvantage at the bottom) but also (by inequality [across the spectrum])〉. [2] Addressing inequality must be a priority, for we humans are social creatures, so society begins to break down (when we see some receiving grapes and others cucumbers).

反論表現　一般論　同格の that　「理由」の for

訳 [1] ペインは，真の問題は不平等ではなく貧困であるという一般的な認識に異論を唱えており，社会を形成するのは底辺層の不利な立場だけでなく，全階層にわたる不平等でもあるのだと説得力を持って語る。[2] 不平等への対処は優先されなくてはならない。なぜなら，私たち人間は社会的な生き物なので，ブドウをもらっている人もいればキュウリをもらっている人もいる様子を見たら社会が崩壊し始めるからだ。

語句 [1] challenge 動 異論を唱える／common perception 一般的な認識／persuasive 形 説得力がある／spectrum 名 分布，範囲，領域／[2] priority 名 優先されること／break down 崩壊する

文法・構文 [1] 1つ目のthatは「同格のthat」で，a common perceptionの内容を説明しています。また，not just *A* but also *B*はnot only *A* but also *B*のonlyがjustに変わった表現で，意味の違いはほとんどないのでしたね（⇒p.213 第4段落）。[2] for ～ は等位接続詞のfor～「というのも～だからだ」です。またand以下は，others {receiving} cucumbersから，重複を避けるためreceivingが省略されています。

10 [1] The breakdown affects not only those [at the bottom], but also the lucky ones [at the top]. [2] Consider baseball: Some team owners pay players a much wider range of salaries (than others do), and one might think 〈that pay inequality creates incentives [for better performance and more wins]〉.

命令文 → 具体例

訳 [1] 社会の崩壊は，底辺層の人々だけでなく，上位層にいる恵まれた人々にも影響を与える。[2] 野球について考えてみよう。一部のチームのオーナーが選手に，他のチームのオーナーたちよりもはるかに幅広い年俸の範囲で支払っている。そうすると，賃金格差によってパフォーマンス向上や勝利数増加を促す動機づけが生まれるのだと思う人もいるかもしれない。

語句 [2] salary 名 給与／incentive 名 誘因，動機づけ／performance 名 パフォーマンス，成果

文法・構文 [1] thoseの後ろには関係詞だけでなく，過去分詞や形容詞句が続くことがあるのでした（⇒p.98（第9段落第4文））。 [2] 2つ目のandは，名詞2つ（better performance／more wins）を結んでいます。

11 [1] (In fact), economists have analyzed the data and found 〈that the opposite was true〉. [2] Teams [with greater equality] did (much better), perhaps (because the players felt a closer bond (with each other)).

訳 [1] しかし実際には，経済学者たちがデータを分析して，事実は逆であることが判明している。[2] 平等性が高いチームのほうがはるかによい結果を残しており，それはおそらく，選手たちが互いにより強い絆を感じていたからだろう。

語句 [2] bond 名 絆

12 [1] (What's more), it turned out 〈that even the stars did (better) (when they were (on teams with flatter pay))〉. [2] "Higher inequality seemed to have a negative effect on the superstar players [it was meant to motivate ϕ], [which is 〈what you would expect ϕ〉 (if you believed 〈that the chief effect of pay inequality was to reduce cooperation and team unity〉)]," Payne notes.

反復表現

訳 [1] さらに，スター選手でさえも，報酬の差が少ないチームに所属しているときのほうがよい結果を残すことが判明した。[2]「不平等性が高いと，そうすることでやる気にさせようとしていたスーパースター選手たちにマイナスの影響を与えるようでした。報酬の不平等の主な影響は協力関係やチームの団結を弱めることであると考えていたら，こんなことは予想できるでしょうがね」とペインは指摘する。

語句 [1]what's more さらに／turn out 判明する／star 名 スター選手／flat 形 平らな，一律の／[2]have an effect on ～ ～に影響を及ぼす／motivate 動 やる気にさせる／chief 形 主な／unity 名 結束

文法・構文 [1]evenは「反復表現」の目印です（⇒p.162（第5段落第2文））。「賃金格差が少ないほうがよい」ということを繰り返し述べています。 [2]it was meant to ～のitは，Higher inequalityを受ける代名詞です。, which is ～ は前の内容を先行詞とする関係代名詞（非制限用法）です。また，the chief effect of pay inequality was to reduce ～ は「～することになっている」を意味するbe to構文ではなく，be動詞とto不定詞「～すること」がたまたま隣り合った形です。

13 [1]Something similar emerges (in national statistics). [2]Countries [with the widest gaps in income], [including the United States], (generally) have worse health, more killings, and a greater range of social problems.

反復表現

訳 [1]似たようなことは全国統計にも見られる。[2]米国を含め，収入の差が大きい国々ではたいてい，（そうでない国々よりも）健康状態が悪く，殺人が多く，さまざまな社会問題が起こっている。

語句 [1]emerge 動 現れる／national statistics 全国統計

文法・構文 [1]反復表現similarに注目して，類似内容の繰り返しだと判断できます。次の文でも，「賃金格差が少ないほうがよい」という内容が述べられています。

14 [1]People seem to understand this truth (instinctively), for they want much less inequality (than we have). [2](In a study of people [in 40 countries]), liberals said 〈company presidents should be paid (four times as much as the average worker)〉, (while conservatives said five times). [3](In fact), the average president [at the largest American public companies] earns (about 350 times as much as the average worker).

訳 [1]人々はこの真実を直感的に理解しているようだ。なぜなら人々は，現在よりも不平等が大幅に減ることを望んでいるからだ。[2]40か国の人々を対象にした研究で，自由主義者は，企業の社長は平均的な労働者の4倍の給料をもらうべきだと回答した一方で，保守派は5倍もらうべきだと回答した。[3]ところが実際には，平均的なアメリカの最大手の公開株式会社の社長は，平均的な労働者のおよそ350倍も稼いでいるのだ。

語句 [1]instinctively 副 直感的に／[2]liberal 名 自由主義者／conservative 名 保守派

文法・構文 [1]for ～ 接続詞「というのも～だからだ」です。 [2]while以下は，while conservatives said five times {as much as the average worker}.から，重複を避けるためas much as ～ が省略されています。

15 [1] (Presented with unlabeled charts [depicting income distributions of two countries]), 92 percent of Americans said 〈they would prefer to live (with the modest inequality [that exists in Sweden])〉. [2] Republicans and Democrats, rich and poor alike, all chose Sweden (by similar margins).

訳 [1] 2か国の収入分布が描かれた図表を国名を表示せずに見せられると，アメリカ人の92パーセントが，スウェーデンのような不平等の少ない国に住みたいと答えた。[2] 共和党支持者も民主党支持者も，裕福な人も貧乏な人も同様に，皆似たような比率でスウェーデンを選んだ。

語句 [1] present 動 提示する／unlabeled 形 分類されていない，標識されていない／depict 動 描く／distribution 名 分布，配分／modest 形 控えめな，適度の／[2] Republican 名 共和党支持者／Democrat 名 民主党支持者／margin 名 比率，差

文法・構文 [1] Presented with ～は92 percent of Americansを意味上のSとする分詞構文です（「アメリカ人の92%が図表を提示される」という関係なので過去分詞で始まっています）。

16 [1] "(When the level of inequality becomes too large to ignore), everyone starts acting (strange)," Payne notes. [2] "Inequality affects our actions and our feelings (in the same systematic, predictable fashion) (again and again)."

訳 [1]「不平等の度合いが無視できないほど大きくなると，皆が奇妙な行動をするようになります」とペインは言う。[2]「不平等は，私たちの行動および感情に，規則的で予想可能な同じ方法で何度も何度も影響を与えるのです」

語句 [1] strange 副（動詞のあとで）奇妙に／[2] systematic 形 規則的な，体系だった／predictable 形 予想可能な／fashion 名 方法（今回は「流行」などの意味ではないので注意してください）

17 [1] "It makes us believe odd things, (superstitiously clinging to the world [as we want it to be] rather than [the way it is])," he says. [2] "Inequality divides us, (splitting us into camps not only of income but also of ideology and race), (eating away at our trust in one another). [3] It generates stress and makes us all less healthy and less happy."

訳 [1]「それによって私たちは奇妙なことを信じるようになり，実際の世界ではなく，そうであってほしいと願うような世界に迷信的にすがりつくようになります」と彼は言う。[2]「不平等は私たちを引き裂き，収入だけでなくイデオロギーや人種によっても異なる陣営に分断し，相互の信頼を食いつぶしていきます。[3] 不平等はストレスを生み，私たち皆の健康や幸せを損なうのです」

語句 [1] superstitiously 副 迷信的に／cling to ～ ～にすがりつく／*A* rather than *B* BよりむしろA（AとBには文法上対等の語（句）がくる）／[2] divide 動 引き裂く，分断する／

split *A* into *B* AをBに分裂させる／camp 名 陣営，立場／ideology 名 イデオロギー／race 名 人種／eat away at ～ ～を食いつぶす

文法・構文 [1]as we want it to be は「名詞限定のas」，the way it isは形容詞のカタマリで，どちらもthe worldを修飾していると考えられます（このようにthe way S′V′のカタマリが名詞を修飾することもあります）。[2]主節に分詞構文2つ（splitting us into ～／eating away at ～）が続いた形です。

18 Think of those words (in the context of politics today): Don't the terms "stress," "division," and "unhappiness" sound familiar?

命令文 → 具体例

訳 これらの発言を，今日の政治に照らして考えてみよう。「ストレス」，「分断」，「不幸」などよく耳にする言葉ではないだろうか。

語句 in the context of ～ ～に照らして

19 [1]So much of the national conversation gets focused on individuals [such as Donald Trump] — (for understandable reasons). [2]But I suspect 〈that such people are a symptom as well as a cause〉, and 〈that (to uncover the root of these problems) we must go (deeper than politics, deeper than poverty, deeper than race), and confront the inequality [that is America today]〉.

訳 [1]無理もないことではあるが，国内の話題のこんなにも多くがドナルド・トランプのような個人に集中している。[2]しかし私は，そのような人々は原因であるとともに，兆候でもあるのではないかと思っており，そういった問題の根底を明らかにするためには，政治よりも，貧困よりも，人種よりも深く潜って，この不平等――今日のアメリカは不平等そのものである――に立ち向かわなくてはいけないのではないかと考えている。

語句 [1]understandable 形 もっともな，無理もない／[2]symptom 名 現象，症状／uncover 動 明らかにする／root 名 根底／confront 動 立ち向かう

文法・構文 [2]1つ目のandは，2つのthat節（that such people are ～／that to uncover ～）を，2つ目のandは，動詞2つ（go deeper ～／confront the inequality ～）をそれぞれ結んでいます。そして，mustはgoとconfrontの両方にかかります。また，the inequality that is America todayは，直訳「今日のアメリカである不平等さ」ですが，和訳では「今日のアメリカは不平等そのものである」と文に転換して訳してあります（意味は通じますが，英文の構造としてはあまり綺麗ではないので，英作文などでは似た表現は避けたほうがよいでしょう）。

音読をしよう！ 12

Monkeys were taught in an experiment / to hand over small stones / in exchange for cucumber slices. // They were happy with this deal. //

Then the researcher randomly offered one monkey // — within sight of a second monkey — // an even better deal: // a grape for a stone. // Monkeys love grapes, // so this fellow was thrilled. //

The researcher then returned to the second monkey, // but presented just some cucumber for the pebble. // Now, this offer was insulting. // Some monkeys would throw the cucumber back at the researcher / in anger and disgust. //

In other words, // the monkeys cared deeply about fairness. // What mattered to them was not just what they received // but also what others got. //

It is not only monkeys that are offended by inequality. // For example, // two scholars examined data from millions of flights / to identify what factors resulted in "air rage" incidents, // in which passengers become angry or even violent. // One huge factor: // a first-class cabin. //

An incident in an economy section / was four times as likely if the plane also had a first-class cabin; // a first-class section increased the risk of a disturbance / as much as a nine-hour delay did. // When there is a first-class section, // it is at the front of the plane, // and economy passengers typically walk through it / to reach their seats. // However, // in some flights, // they get on in the middle of the plane. // Looking at these two scenarios, // the researchers found that an air-rage incident in economy / was three times as likely when economy passengers / had to walk through first class / compared with when they bypassed it. //

Keith Payne, // a professor of psychology at the University of North Carolina / at Chapel Hill, // tells of this research in a brilliant new book, // *The Broken Ladder,* // about how inequality destabilizes societies. // It's an important, // fascinating work / arguing that inequality creates a public-health crisis in America. //

The data on inequality reveals the shocking truth. // The top 1 percent in America / owns more than the bottom 90 percent. // The annual Wall Street bonus pool alone / is more than the annual year-round earnings / of all Americans working full time / at the minimum wage of $7.25 an hour, // according to the Institute for Policy Studies. // And what's becoming clearer / is the weakening of the ties that hold society together. //

Payne challenges a common perception / that the real problem isn't inequality / but poverty, // and he's persuasive that societies are shaped / not just by disadvantage at the bottom / but also by inequality across the spectrum. // Addressing inequality must be a priority, // for we humans are social creatures, // so society begins to break down / when we see some receiving grapes / and others cucumbers. //

The breakdown affects not only those at the bottom, // but also the lucky ones at the top. // Consider baseball: // Some team owners pay players / a much wider range of salaries than others do, // and one might think that pay inequality / creates incentives for better performance / and more wins. //

In fact, // economists have analyzed the data / and found that the opposite was true. // Teams with greater equality did much better, // perhaps because the players felt a closer bond with each other. //

What's more, // it turned out that even the stars did better / when they were on teams with flatter pay. // "Higher inequality seemed to have a negative effect / on the superstar players it was meant to motivate, // which is what you would expect / if you believed that the chief effect of pay inequality / was to reduce cooperation and team unity," // Payne notes. //

Something similar emerges in national statistics. // Countries with the widest gaps in income, // including the United States, // generally have worse health, // more killings, // and a greater range of social problems. //

People seem to understand this truth instinctively, // for they want much less inequality than we have. // In a study of people in 40 countries, // liberals said company presidents should be paid / four times as much as the average worker, // while conservatives said five times. // In fact, // the average president at the largest American public companies / earns about 350 times as much as the average worker. //

Presented with unlabeled charts / depicting income distributions of two countries, // 92 percent of Americans said they would prefer to live / with the modest inequality / that exists in Sweden. // Republicans and Democrats, // rich and poor alike, // all chose Sweden by similar margins. //

"When the level of inequality becomes too large to ignore, // everyone starts acting strange," // Payne notes. // "Inequality affects our actions and our feelings / in the same systematic, // predictable fashion / again and again." //

"It makes us believe odd things, // superstitiously clinging to the world as we want it to be / rather than the way it is," // he says. // "Inequality divides us, // splitting us into camps / not only of income / but also of ideology and race, // eating away at our trust in one another. // It generates stress / and makes us all less healthy and less happy." //

Think of those words in the context of politics today: // Don't the terms "stress," // "division," // and "unhappiness" sound familiar? //

So much of the national conversation / gets focused on individuals / such as Donald Trump // — for understandable reasons. // But I suspect that such people are a symptom / as well as a cause, // and that to uncover the root of these problems // we must go deeper than politics, // deeper than poverty, // deeper than race, // and confront the inequality that is America today. //

MEMO